Physical Being

WAYS OF BEING

Social Being
Personal Being
Physical Being

PHYSICAL BEING

A Theory for a Corporeal Psychology

Rom Harré

Indexed in

I∧IOM

BLACKWELL
Oxford UK & Cambridge USA

Copyright © Rom Harré 1991

First published 1991

Basil Blackwell Ltd
108 Cowley Road, Oxford, OX4 1JF, UK

Basil Blackwell, Inc.
3 Cambridge Center
Cambridge, Massachusetts 02142, USA

British Library Cataloguing in Publication Data
A CIP catalogue record for this book is available from the British Library.

Library of Congress Cataloging in Publication Data
Harré, Rom.
Physical being: a theory for a corporeal psychology/Rom Harré.
p. cm.
Includes bibliographical references and index.
ISBN 0-631-13421-2
1. Mind and body. 2. Body, Human – Psychological aspects.
3. Body, Human (Philosophy) I. Title.
BF161.H28 1991
150.19'8 – dc20
90-20581
CIP

Typeset in 10 on 12 pt Times
by Graphicraft Typesetters Ltd., Hong Kong
Printed in Great Britain by T.J. Press Ltd Padstow, Cornwall

CONTENTS

ACKNOWLEDGEMENTS

I am grateful to the editors of the following journals and books for permission to make use of material already published therein:

I would also like to record my thanks to Oxford University for the sabbatical leave that made the completion of this study possible, and my appreciation to the State University of New York at Binghamton and to Georgetown University for providing many opportunities to test out the ideas sketched in this book. I am particularly grateful to David Barnum and Ann Shackle for their loyal and efficient efforts at the word processor.

Rom Harré

Linacre College, Oxford
Georgetown University, Washington D.C.

But if it impossible by any means to maintain this proposition, namely, that any being, with the exception of the Father, Son and Holy Spirit, can live apart from a body, then logical reasoning compels us to believe that, while the original creation was of rational beings, it is only in idea and thought that a material substance is separable from them, and though this substance seems to have been produced for them or after them, yet never have they lived or do they live without it, for we shall be right in believing that life without a body is found in the Trinity alone.

Origen, *First Principles*

In some ways she thought of her body as a favourite or only child.

Alison Lurie, *Love and Friendship*

GENERAL INTRODUCTION

To the total body counter.
Notice in John Radcliffe Hospital, Oxford

The roles played by our bodies in the ways we live cannot be well understood if the human body is considered only from the perspective of the medical and biological sciences. We must come to see our bodies, their states, functions and uses, as complex clusters of cultural constructions. Body concepts are given meaning, and so made relatively determinate, in a variety of ways in different environments of thought and action. From among the vast array of ways our bodies and their nature and condition enter into our lives I have taken only three. *Metaphysically* the concepts of body and of person are intimately interrelated. This is the most important fact about the concept of the human body as it is put to use in the contexts of everyday life. It exerts a ubiquitous influence on the ways we think about the bodies of ourselves and others. Then bodily form and bodily function are the subjects of all sorts of normative judgements and public and private *evaluations*. The moral protection given to the human body as the material vehicle of personhood sharpens the ethics of all body-directed action. I shall also try to show that it is not only bodily form that is a matter of aesthetic judgements, but also those bodily conditions we call 'health' and 'illness'. In my third context the body and its parts and functions are looked at in the light of their use both as signifiers, systems of signs and as blank surfaces on which significance is 'inscribed'. These are the metaphors of corporeal *semantics* (O'Neill, 1985).

This is the third study in a group of conceptual explorations, concerning the ways of being human. One has a social, a personal and a physical being. Each of our ways of being is implicated in, and partially defines, the others. I have proposed these explorations as theories for social, personal and corporeal psychologies respectively. It is important to be clear about the sense of 'theory' that I have had in mind in defining my project in that way. Academic psychologists tend to use expressions like 'theory' and 'model' both interchangeably and vaguely, conflating several different kinds of conceptual projects.

In the physical sciences two very different meanings for 'theory' are easily discerned. In the first sense a theory is an open set of necessary propositions expressing the interrelationships of a cluster of concepts to be used for describing a certain roughly demarcated class of phenomena, which the concepts of the cluster themselves partly define. Theories, in this sense, can be 'open textured', in Waismann's famous phrase. Some of the conceptual connections are revisable, incomplete and so 'open'. Examples of this kind of theory abound in elementary physics, for example kinematics, the laws of electric circuitry and many others. It would not lead us too far astray to call these theories 'grammars', in the broad sense in which Wittgenstein came to use the word. In existing ways of studying human life open-textured theories can be found in hermeneutics and other interpretative psychologies and sociologies.

In another important sense 'theory' refers to that kind of explanatory discourse in which the generative mechanisms thought responsible for a certain class of phenomena are described. More often, in practice, a theory of this sort describes only a model or analogue of a possible generative mechanism that could be productive of the phenomena of interest. Thus a description of the dance of the molecules in kinetic theory is an account of a model or analogue of the true nature of gases. It serves as a sketch of a possible mechanism that might be responsible for the characteristic patterns of behaviour of gases in bulk.

Theories in the first sense do not enlarge our ontology. They are not used to propose a hidden realm of active beings producing what we observe. In this respect they are in the sharpest possible contrast to theories in the second sense. The invention of explanatory theories has served in the exploration of nature in depth, opening up new realms of being. Wittgenstein warned against the tendency to theorize in the second sense when confronted with patterns of human thought and action. Many of his case studies were designed to bring out the ways that mistaken grammatical models lead the uncritical to assume the existence of all sorts of bogus objects, which then tend to be offered as the ontological basis of explanations. In clearing out this zoo of fabled monsters one by one, he leaves us with the impression that there may be no place at all in psychology proper for theories in this second sense. 'Cognitive science', the latest effort of psychologists to theorize in the explanatory manner, is seemingly replete with such constructions. I am inclined to think that one could show, step by step, that the 'cognitive' entities and processes cognitive scientists propose are either disguised presentations of prescriptive grammars for talk about patterns of thought and action or obliquely presented sketches of the formal structures of some relevant fragments of neurophysiology. In this study into the way the concept of the body appears in human ways of being, the project of setting out a 'theory for a corporeal psychology' is to be read in the first sense of 'theory'. It is to be taken as an attempt at a grammar of the conceptual resources involved in, and necessary to, those patterns of thought and action in which the human body figures either as target or as topic or both.

In this collection of studies I am concerned with questions as to how people use their bodies and how they use body concepts in the conceiving, planning and accomplishment of the ordinary tasks of everyday life. In the whole of human life there is the duality of the lived and the told, the acted and the spoken. In many instances a task can be accomplished in either 'modality'.

I have called this project a theory for corporeal psychology. By a 'psychology' I mean primarily an account of certain kinds of human practices, particularly discursive practices. Dominant amongst these practices are the giving of reasons, anticipating the future and the making of judgements according to criteria and norms. I am well aware that this agenda may seem ethnocentric. I hope that this collection of studies may encourage others centred on a different point of origin in another framework of the commonplace. I should emphasize that I do not regard the giving of reasons as a way of sketching in the outlines of a cognitive psychology of action. The warranting of action is itself action. There are many instances of premissless judgements in the actions of everyday life, the antecedents of which are just neurophysiological. For instance, the important skill of seeing things *as* some specific entity or other is, I believe, a premissless judgement realized in a definite perceptual experience. In this book the bodily enactment of certain important kinds of premissless judgements will be central to one branch of the discussions of bodily evaluations. Emotions and aesthetic responses are just such judgements. A corporeal psychology will be a collection of accounts of those discursive practices in which the fact of embodiment plays a central role, whether accomplished by the body itself or by body-centred talk. In just the same way social psychology should be a collection of accounts of those discursive practices in which the fact of the recognition of other persons in joint action is central. Personal psychology focuses on those discursive practices that depend on the fact of reflexive self-awareness. Nowhere in psychology can the boundaries between lay accounts and those offered by specialists and academicians be firmly drawn. The problem is always to make some form of human action intelligible.

I am not aware of any previous attempt to use analytical techniques to construct the conceptual underpinnings for a corporeal psychology. Sociologists have been more adventurous. Turner (1984) and O'Neill (1985) have proposed schemes of sociological categories that can be specified as defining occasions for the use of body concepts. Turner identifies four social tasks – reproduction, restraint, regulation and representation – in aspects of which the human body plays a central role. O'Neill's 'five bodies' are, like Turner's four 'tasks', sociological 'slots' into which a body can fit. Only Frank (1989), using the metaphor of a 'self-questioning body', which for me would be an embodied person, produces a corporeal psychology. He identifies four bodily aspects of action – control, desire, relatedness to others and self-relatedness – in each of which a social dimension can be discerned and eventually researched. It would not be difficult to adapt his scheme to a corporeal psychology. We might ask how patterns of thought and feeling, emerging in body-related discourses, are involved in those aspects of action he has picked out.

Closer still to my concerns is the 'prolegomenon' for a genuinely corporeal anthropology of Scheper-Hughes and Lock (1987). They develop their scheme around a trio of root uses of body concepts. There is the 'body-self', the human body as we experience it; the 'social body', by which they mean the uses of the body as a natural symbol; and finally the 'body politic', the body as conceived and utilized in practices of social control. Their scheme bears an encouraging similarity to the one that I shall be developing in what follows. Indeed it would not be an exaggeration to say that their work serves to introduce a kind of multicultural corporeal psychology that, given the social-constructionist slant I propose to adopt, ought to fit nicely on to many of my own analyses.

REFERENCES

Frank, A. 1991: 'For a sociology of the body: an analytic review' in *The Body*, edited Featherstore, M., Hepworth M., and Turner B. S. London: Sage.
O'Neill, J. 1985: *Five Bodies: The Human Shape of Modern Society*. Ithaca and London: Cornell University Press.

Scheper-Hughes, N., and Lock, M. M. 1987: The mindful body: A pro-legomenon to future work in medical anthropology. *Medical Anthropology Quarterly*, 1, 6–41.

Turner, B. S. 1984: *The Body and Society*. Oxford: Blackwell.

Wittgenstein, L. 1953: *Philosophical Investigations*. Oxford: Blackwell.

For a general review of the role and significance of the human body see Frank A. 1991 *At the Will of the Body* Boston: Houghton Miflin.

PART I
Metaphysics

Philosophy has succeeded, not without a struggle, in freeing itself from its obsession with the soul, only to find itself landed with something still more mysterious and captivating: the fact of Man's bodiliness.

F. Nietzsche, *The Will to Power*

... to the extent that humans do indeed differ from other organic and inorganic beings, this is due not *to their having some distinctive non-bodily features, but rather to the distinctive character of their bodies.*

Russell Keat

What metaphysical problems could there be about human bodies other than those they share with all material things? Unique among the things of the physical world human bodies sustain persons. There are two salient facts about people that have a profound significance for the concept of the human body and its various manifestations in the acts of human life. People are aware of themselves as embodied, and they manage their lives as embodied beings within diverse frameworks of historically modulating moral and aesthetic evaluations. Bodies are identified as this or that embodied person. And people are individuated in part by reference to the uniqueness of their bodies as material things. But human bodies are not *just* things.

However, they are things, so questions as to how their varieties and kinds are arrived at must present themselves. In the natural sciences classificatory schemes are grounded in theories about the nature and origin of the things classified. Something comparable can be discerned in the ways human bodies are sorted into kinds and dismembered in thought. But it is social, and even political, considerations that serve to fix body-kinds rather than theories as to the nature and origin of their discernible differences. Similarly the parts and states of bodies are not picked out by anatomical criteria alone. Indeed such criteria often play quite a small part in working conceptions of the fine structure of human bodies.

Matters are yet more complicated. The human spatio-temporal universe, our *Umwelt*, is divided, for each human being, into two basic regions. Within the body's bounding surface we can be aware of physical states in two quite different ways. In principle I can be aware of the state and condition of my body in much the same way as I can be aware of the state of any material thing, namely by observation. Yet the state and condition of at least some parts of my body are also presented to me through human sensibility. Outside the boundary of my body there is only observation. Among the dominant features of sensibility are pain and pleasure. They can be adapted to the management of human affairs and so take on not only moral, but political, significance.

Concerning its kinds, parts, states and conditions the human body appears to us through a conceptual structure that is elaborated far beyond that needed to comprehend and manage a thing, even a special kind of thing. As the necessary, but material, seat of personhood, each human being appears as a nexus of a complicated web of social obligations and interpersonal meanings from which each and every one of us draws the significance we assign to our bodies and their parts, each according to his or her own tribal customs. I owe to Nick Rengger the reminder that how the ubiquitous tie between moral principles and the corporeal conditions for the preservation of persons is actually forged is enormously culturally and historically variable. For instance, is it forged through pleasure or through pain?

CHAPTER 1

EMBODIMENT

What is deepest in a human being is the skin.
Adapted from Paul Valéry

INTRODUCTION: THE COMPLEXITY OF
THE BODY CONCEPT

What is a human body? One answer can be found in the sciences of
anatomy and physiology. A human body is an organism. It has distinctive characteristics of form and function. The biological features of
human bodies will never be wholly irrelevant to the various parts of
this study. However, it will turn out that the way the body concepts
enter into the way we manage ourselves, experience ourselves and
think about ourselves in all sorts of contexts cannot be explained in
biological terms alone. This ubiquitous feature of the uses of body
concepts reflects the fact that human bodies are potentially, actually or
formerly the bodies of persons. The analyses to follow are directed to
elucidating the nature and consequences of personal embodiment. In
the first part of this chapter I shall focus on the ontological question
'Is a human body just a rather special kind of material thing?' Looked
at from one point of view, human bodies are obviously things. They
are spatially located and temporally enduring, tracing out continuous
trajectories in the manifold of space-time. They have weight, colour
and texture. They have causal powers through which changes in other
material things can be brought about. The 'thingness' of our bodies is
evident in such commonplace events as sitting on an overfull suitcase
to close the lid. Nevertheless we shall see that typical human bodies
are not typical things. Much that is unique to human bodies depends
on the fact that they are the embodiments of persons. They are the
means by which we display the kind of social beings we are. They are

morally protected in various ways. But that is true too of a person's most intimate and precious possessions. How does a person's body differ then from any other cherished item? Is my body just one of my things? According to some religions I, the person, could exist even without a body. 'Cartesianism' is not a monopoly of modern Christianity.

As we shall see, the body, as a unique material entity, plays an indispensable role in the two ways in which human beings have a sense of identity. Our sense of ourselves as particular individuals is based in part on our sense of the continuous spatio-temporal trajectories of our bodies through which we are located in the material world. But our social identities, the kind of persons we take ourselves and others to be from time to time, are also closely bound up with the kinds of body we believe we have. In the former aspect of embodiment we experience our corporality as personally ruled, while the latter, however we experience it, can be shown to be largely socially ruled (Turner, 1984).

The thingness of bodies cannot be denied. There are similarities between my body and those possessions into which I have, so to say, put myself. A distinction can be drawn by examining the way we get to know our bodies and comparing it with how we get to know even our most precious things. There is one body that I know in a rather special way, namely my own. Short of a better metaphor, I shall call this 'knowing from within'. Things cannot be known from within. To know what is inside a thing or inside another person's body is not at all like 'knowing from within'. Other people's bodies are somewhat like things. But there are ways by which I can, in a sense, have some idea what it is like to be embodied as you are. The resources of language enable people to share personal body experiences in ways that they cannot do with things. We owe our understanding of how this feat is possible to Wittgenstein, who once and for all removed the air of mystery and paradox surrounding our knowledge of how other people experience the intimate flux of bodily feelings.

People do not have unrestricted rights to acquire knowledge about other people's bodies nor can they freely pick up knowledge about other people's things. Those things that are owned by people are protected in various ways and in different degrees from the prying eyes and probing fingers of others much as their bodies are. Clearly there is a complex network of conceptual ties at work in the way we think about these matters and manage our daily lives as embodied beings. I shall explore this network in three stages. In the first I shall try to show how the concept of the 'body as such' can be distinguished analytically from that of 'person' and from that of 'mind'. In the second phase of the analysis I shall display at least some of the complex connections between the concept of 'a human body' and 'a person's things'. In the final step I shall compare the ways of knowing through which we become acquainted with our own bodies, the bodies of other people and the material being of things.

BODIES, PERSONS AND MINDS

The main thrust of my analysis will be directed to evaluating the significance, in all sorts of contexts, of the fact that human bodies are the bodies of persons. I begin this study with a brief exploration of two contrasts – that between a person and their body and that between a person's body and that same person's mind. The contrasts will be brought out by reflection upon how separations between persons, their bodies and their minds are routinely accomplished. I shall show that the routine of separation of a person and their body is a social process, involving, among other things, transfers of responsibility and suspensions of rights. But the separation of body from mind is material – that is, it is a biochemical process, involving deletions or suspensions of functions. I shall call these techniques generally 'separation practices'. In like manner to Merleau-Ponty (1948: Part I) I am not trying to remedy an unfair neglect of the body as opposed to the flattering attention given to the more interesting mind. That tack would preserve Cartesianism. Rather I am engaged in building a conception of human bodies as embodied persons; not accidentally conjoined with personhood, but essentially.

There are many different kinds of separation practices. There are crude material practices like murder, by which a person and their body are separated, never, so far as we know, to be reunited. Exactly what is presumed to have happened when someone has been killed depends on one's religious assumptions. But whether a person is separated from their body by death in such a way that both still exist, or whether it is believed that a mere body has been obtained by extinguishing the person and destroying the mind, there is no doubt that killing is a very primitive separation technique. The subtlety and complexity of the three-way relation between a person, their body and their mind appears only with more sophisticated separation techniques. Imagine now what happens when a patient is prepared for an operation. Anaesthesia is clearly some kind of separation technique. When operating on the body of an anaesthetized patient, a surgeon need not take account of the person usually thus embodied. Neither their dignity nor their right to privacy as a person, nor their usual responsibility for the management of their own body, nor their feelings and sensations as conscious beings need be considered when deciding what to do to the body that lies on the operating table. This though will prove to be a key to the significance of embodiment. Dignity, rights and responsibilities are attributes of persons as social beings, while feelings and sensations are contents of consciousness and attributes of persons as psychological beings.

Let us look closely at the preparation of a patient for surgery. I shall take it as a prime example of separation practices by which the body is detached both from personhood and mindedness. As Goffman (1961) observed, some aspects of the preparation for the operating theatre can be interpreted as ritual acts which accomplish a transfer of responsibility for a particular human body from the person thus embodied to the surgeon and other medical personnel who will take the same kind of care of it, perhaps even more care of it than the person whose body it is. At the same time the normal conventions that define what is and is not humiliating treatment when accorded to a person are suspended. Goffman realized that the ritual separation of a person from their body, in the sense of transfer of responsibility, is accomplished not only in such overt ceremonial acts as the signing of a form giving consent for an operation, but also in some of the medical techniques themselves. Premedications, theatre gowns and so on are metonymic signs of a transfer of responsibility as well as practical actions. Once the change of locus of responsibility has been accomplished, the anaesthetist can proceed to bring about a material 'separation' of body and mind, by suspending mental functions in varying degrees. At last a mere body is presented to the surgeon for treatment.

The fact that there is both the signing of a consent form and anaesthesia is significant when we are working towards an account of the concept of the human body as such. Our understanding of that concept will be achieved partly by seeing it in contrast to the neighbouring concepts of 'person' and 'mind'. Persons are embodied beings who exhibit certain mental accomplishments and sensibilities. But they are also moral beings, centres of responsibility, who owe, and to whom is owed, a certain kind of respect. A human being also appears as a mere body in situations in which consciousness is not suspended. In a massage parlour or in a physiotherapy clinic a person as client no longer takes moral responsibility for what is to be done to their body, nor does a client insist on the moral protection normally accorded to persons through the maintenance of their bodies as sacred territories that may not be invaded by others. A masseur or a physiotherapist decides what is to be done and freely touches and manipulates the bodies of the clients.

After the operation is completed to the satisfaction of the medical team, or the massage or manipulation is over, the separated body must be 'returned' to the person thus embodied. And now the order is reversed. Mental functions such as consciousness, memory and sensibility are first restored, had a 'mind' separation been accomplished. Responsibility for, and moral protection of, the body under care is returned to the relevant person only step by step. Personal responsibility and moral protection may only be fully recovered when the patient is discharged from hospital, and in some cases not even then. Roughly speaking, we can sum up the analysis as follows: the contrast between a person and their body is essentially a social matter, while that between a person's body and a person's mind is drawn functionally. In this study I am not at all concerned with discussing and evaluating the variety of metaphysical theories that have been used to account for the functional differences between 'mind' and 'body' that are evident in routine hospital practice. The focus will be on how persons and their bodies are distinguished and related. Nowhere in this study will such traditional issues as the proper way to understand the mind/brain distinction be discussed.

A human body is a focus of responsibility and the permanent seat of various functions. It is also an object whose value is routinely recognized in the ways it is accorded the protection that pertains to those entities a culture takes to be sacred. In a famous treatment of the concept of human individuality Strawson (1959) invites his readers to extricate the concept of 'mind' and the concept of 'body' from the more primitive concept of 'person'. His technique is to draw our attention to the huge range of attributes commonly taken to be found in persons. His aim is to pick out those attributes upon which a person's sense of their own and others' individuality depends. These attributes are to be found in consideration of the role of the fact of embodiment in the lives of those who have a sense of individuality. In person talk we have M-predicates (used for ascribing corporeal characteristics to human subjects) and we have P-predicates (used for ascribing behavioral, cognitive and moral powers and attributes to human subjects). The thrust of his argument is that mind and body do not differ as two substances differ. 'Mind' and 'body' are words used to pick out different ranges of attributes of the same substance. A person is that sort of being that is properly talked about in terms of both M- and P-predicates.

Looked at this way, a person's body is just a cluster of attributes drawn from the whole range of properties characteristic of human beings. Isn't it enough to say that these are properties that a person shares with material things which are not persons? This will prove to be far too superficial a view of the matter. We have already seen how sanctity and responsibility enter into the relations between persons and bodies. The status of a person's corporeal characteristics are infected through and through by matters of rights and they will differ according to the moral orders in which those rights are variously defined.

There is a third mode of separation, which can be found in certain cults. Each cult has its characteristic range of separation practices and each favours a certain range of experience said to be available to those who abandon their bodies and who then seem to exist in some disembodied mode or 'plane'. In the first two separation contexts I have discussed bodies were left, so to say, depersonalized. But in the third mode persons continue to be present, but they no longer experience themselves as embodied. Among such cults are Australian aborigine 'spirit walking', renaissance cults of ecstasy and the contemporary fringe psychological cult in which adepts strive for 'out-of-the-body' experiences.

I have argued elsewhere and in detail that the sense of selfhood is partly a sense of a continuous trajectory of spatio-temporal locations. This aspect, revealed by a study of the indexical conditions for the use of first-person talk, is tied in with the fact that one has, as an embodied being, a certain point of view in physical space. If there is such a state as ecstasy, it is a separation of the personal point of view from the location of one's embodiment. The same is true of spirit walking and out-of-the-body experiences. The ecstatic person observes, or seems to observe, their recumbent body from a spatial vantage point. Just how a vantage point in space could be a point from which to view material things for a being lacking material sense organs, which have been left in the abandoned body, is never made clear by the cultists. Strawson has argued that the unity of disembodied persons must have originated only in their having once been embodied. It would slowly dissolve once that material point of view was lost. Only by being embodied as a thing amongst things can I have a robust sense of personal identity. Cult separation then leaves the essential locative properties of the sense of self intact and indeed depends for their preservation on the materiality of personal embodiment.

ARE HUMAN BODIES JUST THINGS?

A simple and uncontroversial answer to the question seems irresistible: bodies are material things. Separation practices leave behind mere bodies, depersonalized and deprived of manipulative skills and moral and cognitive powers. They are spatio-temporally individuated and physically identified things. They have neither rights nor dignity nor feelings. What is taken away and restored in separation practices is added to, or taken away from, a mere body in the course of a life course of development and decay.

Ontological questions, such as that posed in the apparently simple query above, can be pursued by an examination of the human social practices by which bodies are identified and individuated, and their comparison with the kinds of practice by which other sorts of material things are picked out. Some instructive differences emerge.

'Identifying the victim': the emotional force of a crime drama is often enhanced by a scene in which a close relative 'identifies the body'. As the distraught parent or spouse, perhaps, is led out of the morgue, the corpse is pushed back into the refrigerator. How very thing-like is the corpse. One can easily imagine a mistake being made. 'I thought at first it was my brother, but looking more closely I see that it isn't.' This picture will do very well so long as the body is his, hers or yours. But it will not do at all if the body under consideration, in some other venue than the morgue, is mine.

I protest at your persistently drinking your coffee from a certain mug. But you convince me that the mug I thought was mine was actually yours. Could I come to realize that the body I had taken all along to be mine was someone else's? I wake up in the morning with this insight perhaps – or you convince me in some manner analogous to the way you proved to me that I was wrong to think the cup was mine, that all along the body had not been mine, but yours. Is my morning glance in the mirror a bit like the scene in the morgue? Is the question 'Is this my body?' in any way at all like the question posed by the Chief Inspector: 'Is this your brother's body?' If not, why not?

I shall use the expression 'metaphysical ownership' for the relation between a person and his or her body. The relation is 'internal'. By that I mean that amongst the conditions for being the very person I am is the fact that I am embodied in just this body. This condition derives from the way that not only my identity and individuality as a person is tied in with my having a definite, unitary and continuous spatial and (with qualifications) temporal point of view in the material world. I am indebted once again to Strawson for his way of putting the matter. According to a strictly Cartesian ontology, in which my thinking self and my body are treated as independent substances, it is ultimately contingent, an accident if you like, that I am embodied thus and so, here and now. Strawson's procedure in advocating the idea of a conceptual link between personhood and embodiment (and it is an 'advocacy', being more like a legal argument than a mathematical proof) is to try out various other possibilities upon which to base an account of principles of individuation, of the techniques of identification and re-identification of person, in a variety of thought experiments. The only plausible account turns out to be based on the thesis that individuation and re-identification of persons are achieved by reference to those persons' materially enduring bodies.

A nice point about this treatment is that the asymmetry between one's experience of one's own identity and one's experience of the identity of other people emerges naturally. One's sense of one's own uniqueness as a person comes from the fact that one has a continuous point of view as a thing amongst things. According to Claparède (1924), 'Mou moi, je le situe d'une façon très exacte dans le milieu de ma tête, au centre d'un plan horizontal qui passe par les deux yeux.' This vantage point coincides via the body itself with the location at which one can exert one's physical powers on other things. One's sense of the identity of other people comes from their distinctive physical appearance, since we are rarely, if ever, able to keep them constantly under observation as they move about the world and endure in time. I have called the special relation between myself and my body 'metaphysical ownership'. To put this epigrammatically: while I do not need to identify myself to know who I am I do need to identify other people. When the sentry says 'Step forward and identify yourself', he is asking me to demonstrate who I am to him. Does this difference extend somehow to ways of knowing human bodies – mine and the bodies of others?

BOUNDARY STUDIES

I shall tackle this problem by contrasting the way I experience my body and its limits with the way I experience the limits of yours.

In a tangle of limbs, for instance in a rugby scrum, I see a knee in front of my eyes. I may not know whose knee it is. Suppose I bite it. If I feel the bite, it is my knee, but if I feel nothing, then either I am anaesthetized or the knee is yours. This ambiguity is settled by your angry reaction. I shall call this test a use of the 'criterion of sensory reach'. I know the 'rim of felt embodiment' for my body by how something feels, but I know the rim of felt embodiment by your physiognomic reaction.

This is a powerful criterion, but it must be qualified. People who have lost some bodily appendage, like a leg, report having feelings as if the limb still existed, even when looking at the stump. It is said that men who have had their genitals removed in a sex-reassignment operation experience this phenomenon. However powerful the illusion of a ghost limb, its illusory status is clear when one tries to use it for some practical purpose. Notwithstanding the evident uselessness of phantom appendages, Sandstrom (1951: 106–8) reports cases of corporeal illusions that have persisted for half a century. The criterion of sensory reach needs supplementing. My experience of my own rim of felt embodiment is refined as I come to use my limbs, teeth and other appendages in practical activities, and acquire a sense of my physical competence and its limits.

This too must be qualified. Descartes pointed out that when I probe the material environment with a stick I feel the shape of things at its distal end as if the stick were another limb. I do not attend to, and am not aware of, the changing tactile sensations that arise in the hand that is holding the stick. Gibson's (1976) theory of direct perception gives some insight into the phenomenon. He demonstrated, in a number of cases, that perception is not the result of cognitive operations performed on elementary sensations. In perceiving something, we are using our perceptual systems actively to explore the flux of energy in which we are embedded. These systems have evolved to abstract higher-order invariants from the flux. The stick simply becomes part of the tactile perceptual system. We can do the same kind of exploration with a finger nail. Unless this qualification to the criterion of sensory reach is further qualified it seems to let in too much. Yet Schilder (1935: 201, 213) assembles impressive evidence for admitting clothing (and even feathers in a hat) to the extended body boundary.

Teeth, finger nails and hair are prosthetic devices which are proper parts of the body while the sticks and rods I use as probes are not. Though insensitive in themselves, the 'natural probes' are one and all undetached body products.

To be *this* finger nail is to be part of *this* body. Given the three criteria, it follows that I could never discover that after all the finger nail I had all along thought to be mine was actually yours. Once the part is detached, then the principles of individuation that are germane to questions of identity change radically. Once the amputated limbs have been tossed into a bucket, the way I would ascertain that one of these limbs was mine would be quite different from how I would do the selection in the usual circumstances. That the connection even of finger nails is intimate is evident in the enthusiasm with which witches hunt for nail clippings and hair trimmings and the care with which such detached body parts are dealt with in traditional societies. Never throw loose hair on the fire in Pakistan, since the air is full of jinn who snuff up the smoke and thus gain power over the people whose tresses these discards once were. Many other body products may seem to have an intimate connection with personal being. What happens to surgical 'offcuts', to post-mortem debris, in those societies that believe that every part of the body is somehow imbued with the human essence? How are body parts disposed of after traffic accidents? I do not know the answers to any of these questions. But I am sure that if one could find out, a kind of gauge for the essentially of the body product or body part would be quite easy to read off the practices of disposal.

We know the outer surfaces of our things by looking, touching and so on and we can come to know their inner structure by dissecting them and looking even more closely. Broadly speaking, the outer surfaces and inner constitutions of unprotected things are known by the same means. However, close scrutiny and dissection of precious things may be forbidden or discouraged. Nowadays we have recourse to penetrating rays that leave the integrity of the thing unaffected. In many ways how I can come to know your body is very like the way I can come to know the physical being of a protected or precious thing. I can see your blue eyes, feel your clammy palms, hear your intestinal gurgle and X-ray you for gallstones. There remains one kind of knowledge of your body that I can never have. I can never know by acquaintance how it feels within your rim of sensory embodiment. My knowledge of your 'subjective' states is only discursive.

The asymmetry between my way of acquaintance with my body and my way of acquaintance with yours is not absolute. Sometimes I have to treat my body as if it were someone else's – that is, like a precious thing. For instance, when I am sitting close to you I may have difficulty in deciding whose tummy is rumbling – yours or mine. My acquaintance with my internal physical states is, in many cases, as much through external signs as is my acquaintance with yours. Doctors, on expeditions, have sometimes had to carry out exploratory surgery on themselves (with the help of mirrors) to determine the physical cause of a persistent pain. I do not propose to analyse this sort of case any further here than to say that we know the lesion through the pain. Pain talk is a physiognomic language game.

Empirical studies of the sense of embodiment have brought out several distinctions with which the foregoing analysis of the body-boundary concept can be elaborated. In Schilder's (1935) classic study, boundary phenomena, through which one's rim of felt embodiment becomes determinate in relation to inanimate material things, are contrasted with those in which bodily limits are experienced in relation to other people as embodied conscious and active beings. For instance, one's body boundary is more sharply defined in case of touch when it is known to be by part of a person than if believed to be by a similar inanimate contact.

The rim of felt embodiment consists, apparently, of two main components. There is a sense of the body surface as a barrier and, in contrast, a sense of its penetrability. Fisher and Cleveland (1968) showed how a weakening in the sense of the boundedness of the body, expressed in terms of 'barrier' and 'penetration', came about in the course of several kinds of life change. It weakens during pregnancy, but also as a result of sensory deprivation and in schizophrenia. Schizophrenics may largely lose the sense of bodily boundedness. The methodology employed in these studies (at first glance more than a little suspect) threw up a remarkable and puzzling phenomenon. The authors used inkblots as the objects whose boundedness was assessed by their subjects. Why, they asked themselves (pp. 57–8), should boundary reactions to inkblots match (or perhaps better, be indicative of) those of reactions to the integrity of one's own rim of felt embodiment? Somehow one's own body becomes the (metonymic?) source of one's attitudes to the materiality of all else in the universe. This suggestion opens up an important vein of research, not further exploited, to my knowledge. Fisher and Cleveland (1968) themselves went on to tie the sense of embodiment to personality and character – for instance, they reported a correlation between the degree to which one experienced one's own body as strongly bounded (favouring concepts like 'wall' in describing the rim) and what one might roughly call 'strength of character' – metonymy meets metaphor!

The rim is a surface enclosing a volume and a mass (Hartmann and Schilder, 1927). The body surface becomes more determinate when it is touched, and that touch is, for normal people, somewhere on the body surface. Thus touch sketches out the rim of felt embodiment. This is the phenomenon of localization (Head, 1920, quoted in Schilder, 1935). It has also been demonstrated that the sense of body volume is, at any moment, relative to the perceived circumambient space and the determinateness of the boundary as experienced just at that moment. The felt volume of one's body expands in open-extended space and shrinks when one is in a closed and confined space, and when one's boundary is made more determinate by touch.

Head showed that the body percept must be further differentiated into a sense of boundary localization and, independently, a 'body-image', a somewhat misleading term for one's momentary sense of posture. The posture schema includes beliefs about how one's body parts are located with respect to other material things and to one another. Schilder (1935: 124–5) added a further root idea to the concept of 'body-image', namely the momentary state of sensibility of the various body openings – including those for ingesting and excreting physical matter and those taking in energy (ears, eyes, heat receptors) and those giving energy out (larynx and throat). Not only is there the ever-changing tactile-kinaesthetic schema, but there is also an independent optical schema. The various claims for 'independence' in this paragraph are based on massive clinical evidence that one or more of these 'senses' can be disordered while others remain intact in various pathological conditions. For instance, Sandstrom (1951: 182–3) showed that one's sense of how body parts are oriented in space is independent of the degree of their localization.

The sense of one's rim of felt embodiment turns out to be a complex synthetic cluster of independent elements. Are these sensory components? Not in any obvious way. They are clearly concept led and so more like Wittgenstein's 'seeing an aspect' than Russell's 'experiencing a sense datum'. Mosher (1967) reports that prisoners with tattoos, emphasizing the skin as an outer body surface, show a stronger sense of the boundedness of their bodies than those inmates who lack such epidermal decoration.

EXPLORATIONS

One can find out about the observable properties of human bodies, such as their colour, weight, height and so on much as one would find out about the observable properties of other material things. Concerning the discovery of these bodily matters the metaphysical owner and the 'other' are more or less on an equal footing. I tell whether I look pale after a sleepless night in much the same way as I tell whether you do. Concerning sensory reach and the rim of felt embodiment, however, the asymmetry between the metaphysical owner and 'other' is apparently radical. Since the sensory rims of bodies cannot overlap, it might look as though I could never know your feelings, and so perforce would be inclined to treat your body as just another thing. But there is more than one way of knowing.

English is poorly equipped to mark the distinction between knowing intellectually (Spanish *saber*) and knowing in the sense of being acquainted with (Spanish *conocer*). I cannot be acquainted with how matters stand within your bodily rim, yet I can come to know how you are feeling. Wittgenstein drew our attention to the central role played by natural expressions of feeling in making discursive knowledge of the bodily sensations of others possible. The Hintikkas (1986) have called these expressions 'physiognomic' behaviour. Though necessary to the acquisition of a meaningful vocabulary of feeling, physiognomic performances do not open a transparent window into the consciousness of others. Feelings can be faked, and our judgements of the experiences that other people have may be wide of the mark. However, pretending to be suffering can only succeed against a background of what is taken to be reliable knowledge of the real thing, since it must be through public physiognomic expressions and responses that one learns to name, and so to identify and even to individuate, one's own bodily sensations. In the very act of my coming to know about your feelings I must acknowledge your personhood. I must accept you as a being who knows the rim of its body according to the three criteria sketched above. Otherwise, whatever I may think I am doing, I am merely reporting your behaviour.

Do I know some of my bodily feeling through their natural expression? It is only thus, as Wittgenstein points out, that I come to know what these feelings are – that is, where to fit them into some cultural constellation of body experiences. I am inclined to think that some feelings only become determinate in such moments. Yet for all this, we do think – and rightly – that there is a sharp line drawn with bodily feeling on the one side and public displays on the other. Pleasure and pain will occupy my attention again in later chapters.

The rim of felt embodiment involves a static characterization of human corporeality. Only when we reflect on bodies in action does it become clear how important are our bodily powers and capacities in the everyday conception of the corporeality of ourselves and others. In everyday talk we tend to reserve the word 'disposition' for describing someone's personality and character. So I shall eschew the standard philosophical terminology of dispositions for plain English. In knowing bodies we are much concerned with finding out what a person is capable of. I shall refer to human capabilities as 'personal powers'. By consideration of its powers, a human body can be thought of as a prosthetic device which someone can use for practical purposes. The metaphysical owner exercises a natural right over such utilizations.

Just another prosthetic device? Is it accidental that people usually play tennis with their bodies equipped only with a tennis racket? Could I enjoy a wine tasting or win a prize at it if I brought along my portable chromotography equipment? That it is my body that I use somehow ensures not only that I have the sensory experiences proper to the occasion, but that I earn the merits or demerits for the quality of my performance. We could stage a robot Wimbledon, but then the players would be judged on how well they managed their machines (as we now judge them on how well they manage their tennis rackets) and we would, as in Grand Prix motor racing, try to ensure that the robots were in all relevant respects identical.

The powers, capacities and liabilities of human bodies are importantly distinguished by whether they are controllable and to what degree. Techniques of extending the domain of such control or of loosening it (say with alcohol) have, for millennia, been part of all human cultures. A rough three-way polarity can be constructed. At one pole are instrumental powers, such as physical strength, which are more or less under the control of the metaphysical owner of the body to which they belong. That that control is never absolute is recorded in such commonplace remarks as 'He doesn't know his own strength.' At the second pole are a cluster of various cases, including manipulable, but finally uncontrollable, capacities such as sneezing or orgasm. At the third pole are liabilities – almost wholly uncontrollable bodily tendencies such as indigestion or the growth of a cancer. In a diagrammatic form we have a scheme like this:

$$\text{controllable powers} <\begin{array}{l} \text{manipulable capacities} \\ | \\ \text{uncontrollable liabilities} \end{array}$$

Technologies of body-self management aim at reducing the two right-hand poles to that on the left. We shall have occasion to revisit this conceptual scheme in studying the aesthetics of bodily function (health and illness) and of bodily form (cults of body building).

In this introductory survey we have frequently come across limitations on the freedom of exploration of bodies. Getting to know about a human body involves examining and exploring it, manipulating it and getting it to react to tests of its powers and capacities. I can look for your scars and test your strength by arm-wrestling with you. How are limitations drawn? May I look in your mouth? Test your pupillary reflexes or open up your abdomen? Put you on an exercise bike or put my hand between your legs? The moment the latter group of questions is put, the issue of rights and permissions to undertake examinations, explorations and tests of your body and its capacities becomes only too obvious. Dentists, surgeons, coaches and tailors can do the things they do because the metaphysical owner has conceded a right of body access by entering into a specific relation with the person so licensed. Medical examinations of conscripts is a somewhat more complex case, since the state presumes an overarching right to ascertain the bodily condition of its citizens. We shall return to this issue in considering the medical profession's powers over the bodies of persons other than their own in discussing matters of health and illness.

Plainly there are limits on interpersonal access to bodies and hence on what may be known by exercising rights of access. I shall at least start with the assumption that a person, as the metaphysical owner of their body, has unlimited rights of access to any knowledge of it that may have been acquired by others. The assumption too will have to be re-examined in the discussion of medical practices.

To see the source of the limitation on access and the roots of the moral protection of bodily privacy, we can compare the human case with that of access to animal bodies. So far as I can tell, animals have no grounded bodily privacy whatever, subject to constraints on manipulations that are ruled out on grounds of cruelty. Animal-rights activists, have never, to my knowledge, argued for a general animal right of bodily privacy, only for an animal's right to be protected from suffering. Much the same goes for the bodily privacy of children, with manipulation being further limited to protect children from sexual interference. Where does the adult human right to bodily privacy come from? The short answer must be that it derives from the fact that living and healthy human bodies embody persons. In so far as persons have rights of privacy, their bodies fall within the sphere of what is intrinsically protected from prying eyes and probing hands. The boundary of what I know of and about someone else's body is determined by a combination of local constraining custom and law, suspension of which can sometimes be obtained by the giving of specific personal permission.

In most cultures there are limitations on looking. In traditional Islam a man may not see the faces of women outside his family circle. In our culture women may object to men looking too pointedly at their bodies. 'Undressing her in public' is an offence of the eyes. In all cultures, so far as I know, there are severe restrictions on how much of someone else's body one can look at or explore by touch. All of these boundaries may be dismantled for some specific purpose, usually with the permission of the person whose body is to be scrutinized. Such permission is usually sought by people with some special relationship to the person whose body is to be explored or given to someone with a professional skill that cannot be put to use without the exploration. Custom may lead to some surprising limitations on knowing. For instance, in the nineteenth century a curious custom of bodily concealment spread throughout the English middle class, so that even married couples did not see one another's bodies.

OWNERSHIP

In the light of these observations we can turn again to the question of how far our bodies differ from other precious possessions. Anything one owns is surely morally and legally protected from prying eyes and exploring fingers. I am not permitted to fossick around in your pockets, read your correspondence, stroll into your house, disport myself on your lawn or ride your bike without your express permission. By entering into a particular social relation with me you can concede some of these rights of access to me, just as you can in the case of your body. Is metaphysical ownership then really no different from legal ownership? Is a person's body then only one amongst their items of privileged private property?

There is another aspect of ownership, apart from the moral protection it affords, already introduced into the discussion, which can help to bring out a difference between ownership of bodies and of things. It is the matter of the individuating criteria of personhood. As the metaphysical owner of my body, my personhood is partly created by the individuating powers of that body's thing-like status. Without just *that* body I wouldn't be me. It is not that I might be someone else. I would not be at all. The same is not true of any of my other material possessions. Deprivation of them might be painful. It might cut deeply into my self-image. But it could hardly be fatal to my personhood. That kind of ownership, which I have called 'legal ownership', is never individuating. To be picked out as 'the one who owns all those vintage cars (that house)', I must already be someone, embodied thus and so.

Yet another argument for distinguishing the human body from things can be developed from the fact of embodied skill. There are many kinds of practical knowledge that cannot be expressed verbally by those who have it. The claims for such people to be in possession of practical knowledge can be certified only in what they do. Practical knowledge can be shown, but it cannot usually be expressed in words. It is learned by practice and it is improved by trial and error. We could say that practical knowledge is *in* the bodies of those who possess it. I owe to Albert Moseley the idea of using this commonplace observation as the basis of an argument for the proposition that human beings are not things. Things are not skilled, no matter how 'cleverly' they perform as gadgets. This remark is not a report of a study project in which several different kinds of thing were examined and all found to lack skills. It is a comment on the grammar of the concept of 'skill'. Only people can be said to be skilful or unskilful, competent or incompetent, knowledgeable about how to carry out a manual task or ignorant of the necessary know-how. Skills belong to members of the species *Homo sapiens*.

To fill out these remarks into an argument, the conceptual link that ties personhood to skill needs to be uncovered. The distinctiveness of human bodies is rooted in the fact that it is persons who are so embodied. Since the skills that our bodies have are just those the executive principles of which we are not aware of, the link we are looking for cannot be through the conceptual relation between personhood and consciousness. However, the concept of 'person' involves another root idea of equal criterial depth – namely, agency. Only agents have those executive powers that we can call bodily skills. The weaver bird can make nests, but so far as we know, this activity is not monitored or managed in the way that the work done by a skilled lacemaker of Bruges is monitored and managed. Such a claim would have to be instantiated in detail by looking into how the skill was acquired, how the active user of the skill responds to, and introduces, innovations and so on. While 'knowing that' is conceptually tied to consciousness and the discursive production of propositional knowledge, 'knowing how' is conceptually tied to agency and the manipulative production of skilled performances. To put this another way: as persons, while we may consciously will the end, in many cases the means for the realization of an envisaged or declared end is an embodied skill, which as active agents we merely exercise. 'Now I know how to go on' as Wittgenstein taught, is not a description of some state of mind. An interesting variant on this theme has been proposed by Streets-Johnstone (1981: 400) in the idea of dance improvisations as acts of thinking in their own right. 'In such thinking, movement is not a medium by which thoughts emerge but rather, the thoughts themselves, significations made flesh, so to speak.' She compares two ways in which a person can think actions – '. . . thinking in movement and thoughts of movement are two quite different experiences.'

Many of the distinctions introduced in this chapter will be elaborated and qualified in later sections. My aim has been to establish certain fundamental guidelines that will shape all that follows. At the root of my treatment of bodily matters is the notion of metaphysical ownership. The distinction between persons and their bodies is made in all kinds of ways, but one and all of these ways are conceptual. This is because through the conditions of individuation it is a conceptual relation that unites them. To think of you as a person I must think of you as embodied thus and so, but for certain purposes I can think of your body as a thing, but even when I do so its personhood intrudes in the ways that it is morally protected.

DEATH: TERMINAL CONSEQUENCES OF EMBODIMENT

Bodies are alive or they are dead. Students of medical ethics pursue the question of the appropriate criteria for making a judgement one way or another between these apparently exclusive alternatives. But bodies die as persons' bodies. They do not perish as things in the moment of the death of the impersoned body. Dismemberment, the breaking up of the body as a thing, can be carried to considerable lengths without that body being declared dead. There are limbless people, people without eyes, ears or noses and so on. Provided that they can express themselves in something akin to our way and on matters akin to those we express, there is no ground for abrogating their personhood. Precious things are much more susceptible to radical loss of self-identity, should certain parts by removed. A Type 33 Bugatti without wheels or suspension is a poor thing, scarcely meriting the name of 'car', even by courtesy. Yet it might be able to be restored, even if the new parts are not authentic.

It has recently been revealed that 'dead' bodies are being kept going on 'life'-support systems to provide a bank of nice fresh organs for transplant surgery (*The Times* (London), 20 March 1990). Here is a paradoxical ontological status in which a material entity can be suspended indefinitely in a categorial limbo – neither embodied person nor corpse – but certainly not both person and corpse.

Clearly one's physical being ceases with the termination of just those bodily functions that sustain the physiognomic displays in which our personhood is manifested. One's personal being may have already perished in the disintegration of the sense of identity that is constitutive of it. The agonizing problem for those responsible for the continuance of the vegetative life of the seemingly brain dead concerns the tantalizingly opaque and indeterminate empirical question of whether the *powers* of thought and action that distinguish embodied persons can be recovered or restored. One's physical being consists in just the necessary organic conditions for the actual possession of those powers. But, as I have argued in *Social Being*, one's social existence may persist into a post-mortem future just as it may have pre-existed personal, and even physical, being in a pre-partum past. It is only as a social being that one necessarily attends one's own funeral.

In a universe in which dispositions and powers are the basic particulars, the distinction between a person and a corpse is ontological. A corpse is a different kind of thing from a person's body, even though to be a corpse, a material thing must have once been a body. Corpses are morally protected, but only as the seats of former persons. By disinterring and hanging his corpse, the triumphant royalists heaped retrospective humiliation on Oliver Cromwell. When Churchill's body was borne in a gun carriage, the man was honoured. The thing that is a corpse had in both cases been subjected to manipulation and interference that would have been unthinkable in life. The termination of some aspects of the moral protection of bodies arrives with the death of the person. The body at the funeral, whether subject to execration or praise, exists there as a kind of 'figure of speech'. It is metonymic of the person it once, as a living being, embodied.

The biological fact of organic death, bodily decay and personal senescence can hardly be totally ignored by human beings. Like every other aspect of our embodiment, death enters life through an interpretation. Interpretations draw on the available cultural resources or occasionally transform them. The interpretation and management of the fact of death is a topic of such magnitude that I can touch on only two aspects that are germane to my studies of the ways of lived embodiment. The body enters into our conception of ourselves not only as the root of individual and personal being, but also as a support of whose vulnerability we are occasionally dramatically reminded. Yet at the same time most people have considerable confidence in the robustness and durability of their bodies. They treat them with scant respect and subject them to considerable abuse. And yet they survive. The body resists the forces ranged against it. With careful cultivation, that resistance can be greatly strengthened, many people now believe. Adherents of health cults are at least partly concerned with the postponement of death. Paradoxically, though, for most people death is both feared and ignored. The second aspect of modern dying I want to touch upon is its transformation from a social event to a scientific-technical problem.

Occasionally the vulnerability of one's body is brought home to one. A near-fatal accident in the fragile hull of an aircraft is a modern *memento mori*. To what is the fear of death directed in modern dying? Of what are the people in the endangered plane afraid? Traditional fears of posthumous judgement have been depicted often enough, but perhaps among the best portrayals is that by Mozart in *Don Giovanni*. Some of these fears linger on, no doubt, but they seem to play next to no role in most people's ways of living and dying. If it is not one's fate in the afterlife that terrifies one, what is it? There remain several possibilities for alarm. One's personal future is an unknown and dark abyss. The very process of dying is an awful prospect. One fears the extinction of one's very personhood. For most people with whom I have talked about this rarely discussed subject it is the second of the possibilities that looms largest. To both of the others they tend to be fatalistically resigned. Unlike the followers of the traditional Christian way of living, modern people seem to have little sense of the possibility of working now to ensure a future state of bliss, or at least so to act now as to stave off the worst fate. At most, people seem to work for a post-mortem future in the thoughts and memories of others. I think

1.   A Victorian death bed scene.
(Reproduced by kind permission of The Mansell Collection, London.)

that we know very little about the structure of the modern resignation in the face of the fact of death. Sometimes people explain their attitude as follows: either one survives as a personal being or one does not. If the future holds only the second alternative one will not be there to regret missing out on immortality. So fear of being dead is quite pointless. Of course there remains the fear of dying, for which this argument offers no palliative.

In the now classic study of modern dying Glaser and Strauss (1964) drew attention to the moral enormities of dying according to the principles of a scientific-technical moral order. The contrast with older ways of managing the last days of a human life was only too stark

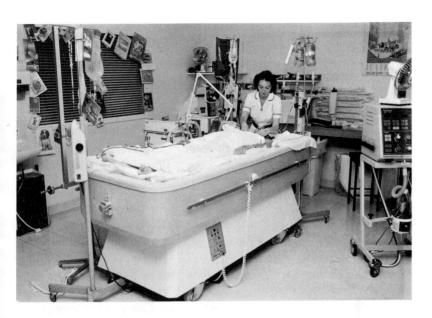

2. High-tec body support.
(Reproduced by kind permission of The John Radcliffe Hospital, Oxford.)

(Enright, 1987). The accompanying illustrations (plates 1 and 2) make the point far better than it can be put in words. In the traditional forms the value of the embodied person is the dominating theme of the management of dying. In the modern way the fate of the organic machinery overarches all else. However, Glaser and Strauss did show how the people themselves co-operated in a desperate attempt to make something of value in the last moments of each of the dying. There are some gleams of light in a dark prospect, namely the hospice movement. But it still remains as difficult to arrange to die at home in the bosom of one's family and in the presence of one's friends as it is to be born there.

THE BODY IN TIME

Spatial aspects of the materiality of the body have been central to the analysis so far. Only simple duration among various temporal aspects of materiality has been assumed in relating the ontology of our mode of embodiment to the metaphyics of personhood. A great part of what it is to be just this person is to be embodied as just this material thing.

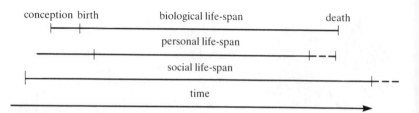

Individuation and continuous self-identity as spatially unique beings are generic properties of a huge variety of solid, bounded material bodies. Had the human mode of embodiment been liquid or gaseous or somehow in pulses of energy (as in Strawson's auditory world), persons would not have been individuals in the robust sense that characterizes our form of life. Neither rain drops nor electrons can merge with a crowd of fellow citizens and come out as numerically self-identical. Considered with respect to endurance, to the possibility of re-identification as the same beings, drops and pulses are more weakly individuated than are people as we know them. But considered with respect to the durability of diamonds, human individuality can seem fragile and ephemeral. The sense of durability we may have of our lives in time depends on the kind of beings with which we compare our life-spans. This has long been the basis of a literary device through which we can be called to reflect on the fragility of human life. It is an ancient tradition:

> ...for the breath in our nostrils is as smoke, and a little spark in the moving of our heart: which being extinguished, our body shall be turned to ashes, and our spirit shall vanish as the soft air...and our life shall pass away as the trace of a cloud, and shall be dispersed as a mist, that is driven away with the beams of the sun, and overcome with the heat thereof. (Wisdom of Solomon 2: 1–5)

Our bodies endure, but as material beings that mature, persist for a while and then decay. Our mode of embodiment imposes a life-span on all of us. By the same token, for humanity to endure, the finite life-span of individuals must necessarily be complemented by the re-production of new people to take the place of the old. Sex and death are internally related to one another. When the Ik despaired and gave themselves over to the conviction that they must vanish as a people, sexual activity and the search for food ceased together (Turnbull, 1984).

The temporal span of lives and of persons are knitted into a complex weave of three interrelated strands. There is a biological life course, a social life course and a personal life course for every human being, each with its own beginning and end. The temporal correlation between these strands can be seen in figure 1.1. I have discussed the human social life-span in *Social Being* (1979: Part IV) and the human personal life-span in *Personal Being* (1983: Part III). A person's social identity may well begin before their bodily identity has taken shape in the parental definition of the child to come. And it may persist long after bodily identity has perished by the dissolution of death and decay of the body in funereal celebrations and, in some cases, in enduring monuments. But these too, however massive and adamantine, have a finite life-span. Ozymandias' vast memorial was but a heap of rubble when Shelley imagined its deserted remains. One's personal identity fits within the time frame of one's bodily or physical being. One's sense of oneself, compounded of spatio-temporal point of view and reflective consciousness, begins in late infancy and often ends in the chaos of senility, sometimes well before the dissolution of organic unity. As a physical being, one's conception and often one's death lie outside the span of reflexive and reflective self-knowledge. The body's life course is, one might say, relative to the main acts of the drama of a life as it is lived, merely 'noises off'. Paradoxically, though conception and death are absolutes in the human time frame, they are external to our sense of ourselves and stand outside both social and personal being. To most people who have reflected on these matters they seem to be imposed, even cruelly imposed, from outside on an essentially timeless consciousness. There seems to be nothing necessary about the inevitable cessation of personal experience and social identity, nothing that flows inexorably from the very forms of those experiences themselves. Only considered with respect to physical being, defined with respect to the exigencies of earth-bound biology, does the concept of life include that of death.

The temporality of the body also enters into our social and personal lives in quite another way. It appears as cycles and rhythms, driven by biological clocks known to us only in their effects. Daily, monthly and annual cycles appear to us as hunger, depression, lust, elation and so on. Biological science reveals tidal flows of hormones, fluxes and refluxes of blood sugars and metallic ions, the extraordinary effect of very bright light on the setting of biological 'clocks' and so on. Light therapy can work wonders with those who become depressed as the seasonal changes of winter come on. There are several excellent summaries of the biology of organic cycles, for instance that of Hughes (1989). But from the point of view of this study the salient issue is the way that meanings are drawn from the social and personal environment through which the bodily feelings brought about by the cyclical changes in body states are made sense of. A most striking example is the way that women draw on their immediate social situation and immediate personal predicaments and troubles to give meanings to feelings of premenstrual tension. Anger with people and resentment at situations arise through misplaced assignments of causality. Hunger and other feelings arising from bodily deprivations can also be interpreted with respect to social and personal environments. Feelings of mysterious origin can find external interpretations in influences from the extra-mundane realms of gods. Rhythms and cycles of the body exhibit the characteristic features of all corporeal psychology. Meanings must be found in the social and personal relations of the human *Umwelt*. Only in that way can bodily states of any kind find their way into the ordinary life worlds. Corporeal personhood is then bounded in space, enduring in time and sequential in its rhythms.

REFERENCES

Brown, P. 1988: *The Body and Society*. New York: Columbia University Press.

Claparède, E. 1924: Note sur la localisation du Moi. *Archives Psychologiques de Genève*, 19, 174.

Enright, D. J. (ed.) 1987: *The Oxford Book of Death* (pp. 43–81). Oxford: Oxford University Press.

Fisher, S., and Cleveland, S. E. 1968: *Body Image and Personality*. New York: Dover.

Gibson, J. J. 1979: *The Ecological Approach to Visual Perception*. Boston: Houghton Mifflin.

Glaser, B. G., and Strauss, A. L. 1964: *Awareness of Dying*. Chicago: Aldine.

Goffman, E. 1961: *Encounters*. New York: Bobbs Merrill.

Harré, R. 1979: *Social Being*. Oxford: Basil Blackwell.

Harré, R. 1983: *Personal Being*. Oxford: Basil Blackwell.

Hartmann, H., and Schilder, P. 1927: Korperinneres und Korperschema. *Zeitschrift ges. Neurol. Psychiat.*, 109, 666–75.

Head, H. 1920: *Studies in Neurology*. Quoted in P. Schilder (1935), *The Image and Appearance of the Human Body* (pp. 12–13). New York: International Universities Press.

Hintikka, J., and Hintikka, M. 1986: *Investigating Wittgenstein*. Oxford: Basil Blackwell.

Hughes, M. 1989: *Body Clock* (popular account of biological rhythms). London: Weidenfeld and Nicholson.

Merleau-Ponty, M. 1962: *The Phenomenology of Perception*, London: Routledge and Kegan Paul.

Mosher, D. L., et al. 1967: Body Images in Tattooed Prisoners. *Journal of Clinical Psychology*, 23, 31–2.

Sandstrom, C. I. 1951: *Orientation in the Present Space*. Uppsala: Almqvist and Wiksell.[1]

Schilder, P. 1935: *The Image and Appearance of the Human Body*. London: Kegan Paul (American edn New York: International Universities Press).

Streets-Johnstone, M. 1981: Thinking in Movement. *Journal of Aesthetics and Art Criticism*, 39 (4), 399–407.

Strawson, P. F. 1959: *Individuals*. London: Methuen.

Turnbull, C. 1984: *The Mountain People*: Paladin.

Turner, B. S. 1984: *The Body and Society*: Oxford: Blackwell.

Witkin, H. A., et al. 1962: *Psychological Differentiation*. New York: J. Wiley.

---

[1] I am particularly grateful to Douglas Bennett for this and several other helpful references.

CHAPTER 2

BODY KINDS I: CATEGORIES AND CHARACTERS

And the Lord God caused a deep sleep to fall upon Adam, and he slept: and he took one of his ribs, and closed up the flesh instead thereof; and the rib, which God had taken from the man made he a woman, and brought her to the man. And Adam said, This is now bone of my bones, and flesh of my flesh: she shall be called Woman because she was taken out of Man.

Genesis 2: 21–3

Sex: the fundamental distinction found in most species of animals and plants, based on the type of gametes produced by the individual or the category into which the individual fits on the basis of that criterion.

Dorland's Medical Dictionary, 27th edition

INTRODUCTION: PHILOSOPHICAL FOUNDATIONS FOR THE PRACTICE OF CATEGORIZING

In this chapter I shall begin an investigation of the ways we categorize people, including ourselves, according to the kind of body we take them to have. These categorizations will prove to be fateful, having an enormous influence on how we can live our lives. Every society of which we know anything has categorized people as men and women. Based on the biological sex of the body, the distinctions of gender are loaded with practical and moral implications. I shall call this loading a 'social construction'. I shall be exploring the ways in which the categories of gender, 'man' and 'woman', are socially constructed on the basis of the identification of bodies as 'male' and 'female', the biological distinctions of sex.

But first some analytical tools must be prepared. It is important to be clear about the philosophical foundations of the practice of categorizing generally. A heap of stones can be sorted into kinds in all sorts of ways. A builder might separate those of regular shape from the irregular, and then divide the former into round and square. An explanation of this choice of categories could be sought in the practical uses to which the stones will be put. The builder's classification depends on a particular human interest. Another builder, animated by a different interest and engaged in a different project, might have sorted them by colour. From the point of view of geology, the categories used by the builders are arbitrary.

Geologists would divide the pile of stones up in other ways. A mineralogist might use categories like 'schist' and 'granite', or perhaps 'igneous' and 'sedimentary'. The choice of mineralogical stone categories can be justified by reference of something other than the apparent properties of the stones. It might be by reference to chemical composition or it might be by reference to the way the materials of the stones were formed. The categories of geological classifications are rooted in natural differences, not in human practical interests. They are 'natural kinds'.

Our understanding of the logical structure of classificatory schemes harks back to the ancient distinction between real and nominal essences. To merit selection as shale, and so to be properly named as such, a specimen of rock must have certain observable characteristics. Together these properties constitute the nominal essence of shale, and are put to use in practical contexts. However, unless the sample could also be shown to have a certain chemical composition, it would not count as genuine shale. Its chemical composition is something like the real essence of a certain geological kind. Chemical composition is cited in theoretical contexts, for example to explain why the characteristics that make up the nominal essence are always found together. Locke thought that we could never know the real essences of material things since, he supposed, we would never be able to observe their atomic structure. But in this regard chemistry, largely through developing indirect ways of finding out about the inner constitutions of material stuffs, has triumphed over philosophy.

What is meant by the 'social construction' of a category distinction? Social order requires and incorporates means for the reproduction of certain practices, ways of doing things, in which members of a culture systematically and persistently treat each other, in one way or another, as different. In a sense all differences between persons are socially constructed, in that to treat variants in some natural property of body, character or talent as worthy of attention is rarely a spontaneous reaction to the appearance and actions of others. The thesis of social constructionism is meant to place particular emphasis on those distinctions among people that, whether they emerge from natural endowments or not, are loaded with non-biological significance. Such distinctions might be a matter of differences in moral expectations, differential restrictions on social advancement, special role requirements based on body-kind and so on.

Socially constructed differences between people are usually expressed symbolically and registered in language. The biological attributes that serve as a basis on which a social distinction is raised may themselves become the signifiers of social difference. More often than not, socially constructed differences are the topic of clusters of beliefs that people entertain both about themselves and about others. Since beliefs are simply persistent dispositions to act and speak in certain ways, to add 'belief' to the concepts of 'practice' and 'language' is rhetorically convenient, but actually pleonastic. To say that one believes oneself to belong to a certain human category is to say that one routinely adopts certain practices and that one regularly talks about oneself in certain distinctive ways.

Corporeal attributes such as height, skin colour, plumpness, body form, muscular strength and so on show great variability in any human population. However, the ways we talk about, address and judge each other exhibit a characteristic corporeal bipolarity. People are said to be either fat or thin, tall or short, white or black, men or women, children or adults. Differences that shade into one another are sharpened into all-or-nothing criteria for the assignment of people to kinds, unambiguously if possible. Let us call this a 'discursive practice', since it is more fateful than just any casual way of talking. All sorts of social arrangements are built around bipolarities, for instance whether one can see a film, who plays whom at Wimbledon and so on, through a myriad of instances. Above all, the poles of these constructed oppositions tend to become evaluatively loaded in very complicated ways.

There have been two main responses to the social and moral entrenchment of such bipolar oppositions. People, embodied in a discredited or lowly kind of bodily frame, seek, sometimes desperately, to change their bodily attributes to those of one of the more socially favoured kinds. (It is instructive to realize how far back in European history one can find recipes for blonding hair: e.g., della Porta, 1560.) Fat people want to become thin, hunchbacks want to become straight, skinny people want to develop a massive musculature and so on. These are not treated as mere accidental attributes. They are taken to be definitive of contrasting kinds – the obese and the anorexic, the ugly and the beautiful, the weak and the powerful. As soon as we move to the use of kind terms the evaluative aspect is disclosed. The urge to change hardly needs explanation. However, which direction of change is taken to lead to an improvement is amongst the many aspects of body thought I shall be trying to account for. The other response is to attack the relevant polar opposition. One can resist the evaluative loadings of the pair of complementary categories while leaving the opposition in place. More radically one can set about 'deconstructing' the distinction, for instance by showing how the bipolarity is produced out of mere tendencies. In this chapter I shall look first at the matter of the evaluations and then attempt to deconstruct one of the alleged bipolar categorical oppositions.

TRANSFORMABLE AND NON-TRANSFORMABLE KINDS

Is a person well endowed with fat admirable or pitiable, good-looking or ugly? The way value is loaded on to the corporeal distinction 'fat'/'thin' has changed, even quite recently. It also depends on whether the person is male or female, young or old. Cutting across the evaluational loading of these and a myriad other bodily distinctions is the question of whether the kind distinction in question can be remedied by human effort. Can a fat person become thin? Can a short person become tall? Can a man become a woman? Some kind differences seem to be non-transformable, others clearly can be managed. A first rough classification will give us male/female, dwarf/normal, young/old as normally non-transformable kinds, with fat/thin, slobbish/athletic, grubby/well groomed as normally transformable body-kinds. The qualification 'normal' is needed here not just because of cultural differences in the extent to which these kinds are seen as evaluatively loaded, but also because of the differential access people may have to the technology of change, even when it does exist. One should notice that however superficial, and even artefactual, is the favoured member of one of these pairs, it frequently appears in one guise or another as a kind term.

Techniques abound for achieving bodily transformations towards the currently favoured pole. Some of these will be discussed in detail in the sections on the concept of the body in aesthetic and semiotic contexts. There are commonplace revisions such as circumcision, but there are also such exotica as hypervagination and breast enhancement. At this point in the argument it is enough to point to the continuous development and refinement of methods for bringing about transformations, even in what are apparently the most entrenched body kinds (see Schwartz, 1986, for a survey of the fads and fancies of the last one hundred years). For instance, we have had sex-change techniques developing from the cross dressing practised by transvestites to the sophisticated surgical and hormonal treatments used in contemporary sex-reassignment surgery. But more about that later. Platform soles elevate the short, while sectioning the leg bones has been tried to shrink the overly tall. At present it may be only the polarity between dwarfs and normals that remains wholly intransigent (though I am told that if the abnormality is detected at the foetal stage, hormone-replacement therapy can be effective, operating not on the actual body-kind, but on the kind in potentia). Youth and age, at least as body appearances, have long since become transformable with diet, exercise, clothing, and now with hormone-replacement patches which, adhering to the skin, feed in the required doses of an elixir of life.

ARE 'MAN' AND 'WOMAN' NATURAL KINDS?

Is the distinction 'man'/'woman' anything like the chemical distinction 'acid'/'alkali'? Acids and alkalis are distinguishable not only by reference to their observable behaviour, but also in chemical theory. They differ in atomic architecture or real essence – the outermost shell of electrons having only one member in acids and seven in alkalis. Is there a real essence to manhood and womanhood that grounds the use of genital or primary sexual characteristics as signifiers for dividing people into fundamental kinds for general purposes? The discovery of the genetic mechanism by which the sexual characteristics of human beings are determined might lead one to suppose that in the distinction between XX and XY chromosomes there is a perfect analogue of the distinction between the one outer electron and seven outer electrons that grounds the acid/alkali distinction in a well-defined real essence.

A way of telling how far a distinction is natural, and the criteria for it organized around something like the difference between nominal and real essence, is to see what considerations are advanced to resolve anomalous cases, beings which, on the face of it, fit neatly into neither category. Does sex-reassignment surgery bring about a change in body-kind? Ronald Richards became Renée Richards and James Morris is now Jan Morris. Were these cases of change of body-kind? The two are instructively different. Richards used 'her' body (with its pre-given musculature, acquired when 'she' was a man) for competitive tennis. Women players protested against 'her' appearance in tournaments in the women's division. According to the protesters, Richards had a man's body, despite the surgical mimicry of female genitals. Male muscles confer an advantage in tennis. This was a categorization by something like nominal essence. I have been unable to find any evidence that women journalists or travel writers protested against Jan Morris working in their professions. A male brain, if there is such a thing, does not confer any advantage in intellectual pursuits. In both cases the social location of anomalous individuals is determined by nominal essence alone.

However, there are human beings who are genitally female, but with the musculature of human males. Are they to count as women? If the Richards case is to serve as a precedent, the matter is disputable. Should the brawny Russian contestants in the women's field events be barred from the Olympic Games? The solution that has been universally adopted in athletics is philosophically instructive. Contestants are classified into genders by real essence of sex. Chromosomes are what count, no matter what are the secondary sexual characteristics. Chromosomal endowment works for athletes much as atomic architecture works for acids and alkalis.

But there are further complications. People presenting themselves for sex-reassignment surgery often claim to have really been a man or a woman all along, despite being embodied as a member of the opposite sex. In some sex-reassignment clinics an attempt of sorts has been made to fill out this idea biologically (Garfinkel, 1967). Between chromosal endowment and somatic constitution lies a world of endocrine chemistry, the hormones. These are characteristically distributed according to sex. Are they responsible for gender? Do they make males into men and females into women? In the case reported by Garfinkel Agnes's claim to be really a girl was supported by proof (faked in his/her case) of a hormone profile typical of a human female. Since these chemical messengers are largely responsible for secondary sexual characteristics, such as mammary development, distribution of body hair and so on, their implication in the nominal essences of the sexes is obvious. If female hormones in a male body can make room for doubt as to which gender a person really is, then biological determinism has overtaken social construction as the dominant process in the differentiation of people by gender. To restore the hegemony of the constructionist thesis much more analysis is required. First, however, I need to develop the power of the nominal/real essence distinction to include tertiary sex differences.

Male and female bodies differ in two ways. Sexual dimorphism of the genital organs is sharply defined. In popular conceptions of maleness and femaleness the secondary sexual characteristics, such as skeletal form, distribution of body fat and so on are equally 'dimporhic'. Since the genitals are usually hidden, secondary characteristics take on an emblematic or symbolic role by which a person's sex is displayed. The emblematic role for category assignment played by overall body shape, for instance, is possible only if central cases of a very variable characteristic are taken as typical. A certain size and shape of bosom and of the orientation of the limbs defines the womanly figure. Since 'rightness' of bodily being is defined with respect to central cases, they are subject to deliberate manipulation and control by those on the 'wrong' side of the inevitable variations. Both breast reduction and breast-enhancement surgery are on offer for women, while men can have the loose skin of an ageing belly nicely tucked up. I shall return to a closer study of the process by which such norms are created in the next section.

In true human fashion Ossa is piled on Pelion, and in all societies of which we have any knowledge tertiary sexual markers have been added to those distinguishing characteristics that, with a little help, nature has provided. Men and women adopt different hair styles and dress in different garments. The differences may be extreme, as in the Victorian distinctions between the wearers of trousers and the wearers of skirts. Or it may be subtle, as in the differences in cut and colour of the ubiquitous *shalwa* and *kemis* of Islamic tradition. Many people have succeeded in living as a member of the 'opposite' sex merely by cross dressing. Since the real sex of a human being is defined on the basis of hidden differences in body form and equipment, an illusion of sexual category is easily created by the use of emblematic clothing and the appropriate hair style.

Conceptual clarity in these matters can be assisted by thinking in terms of a double application of the overt-nominal/covert-real essence distinction. Chromosomal difference serves as the real essence of the distinction in sex, the overt manifestation of which in complementary, and in principle visible, genitals is thus nominal. But since the genitals are usually hidden, their differences serve as the real essence of the public manifestation of sex differences, whether in tidied-up secondary characteristics or in manufactured tertiary. The possession of male organs is so uniformaly correlated with the wearing of coat and trousers, short haircuts, an interest in guns and the ability to mend fuses, but a hopeless incapacity for changing babies' nappies, that these tertiary characteristics denote one's sexual category for all practical purposes. The irony is intentional. An equally diverse catalogue could be provided for the female of the species. Why are the socially contrived tertiary characteristics apparently so well correlated with biologically determined primary ones? Is it because, in subtle ways, the tertiary are also biologically determined?

But there are further complications in linking body-kind as nominal essence to a biological real essence through primary – that is, genital –

differences between embodied persons. There are the recently discovered envelope-and-core anomalies, as I shall call them, which must be accommodated in any scheme. It turns out that the primary sex-distinguishing attributes are controlled by two sets of genes, whose activity is normally nicely synchronized. It can happen that while the 'core' of a human body is one sex, the 'envelope' has not developed the sex characteristics to match it. The commonest pattern is a male core within a female envelope. Some cases have been reported in which only the accident of exploratory surgery has revealed a male interior anatomy mismatched to female external genitalia. Most surprising of all is a genetic anomaly discovered in a small Caribbean island. All the members of a certain lineage are born as girls, in so far as external signs of sex are concerned. Half of these children develop external male organs at puberty, turning into functionally perfect males, as they would have done at a very early stage in the course of a normal maturation. All the children are brought up as girls, since the parents have no way of telling which ones will undergo metamorphosis at the critical age. This lineage offers us a living laboratory for testing certain feminist theories about the cultural sources of feminine stereotypes in style of living. As far as I know, no detailed social-psychological studies of these people have been undertaken to explore such matters. However, from the point of view of the analysis, introducing concepts of potentiality into the kinds story has some disturbing consequences. 'Body-kind' begins to look rather less well defined than the usual ways of commonsense thinking would have it.

To sum up: the model of nominal (overt) and real (covert) essence taken from the philosophy of chemical kinds can be applied to sex differences, provided that we are ready to deal *ad hoc* with the complexity of the double application of the overt/covert (displayed/hidden) distinction. 'Male' and 'female' do seem to be body-kinds. But does the same hold true for 'masculine' and 'feminine.'

MAPPINGS: THE CASE FOR INTERPRETING GENDER AS A SOCIAL CONSTRUCTION

To take the discussion far enough to try to answer the question with which I ended the last section, a new distinction is needed. Let us use the words 'male' and 'female' for strict biologically defined difference in sex, and the words 'masculine' and 'feminine' for the psychological and social distinction of gender. The question above can now be rephrased. Is gender determined by sex? It has been argued that not only are the differences in gender socially defined, but they are also

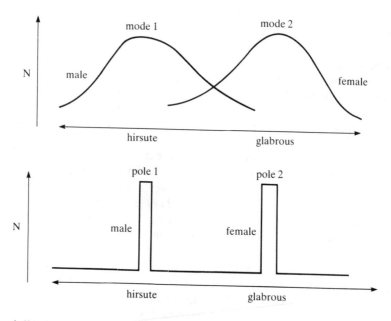

socially determined. Gender is a social construction. People embodied as females are expected to be sweet and neat, kind and good at nursing – that is, to be feminine, while those embodied as males are expected to be rough and tough and good at fighting – that is, to be masculine. I shall call the realization of such a set of expectations a 'mapping' between sex and gender. The matter is complicated because of the role that secondary and tertiary sexual characteristics play in the gender distinction. Husky, bearded hulks are 'obviously' rough and tough, while dainty, peach-complexioned beauties are 'obviously' sweet and neat. We shall encounter more than one mapping. The tidy fit of masculine- and feminine-people categories to male and female body-kinds is the traditional mapping. Most people at most epochs and in most cultures have taken something like the traditional mapping to be natural, and even divinely ordered.

At birth human infants are only rarely of ambiguous sex. Only about one in 54,000 children is of indeterminate sex. Male and female are therefore clearly bipolar categories. A person is either one or the other, and almost no one is in between. In the traditional mapping the social and cultural norms of gender take on a matching bipolar and exclusive dichotomy.

The first point to notice is that between gender, which is largely tertiary, and sex, which is primary, lies the important range of secondary sexual characteristics. Most secondary characteristics such as body form (womanly hour glass or manly inverted triangle), distribution of body hair, height, distribution of body fat and so on are not bipolar. They are bimodal. That is, while the majority of female human beings are less hirsute than the majority of males, there are some females who are hairier than some men and some males are more glabrous than some females. Graphically these distributions appear as in figure 2.1. In a bipolar distribution assignment to sex/gender on any secondary variable is sharp and dichotomous (see figure 2.2). Unmodified by cultural norms, it is true to say that all secondary characteristics are bimodal. Since secondary sexual characteristics are serving as emblematic nominal essences (Perper, 1985) for the primary, it is easy to see how a mapping of secondary on the primary is necessary. Ambiguities in secondary characteristics should be remedied to conform to a the strict bipolarity of primary sex. The bodies of men and women should be polarized in all their characteristics. They should appear as such even in messages to extra-galactic civilizations (plate 3). A socially enforced technology of stays, padded brassières, hair pieces, padded shoulders, built-up heels, lady shavers, depilatories and so on is made available to remedy the biologically given bimodality of secondary sexual characteristics. Tertiary characteristics, prime candidates for an iconography of bipolar primary sexuality, such as styles of clothing, can be made bipolar from their moment of introduction, since they are artefacts.

But what of character, personality, intellectual and practical capacity and talent? Should it too be polarized to fit neatly onto the polarity of sexually defined body-kinds? The mappings between primary and secondary have in fact been repeated in almost all aspects of life. People are assigned to polarized ways of being, to the masculine or the feminine gender. Embodiment is socially fateful.

Men and women have been found to judge other people's actions and to assess their own conduct according to very different styles of reasoning. Carol Gilligan (1982) showed that at least some men tend to adopt a form of self-definition that lays 'out across the coordinates of time and space a hierarchical order in which to define one's place, describing himself as distinct by locating his particular position in the world' (p. 35). But a woman 'counterposes an ideal of care, against which she measures the worth of her activity' (ibid.). Feminine actions are made determinate within a framework of obligations and duties that serve to nourish and sustain a network of concrete social relationships, which often tend to take precedence over abstract moral principles.

The obviously pejorative implications of terms for those who have made various cross-mappings illustrate the social force with which

3. Cosmic messenger body images.
(Reproduced by kind permission of NASA.)

conformity to traditional patterns of behaviour is exacted. If a person embodied as a female adopts some of the characterological attributes as tertiary markers of manood, she is a 'tomboy', 'mannish' or 'butch'. If anyone embodied as a male takes on any of the characteristics of femininity, he is 'effeminate' or a 'pansy'. However contingent the traditional mapping may appear in thought and in the political prospectus of feminism, it tends to be sharply defined and firmly maintained in everyday life.

Challenges to the seeming inevitability and apparent 'naturalness' of the traditional mappings have come from two quarters. Feminists have argued that when women are released from social bondage, whether they have abandoned the traditional feminine virtues or no, they can do anything that had previously been reserved for men on grounds of their masculinity. Therefore distinctively feminine behaviour, capacities and achievements are nothing but the results of a socially driven imposition of conventions on an essentially common humanity.

The assumption that the traditional mapping from polarized bodies to polarized social and intellectual characteristics is natural has also been queried by developmental psychologists (Lloyd and Duveen, 1990). They have suggested that infants are taught to be boys and girls, to be masculine and feminine, albeit in subtle and little-attended ways. Not surprisingly, feminists have found this suggestion congenial, since it seems that what man has made woman can unmake.

Arguments about the causality of the mappings have mainly assumed that biological and cultural explanations are mutually exclusive. However, there are other possibilities. Convincing evidence has been found (e.g. Trebarthen, 1979) of pre-programmed infant behaviour that seems to trigger off certain mothering routines, perhaps pre-programmed in women. It has also been suggested that a baby's body shape, particularly that of the head, can also have such an effect. These mothering routines elicit, in their turn, reactions from the infant. It may be that in some such interaction of fixed action patterns the basic differentia that we see as differences in gender are brought about, the traditional mappings would be both 'natural' and also socially constructed, in that an essential interaction pattern is required to complete the cycle.

One could also argue that even if gender differences owe nothing to genetic programming, the bipolarities of masculine and feminine ways of being are conducive to the survival of the tribe and the general biological welfare of human beings. Those cultures that imposed the 'traditional' mappings on their members would develop ways of life through which more infants grew to maturity. Such tribes and their cultures would survive. Those with social practices more vulnerable to biological hazard would disappear and take their cultures with them. A similar line of argument has been proposed by Reynolds and Tanner (1983), linking religious practices to long-term biological advantage. If there is anything in this argument, it would call for a different style of feminism.

Ajudicating between these positions is impossible in the present state of our knowledge. Objective discussion of the nature of the 'traditional' mappings has been made more difficult by the politicization of body-kinds in some contemporary feminist writing. It is worth remarking that feminist reform of social restrictions on the activities of women could be based on the bimodality of actual distributions of powers and skills between the sexes: the distribution of all those characteristics that I have comprehended under gender overlap.

One way of establishing the mere contingency of a correlation is to build up a repertoire of thought experiments in which other correlations among the relevant variables are shown to be possible. Suggestions for mappings other than the traditional one-to-one correlation between sex and gender have come from several feminist authors.

1.   the androgynous mapping aims for one universal human social-behavioural type, on to which both male and female embodiments are to be mapped. The masculine/feminine distinction would necessarily disappear in the new social order.

2.   The radical-feminist mapping is formally identical with the traditional way of socially stereotyping embodiment, but calls for a reversal of the social evaluation of the masculine and feminine as person kinds. It is argued that the feminine stereotype ought to be celebrated as morally superior and psychologically 'healthier' than the masculine.

3.   Post-feminists, like radical feminists, do not argue for the abolition of the masculine/feminine distinction, but for a dismantling of the social processes by which that distinction is rigidly mapped onto the biological dichotomy of persons embodied as males and females. Thus, it is argued, any human being can, and should, be enabled to adopt a masculine or feminine mode of life regardless of natural genital endowment. This is the position of authors like Davies (1990).

4.   Finally, a fourth position has emerged, most notably as advocated by J. Kristeva (1981), if I have understood her somewhat delphic pronouncements aright. The radical and post-feminist positions remain in her scheme as necessary stages in personal/social development, to be transcended at a third stage when there comes to be a social order in which there are no dichotomous distinctions isomorphic with biological gender.

Could these alternative mappings serve as the foundations for possible ways of life? We must bear in mind that the Western tribe is no longer in danger of biological extinction – rather the contrary. No woman need devote more than a small part of her total life-span to reproducing the human race, biologically and culturally. She can be confident that nearly all her offspring will survive to maturity.

Objections to androgyny have been assembled by Morawski (1982) in the context of a general critique of what one might can 'classical' feminist sex-role psychology. Citing a variety of sources (it must be admitted of variable quality), she points out that at least five major assumptions of the tradition should be questioned. These challenges are almost a roll-call of the high points of the third-level feminist standpoint. Thus the traditional treatment assumed that in the world they were investigating there actually was (1) evaluative opposition of sex roles; (2) evaluative preferences for the masculine; (3) covert prescription of sex-roles as developmental ends; (4) no role flexibility nor role change; (5) context independence. These challenges lead to a theory of a kind of base-level androgyny against which historically situated and context-sensitive sex-role acquisition and display could be studied. But as Morawski points out, 'androgyny' has itself taken on a pro-evaluation for some of these investigators and the fact of its historical location is ignored. Furthermore, the concept of androgyny has been used in a context-insensitive way. This critique can be taken further. Post-feminists of a certain variety (Paglia, 1990) would now argue that in fact the reproduction of a society of well-adjusted people requires the nuclear, or better the extended, family, with complementary styles of parenting, caring, etc. Hence the historical survival of these styles as gender roles, and of course the desirability of somehow preserving them, even if the rigid mappings of the traditional system are relaxed.

A philosophical basis for radical feminism could be devised by taking account of what one might call 'obligations to humanity'. In giving absolute priority to the feminine ways of life, not only do women take on the obligation to maintain the human species, but they could also claim to act as repositories of a morally superior form of life. Thus women are endowed not only with obligations, but with the right to claim a certain moral hegemony. In this way radical feminism differs sharply from androgyny. In taking up the masculine way of life, which is what political androgyny amounts to in practice, women also take on the masculine moral order. It has also been suggested that the feminist ways of being are spreading in Western societies through a subtle and non-political development. There has been a remarkable rise in the number of small-scale service industries, managed predominantly by women. Success in such businesses demands just those qualities of character and styles of action that are immanent in Gilligan fashion in the 'woman's voice'. In the end the shift from the production of goods to the provision of services may change the social order quite radically. But it will be in the direction of the 'traditional' mapping. What will change will be the tendency to give political and moral priority to the 'man's voice'.

In considering the viability of the world conjured up in the Davies–Kristeva thought experiment, we are driven back to technical questions of sociobiology. Accepting that the complementary forms of life, traditionally polarized between the male and female sexes, are both desirable and of equal value, the viability of their proposal turns on the explanation of the evident bimodal distribution of Gilligan's 'voices'. This distribution has been confirmed in a very interesting way by a study of men's and women's conversational patterns (Tannen, 1990). A movement to revive 'traditional values' in a modified form seems to be gaining ground among middle-class women. For instance, there seems to be growing support for events like Christine Vollmer's 16th International Congress for the Family (1990) (cf. the report in *The Times* (London), 4 July 1990, p. 20).

Discussion of this matter has been clouded by feminist political rhetoric and outbursts of moral indignation. The only works, among the many I have skimmed, that address the issue reasonably dispassionately are Tiger and Shepher's (1975) *Women in the Kibbutz* and Mary Midgeley's (1978) *Beast and Man*. Tiger and Shepher's results were at best equivocal. While there can be no doubt that many Israeli women have returned to traditional gender roles from the egalitarian beginnings of the kibbutz movement, there are other possible explanations than the 'gentle pressure of the genes'. For instance, throughout the period they describe, large numbers of immigrants have arrived bringing with them traditional social assumptions and gendered ways of life. Moral right or wrong and social or biological origin are two independent disjunctions.

THE MECHANISMS OF ASSIGNMENT OF BIOLOGICALLY CATEGORIZED HUMAN BEINGS TO SOCIALLY DEFINED KINDS OF PEOPLE

Having arrived at a fairly well-specified conceptual system for discussing body-kind judgements based ultimately on sex, as the doubly hidden real essence of body-kind, the question of the mechanisms of the formation of gender identity out of sex can be raised. How do the mappings of social-cultural identities (man/woman) onto biological sex (male/female) come about? Feminists sometimes talk of a 'cultural process' and sometimes, particularly in French writing, they call upon Freudian psychodynamic accounts. Freud's theory of the formation of sexual identity can be summarized in short compass. It depends on the assumption that there are quite specific attitudes that very young children are supposed to take up to their own genitals, and to those of the other sex. Freud presupposes that small children both know that there is another sex, and in some detail what the alternative equipment is actually like. Boys become masculine by the resolution of castration anxiety, while girls become feminine through the resolution of penis envy. These resolutions are accomplished, it is supposed, through complex psychological processes in which the child's relations to each parent as not only a gendered, but also a sexed, being are the salient matters.

Infantile sexuality is the same, he asserts, in boys and girls, and is active in both, realized in masturbation. This mode of realization is a simple consequence of the biological arrangement of the genitals in both sexes. Transition to a more mature sense of differential embodiments, which Freud saw as masculine and feminine – that is, the embodiment of people as men and women – requires a psychological repression of the active aspect of genital sexuality by girls alone. Boys remain active in relation to their sexuality throughout their development. The repression required of girls is tied in with the alleged physiological change in the 'leading genital zone', which occurs only for women. According to Freud, in the course of this alleged transformation the sexual salience of the vagina (passive sexuality) is substituted for that of the clitoris (active sexuality) as the focus of sexual feeling. The former awaits the active male while the latter is actively stimulated by the female herself. Thus the psychological stereotype of feminine passivity is grounded, so says Freud, in the physiological imperative (Freud, 1953 (1905): 219–24, 235). Thus men, as embodied in the masculine mode, are the direct heirs of boys, and retain their active sense of sexuality.

That this is the most arrant nonsense is easily seen from historical studies, for instance that of Gillis (in Stearns and Stearns, 1988). The idea that a feminine mode of embodiment entails a necessarily passive role in the relation between the sexes is a late-historical transformation, whose aetiology can be traced step by step. According to Gillis (p. 93), 'men as well as women [before the Napoleonic era] were taught from childhood to think of themselves as connected interdependent parts of a larger whole, whether it be the family or community.

Boundaries between persons [considered as essentially embodied] were viewed as porous.' As Gillis says, *sōma* and *psychē* were not separated in early-modern people. It is of the greatest importance to realize that in these fundamental respects there were no important differences between the modes of embodiment of men and of women. Each sex was embodied in the same way. 'The body was simultaneously the symbol of their [that is young people's] connectedness and the means through which men as well as women managed to secure and repair cooperative achievements' (p. 96).

The appearance of the grounding ideas of the passive feminine embodiment idea assumed universal by many feminists can be traced to the early years of the nineteenth century. Commenting on the new emotionology of the period, Gillis says (p. 107): 'Because men were supposedly driven by stronger inner impulse, they were expected to take the initiative in love as well as in sex. The older forms of courtship, in which women often acted forcefully both physically and symbolically, gave way to a new etiquette in which the male was invariably the suitor.' This transformation had come about through a systematic series of redefinitions in which, to quote Gillis again, 'heterosexual love was redefined as pure feeling ... the old ways of symbolizing love, using the body, became taboo. The body itself underwent a radical sexualization, ceasing to be the vehicle for public performance ...' and becoming the location of private feeling. *Sōma* and *psychē* had been torn apart, never to be reunited in the next one and a half centuries.

Other aspects of Freud's treatment of the psychology of people differentiated by sex and gender need not detain us, since my interest is exclusively in the sources of ideas of body-kinds and their characteristics.

Freud's account of the conceptualization of male and female bodies as kinds, the origin of the masculine/feminine distinction, is based on the assumption of the absolute salience of genitalia. It is the kind of account that a physically idle (non-sporting), urban (no garden), middle-class (no manual labour) intellectual would be inclined to give. But with the breaking out of that cocoon into the world where most people live and have always lived, quite different saliences appear. It seems to me that Connell (1983, 1989) proposes an account of the genesis of the concept of 'male body as being of the masculine body kind' (itself a generic concept with species) that is much nearer the mark, even though his material is drawn from the last bastion of male supremacy, Australia.

Masculinity, in exemplary cults of male physicality, is not sex oriented, but to do with the manifestation of the appearances of power. (See also my account of body building in chapter 9, where the same conclusion emerges.) 'To be an adult male is distinctly to occupy space, to have a physical presence in the world' says Connell (1983: 19). The male sense of masculine embodiment is a combination of force and skill. 'Force, meaning the irresistible occupation of space; skill, meaning the ability to operate on space or the objects in it (including other bodies). The combination of the two is power' (Connell, 1983: 18). Connell's analysis of the genesis of these conceptualizations through which men define their own masculinity shows how thoroughly the process is one of social construction. His own research focus has been on sport as the locus of the formative development of masculinity as a self-definition, but one could equally have focused on the institutions of manual labour, either as a way of earning a living or as a middle-class pastime. The embedding of the body in specific sporting or labouring activities has a profound effect on 'ideal definitions of how the male body should look and work'. These definitions (and they will be multiple because they are tied to specific activities such as football, surfing, basketball, boxing, driving heavy machinery, digging trenches and so on) are radically distinct from maleness simply defined sexually, either absolutely with respect to genital endowment or relatively with respect to what it is to be bodily female. The non-sexual mode of definition has further profound consequences, says Connell (1983: 27). 'It is important that [male-defining properties] are attributes of the body as a whole; they are not focused, even symbolically, on particular parts of it.' Since, according to Connell (1983: 27), 'there is a whole range of ways in which the body can be defined, perceived, etc. as masculine; and a whole range of ways in which, and ages at which, that bodily masculinity can be called in question' – research into origins must be particularistic and its results can only be exemplary, neither universal nor normative. In a recent paper (Connell, 1989) the 'Iron Man' surfing cult provides the setting for an idiographic, but exemplary, study of the details of the social construction of that mode of bodily masculinity. The body-kind, as a species of the masculine genus, is defined not only through the exigencies of the sport itself, but also through the uses the media of television, newspapers and magazines make of an 'Iron Man' as exemplary of just that mode of masculinity. So much for the account of the genesis of the sense of masculine embodiment.

Connell also goes on to comment on the consequences of this for the relations between men and women. Here one is forced reluctantly to part company with him. His material seems to show the separateness of masculinity from femininity, and the marginalization of women within the social order of sport (or heavy labour, for that matter). But

– and perhaps the Australian context is exerting a distorting effect – he links this to the cult of 'hegemonic masculinity' in the book of 1983. However, in the later piece of 1989 he observes that 'oddly childish turns of phrase, etc.' are used by an exemplary Iron Man. This form of bodily realized masculinity does not engender hegemony, even in Australia. My impression is of women tolerating, and even babying, this great infant. The power of small women over huge men is legendary. But further pursuit of this issue is outside my remit. As an account of how one form of masculine embodiment comes about, 'Iron Man' is surely definitive.

In general a social psychology of the female body as a kind is not likely to find a source of most women's sense of their bodies as feminine in sport. It hardly needs emphasizing that the ontology of sports of whatever kind rests on a primary male embodiment of the participants. This is simply a historical fact about the origins of what we now call 'sports'. In so far as women share masculature, cardiovascular capacity and manipulative skills with men, 'sport' is, of course, open to them, in so far as the local culture allows. The distinctive moral orders that, as Gilligan has amply demonstrated, typify men's and women's styles of involvement with one another, must present competitive sport as a dilemma for women. A careful study of the spontaneous rhetoric surrounding the Mary Decker–Zola Budd collision in the Olympics of 1984 might be illuminating. But to pursue this byway is also not germane to my purposes.

There may be all sorts of ways in which women's bodies are classified as feminine. Clearly, in the eyes of men, the female body kind is generic, and its species are defined in relation to local conventions of sexual attractiveness. More interesting are the kind concepts adopted and put to use by women of themselves. In Connell's treatment of the origin of one kind of masculinity as a body-kind we have seen functional or action aspects come to the fore, for which the bodily form is only an enabling condition. These action aspects become salient, or even indeed possible, only within certain socially defined frames of activity, for instance football. A similar suggestion has been made for feminine body-kinds in general.

We have good reason to reject Freud's account of the biological origins of a feminine body-kind characterized by passivity. However, it is not the only theory of the origin of body-kinds to make essential use of biology. I shall set this approach out in such a way as to introduce ideas about both the content of the concept of feminine body-kind and ideas about the process by which a person embodied as a biological female comes to regard herself as embodied in a feminine body and what the body-kind is taken to be. While Freud built his theory around the idea of modes of sexual excitation and the anatomy of the genitals, our second theory adverts only to the maternal function, which could of course be fulfilled without sexual intercourse, given the technical possibilities of embryo implantation and AID. It is built up on quite a different aspect of the sexual biology of gender from that which so obsessed Freud.

According to Grosz (1987), the feminine mode of embodiment is derived from the biological function of maternity – thus to experience oneself as embodied in a feminine body-kind is to experience oneself as a mother or a potential mother. Again, as in Freud's genital account, the feminine or womanly way of life is a mere repetition of an aspect of the biological body-kind, female.

Arguing that this concept of the feminine is just a cultural artefact, Grosz proposes a number of novel possibilities, all of which depend on a specific account of the processes by which the feminine mode of embodiment *concept*, which she takes to be already in place, has been created. This is the metaphor of 'inscription': '... the corporeal may be approached, as it were, from the outside [in contrast to an approach she calls "embodied subjectivity" culled from Freud and Lacan]: it can be seen as a surface, an externality that presents itself to others and to culture as a *writing* or inscriptive surface' (Grosz, 1987: 10).

The metaphor is partially couched in talk of techniques by which a body of some person is 'coordinated, structured and experienced', which include such diverse matters as diet and pleasures, supplemented by reference to techniques that 'constitute, maintain or modify' that body, such as surgery. Grosz goes on to claim, though without citing empirical evidence, that

> the inscription of its [i.e. the body's] 'external' surface is directed towards the acquisition of appropriate cultural attitudes, beliefs and values. In other words, the metaphor of the body as a writing surface explains the ways in which the body's interiority is produced through its external inscription. (p. 20)

Presented in the abstract, the theory is hard to assess, but it might be filled out as follows: women's clothes, which are cut so as to emphasize breasts and hips, 'inscribe' maternity on the bodies of those who wear them. These clothes are presented as the dictates of fashion. However, by wearing them women come to think of themselves as primarily maternal. The fashion is actually, though unintentionally, 'directed towards the acquisition' of the proper female attitude, namely maternal. But one might equally well argue that there already exists an imperative in any society to highlight maternal functions and the fashion will hardly be needed to set it in motion, nor is it likely to stem it. There were very unmaternal fashions in vogue in the 1920s, with little discernible effect on the contemporary emphasis on feminine bodies as mother-worthy. Grosz's idea is interesting, but it is seriously under-researched.

More plausible is the idea of 'inhibited intentionality' (Young, 1980) as the message that is inscribed on the female body and leads to the development of a cluster of beliefs and attitudes towards it, thus defining the concept of feminine embodiment. This theory is offered as an explanation for the seemingly ubiquitous fact that girls, from infancy, are less physically aggressive than boys, readier to step back from bodily confrontations, less willing, apparently, to follow through a physical intention with full-blooded action. It is argued that girls are systematically *trained* to 'inhibit their intentionality'. Battered wives are common, but battered husbands are rare. This commonplace observation derives from early childhood, when girls are expected to be sweet and neat and boys to be rough and tough. Of course this distinction is never better than bimodal, so we need concepts like 'tomboy' and 'sissy' to mark imperfectly differentiated individuals. Drawing on the brilliant analyses of Gillis and Carol Stearns, it becomes possible to see that the term 'inhibited intentionality' does refer to something. But it is the historically contingent separation of *sōma* and *psychē*, and the feminization of feeling that went along with it.

So far as I can see, there is no evidence whatever for the thesis of universal inhibited intentionality as the feminine mode of embodiment. Gillis's study, to which I have already referred, shows that restrictions on the frequency and robustness of bodily contact between persons of different sex are very recent, while Carol Stearns has given us good grounds for thinking that in seventeenth-century Britain and North America violent physical interaction was the norm among excited adults. So much for any suggestion of universality for the phenomenon of inhibited intentionality. One can also query its contemporary application. There is nothing of inhibited intentionality about a woman beating an egg (or a carpet), spitting on a hankie and scrubbing a grubby child, playing a musical instrument, driving a VW GTI down the M40, milking a cow and so on. I, for one, am surrounded by vigorous and physically decisive women. If inhibited intentionality exists, it must be somewhere over the hill.

The Connell–Grosz accounts favour the kind of half-way social-constructionist analysis of the mappings of social and physical characteristics onto the bipolarity of sex to create gender that has been appearing and reappearing throughout this chapter. The mapping brings about a social arrangement conducive to human biological survival. With the threat of extinction gone, new social arrangements, such as those sketched by Kristeva and Davies become biologically possible. We are currently seeing a bimodal distribution of 'masculine' and 'feminine' forms of domestic life appearing. Whether the final transition to a completely free permutation of forms of life among the sexes is possible is a matter of the facts of genetic programming. The evidence is not yet in.

VOLUPTUOUS CONSANGUINITY

The duality of body types so far described is created by the creation of a polarized distribution of secondary and tertiary sexual characteristics on a spectrum of continuously varying body attributes. In the 'Romantic' age, in the late eighteenth and early nineteenth centuries another ideal-body typology appeared, expressed in sculpture and poetry (Hagstrum, 1989). In this scheme there was only one gender, though there were, of course, two sexes. The Romantic movement anticipated certain trends in contemporary thought such as the transcendence of bimodality of gender which gives a privileged and foundational role to sexual dimorphism. But it also serves as a correction to the coarse-grained anachronism of those feminist writers who project an undifferentiated and oppressive 'paternalism' into past centuries.[2]

The Platonic ideal of androgyny is not realizable, according to its author, in the everyday world of appearances. Hagstrum (1989: 78) points out how far the Romantic idea of androgynous beings differed. The new ideal puts its expression in sculpture and in poetry, and is presented as a way in which embodied human beings can *actually* be conceptualized. The legend of Cupid and Psyche captured the interest of both poets and sculptors. In the sculptured rendering of the time the bodies of the lovers are presented as identical in general form, in stature and in the delicate moulding of flesh. Their sexual dimorphism is, one might say, almost incidental.

This change of mapping (which may or may not have supplanted a 'modern' bimodalism) was accompanied by a transformation of the conceptual repertoire with which sexuality was expressed. The new conceptions are everywhere, but they are eminently visible in the poetry of Shelley. To quote Hagstrum again, the Romantic ideal of sexuality is 'compounded of the incestuous, the homoerotic and the narcissistic' – but above all the incestuous. Coleridge treats conjugal love as a mere step from the love of siblings. The apotheosis of love is that which develops between beings as similar to one another as nature will allow. If not between brother and sister, at least it proposes a sexual love between beings of one body form. The corporeal androgyny towards which one might strive in real life could even be idealized further into an imaginary world of doubly sexed 'sexless' beings, hermaphrodites. Politically the Shelleys, Percy and Mary, were not unaware that these ideals of the erotic life had profound implications for the political organization of society around a system of male hegemony and female dependence. In the Romantic period, and indeed one might say, throughout the subsequent century, the form of private sensibility and of public life have never been so far apart, nor at such odds. Hagstrum remarks on the fact that both Comte and Jung, at the beginning and at the end of the Victorian era, idealized a race of beings whose bodily forms were not diversified into the masculine and feminine.

NOTES

1   Richard Hull pointed out to me that there are many cases in which people's bodies come under the dominating control or interference of a collective. Air-traffic controllers and members of other professions are bodily examined for signs of drug taking in the United States, in the interests of the collective. A slightly different case is the Jehovah's Witness mother who is forced to have a life-saving blood transfusion on the grounds of her value to her children.

2   As Estelle Cohen (1989) has argued, the rise of a new form of economic organization in the later eighteenth century led to a situation in which 'women's public status declined at the same time as their sphere of activity contracted to the household. One form of power and influence was traded in for another.'

REFERENCES

Cohen, E. 1989: Medical Debates on Woman's 'Nature' in England and Holland in 1700. Paper read at History of Medicine Seminar, Oxford University.

Connell, R. W. 1983: *Which Way is Up? Essays on Class, Sex and Culture* (ch. 2). London: Allen and Unwin.

Connell, R. W. 1989: An Iron Man: the Body and Some Contradictions of Hegemonic Masculinity. In M. Messner and D. F. Sabo (eds), *Critical Perspectives on Sport, Patriarchy and Man*. New York: Sage.

Davies, B. 1990: *Frogs and Snails and Feminist Tales*. London: Allen and Unwin.

Della Porta, B. (1560) (1658): *Natural Magick*. London: Young and Speed.

Freud, S. (1905) (1953): Three Essays on Sexuality. In E. Jones (ed.), *The*

Complete Psychological Works of Sigmund Freud, Vol. vii. London: Hogarth.

Garfinkel, H. 1967: *Studies in Ethnomethodology*. Princeton: Princeton University Press.

Gilligan, C. 1982: *In a Different Voice*. Cambridge, Mass.: Harvard University Press.

Gillis, J. R. 1988: From Ritual to Romance. In C. Z. Stearns and P. W. Stearns, *Emotions and Social Change: Towards a New Psychohistory*. New York and London: Holmes and Meier.

Grosz, E. 1987: Corporeal Feminism. *Australian Feminist Studies*, 5, 1–15.

Hagstrum, J. 1989: *Eros and Vision*. Evanston, Ill.: Northwestern University Press.

Kristeva, J. 1981: Women's Time. *Signs*, 7, 13–35.

Lloyd, B., and Duveen, G. 1990: A semiotic analysis of the development of social representations of gender. In G. Duveen and B. Lloyd (eds), *Social Representations and the Development of Knowledge*. Cambridge: Cambridge University Press.

Midgeley, M. 1978: *Beast and Man*. Ithaca: Cornell University Press.

Morawski, J. G. 1982: On Thinking About History as Social Psychology. *Personality and Social Psychology Bulletin*, 8, 393–401.

Paglia, C. 1990: *Sexual Personae*. New Haven, Conn.: Yale University Press.

Perper, T. 1985: *Sex Signals: The Biology of Love* (pp. 184–6). Philadelphia: ISI Press.

Reynolds, V., and Tanner, R. F. E. 1983: *The Biology of Religion*. Harlow: Longmans.

Schwartz, D. 1986: *Never Satisfied: a Cultural History of Diet, Fantasies and Fat*. New York: Free Press.

Stearns, C. Z., and Stearns, P. N. 1988: *Emotion and Social Changes: Towards a New Psychohistory*. New York and London: Holmes and Meier.

Tannen, D. 1990: *You Just Don't Understand*. New York: Morrow.

Tiger, L., and Shepher, S. 1975: *Women in the Kibbutz* (chs. I and II), New York: Harcourt, Brace, Javanovich.

Trebarthen, C. 1979: Competition and Cooperation in Early Childhood: A Description of Primary Intersubjectivity. In *Before Speech*, ed. M. Bullowa. Cambridge: Cambridge University Press.

Young, I. 1980: 'Throwing Like a Girl.' *Human Studies*, 3, 137–56.

CHAPTER 3

BODY-KINDS II:
SHAPES AND TEMPERAMENTS

CAESAR: Let me have men about me that are fat;
Sleek-headed men, and such as sleep o'nights.
Yon Cassius has a lean and hungry look;
He thinks too much: such men are dangerous.
ANTONY: Fear him not, Caesar; he is not dangerous;
He is a noble Roman, and well given.
CAESAR: Would he were fatter! ...

Shakespeare, *Julius Caesar*

I'm not a short man, I'm a tall dwarf!

Anonymous

INTRODUCTION: BODY FORM AND CHARACTER

The transformation of sex into gender is not the only way attributes of one's body can be fateful. In this chapter I turn to the study of other distinctions in body type that are, in their own way, as fateful as the gender mapping. Height, girth and body form are all tied to specific characterological assumptions. Any of these assumptions can be manifested as peremptory social demands on one's style of public presence and performance. The social advantages of being tall are well known and very thoroughly researched (Argyle, 1969). Their origin and nature remain obscure, however. Is height advantage a visual metaphor of superiority? Is it metonymic of an excess of power? Do we have to learn the meaning of body height? Whatever light has been cast on these matters only serves to emphasize our ignorance (Keyes, 1980).

In addition to the rich seam of traditional and everyday doctrine associating body form and character there have been important attempts to arrive at 'scientifically' established sets of relationships. Kretschmer's studies have been refined and extended by other workers. One cannot help being impressed by the feeling that 'there is something in it.' But, so far as I can tell, the question of the priority of nature or culture is far from settled. Is it the expectations of others that draws forth a particular habit or style of behaviour from persons of distinctive body form? If Pistol and Nym and Mistress Quickly expected Jack Falstaff to be jolly, what option had he? Personal acquaintance with chondrodysplastic dwarfs does suggest an optimistic and upbeat temperament bubbling up from within. Yet, growing up as a dwarf, a person may seize on this style of life as a strategy to cope with their relationships with potentially patronizing others (Keenahan, 1990).

BODIES OF MENACE AND REGARD: DWARFS AND GIANTS

I have treated the masculine/feminine distinction as dichotomous, a bipolarity imposed upon a bimodality. There are hermaphrodites, but they play a very small role in our society – indeed their body type does not appear as a social category of embodiment at all. This has not always been true, nor is it true in other contemporary societies, such as that of the Indian subcontinent. But the distinctions in height that are made determinate as kind distinctions are trichotomous. There are dwarfs, normals and giants. Of course this trichotomy is hacked out of a weakly trimodal continuum. In this section I want to follow the patterns of culture that engender this trichotomy and to look briefly at the same issue of personhood, character and endowment and body-kind that became central in discussing the relationship between gender and sex. However, there is one great difference. In the case of human height there is no trichotomous biological category on which the claim to a social trichotomy can be rested. Biological gender, taken as primary differentia, is to all intents and purposes bipolar, while secondary characteristics are bimodally distributed. There is no underlying tripolarity in height. Height is always a secondary characteristic, not because there is something else more primary, but because there is no primary distinction in this modality at all. Yet we shall find that personhood is differentiated around height in much the same way as it is around sex (Argyle, 1969).

According to tradition, dwarfs have power and skill and access

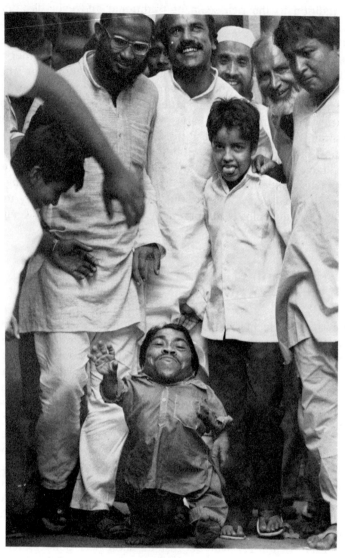

4. Pakistani dwarf.
(AP WIREPHOTO.)

to precious objects. They are often presented as superior to human beings in certain ways. They are usually benevolent and well disposed to people of normal height. If they are portrayed as hostile towards anyone, this is usually in fulfilling the role of guardian or servant. Giants are generally shown as clumsy and stupid. They appear coarse in their tastes and simple in their habits. They are usually malevolent. But they are easily outwitted and brought to humiliating ends by clever normals. There are 'gentle giants', but they are rare in folk-tales.

These are literary and folkloric stereotypes. How far are they realized in contemporary life, either in the way normals treat dwarfs and the very tall or in the way such exceptional folk think of themselves? We should remind ourselves that while dwarfs like the ones who formed Snow White's entourage do exist, there are not really any giants like the creature who chased Jack down the beanstalk.

Some people are very short, and some very, very short. This may be for three main reasons; the inherited or constitutional shortness of midgets who retain adult proportions; glandular disorders, the source of chondrodysplastic dwarfism, the typical proportions of the miners who looked after Snow White; hunchback, a condition in which shortness is due to enfolding of the spine, often brought on by tuberculosis. The dwarfs with whom I am concerned are little people of the second type. These are the people who have figured in the history and legend of Europe and to whom I shall devote almost the whole of this section.

First of all it will be worth setting out what we now believe on the basis of psychological testing, for what that is worth, of the personal characteristics of chondrodysplastic dwarfs. Stabler and Underwood (1986) sum up much of the current opinion as follows:

> ... early reports [by psychologists] would lead one to believe that short individuals are chronically depressed, dependent on others, socially isolated and emotionally immature. These findings, which reflected the philosophical and theoretical orientations of the investigator [and their profound historical ignorance] have proved not to be applicable to most short patients. (p. xiii)

And it is further reported in the book that 'results indicate that overall intellectual development is not retarded in conjunction with delayed physical maturity [in so far as that is indicated by height].' The most telling article is that of L. P. Sawisch, himself a dwarf, which for its ebullience, optimism and unfailing good humour shows all the character and personality attributes of the typical dwarf (see plate 4).

The history of dwarfism can be traced in some detail. Dwarfs have been prominent in the entourage of royalty from Egyptian times.

Medieval and Renaissance courts were well supplied with dwarf retainers and they figure regularly in romances of the period. Some taxonomizing will be necessary to reach a clear idea of the body-kinds subsumed under the general category of 'little people'. Generally in Celtic tradition, both in Wales and in Brittany, one finds frequent mention of a legendary kingdom, inhabited by a race of people of great physical beauty and extremely short stature. Rich in gemstones and generally well disposed to normal human kind, these dwarfs live in a subterranean world only rarely accessible to ordinary people. So far as one can tell, the image of the little person at the heart of these tales bears little resemblance to the form of the chondrodysplastic dwarf with which we are familiar. As Hayward (1958) puts it, the inhabitants of these hidden kingdoms are closer to the fairies than to the dwarfs of medieval courts. Nevertheless it is worth remarking that they are held in high regard and their attitudes are generally benevolent. But like the dwarfs of Snow White, they work underground and are likely to be well endowed with the products of the mine.

In Arthurian romances, however, the more familiar form appears, with large head, powerful torso, short arms and legs, playing the role of retainer to some lord. Such dwarfs can be benign as jesters or threatening, and even dangerous, as guardians and porters. There can be little doubt that the figure of the dwarf in medieval literature is drawn from life, from the dwarfish retainers of the courts of France and England. It is evident in the roles assigned to these people that the dwarf retainer is a person of some honour. There are well-documented instances of sumptuous gifts, particularly costumes, presented to the court dwarf. It has been suggested, with some plausibility, that these clothes were often the costume needed for the dwarf to play a role in the acting out of a courtly romance. For instance, Hayward cites the case of a jousting tournament organized by King René of Anjou in which there was in the royal train, 'Un nain vestu a la turque, sur un beau cheval richement caparaconne'. Embodied as a dwarf, one had certain duties and obligations, and it can be hazarded that so embodied, one aroused certain expectations as to character. These characteristics, a certain reckless cheekiness and aggressive bonhomie, can be found in dwarfs in contemporary society, and the stereotype reappears in dramas. One need only recollect the gang of 'time bandits', in the film of that name, led by the redoubtable David Rappaport.

So much for the dwarf as jester. There is another role, also adumbrated in the medieval romances. Dwarfs can be malevolent. They can be set to spy on people, and they can be dangerous. It is in this guise that dwarfs appear in some of these tales utilizing these attributes on behalf of their masters. In this social role the body type of the chondrodysplastic dwarf takes on a sinister, and even hideous, appearance. For instance, in *Fergus et Galiene* the hero encounters 'a hideous black-skinned dwarf three feet high and humped like a camel. He has a large head, flat forehead, catlike nose with flaring nostrils, and bristly black hair.' Typically we find him guarding the entrance to a tent. This dwarf aesthetic is repeated in many ancient and modern tales. The dwarf guardian is frequently portrayed not only as ugly, but also as truculent and abrasive in manner. Similar too is the 'spying dwarf', a type that Hayward sees as modelled on the court dwarfs, who no doubt acted as informants for their noble masters. On the other hand the dwarfs that accompany noblewomen, and they do not do so as menials, are notably handsome, noble and skilled in music. However for the 'cute' dwarf, built on lines similar to the hideous-dwarf guidelines, but seen as attractive in the manner that a baby might be, we must await the fairy-tale tradition from which the companions of Snow White emerged into contemporary folklore.

Is the ebullient temperament that seems to go with chondrodysplastic dwarfism a social construction? Are the characters of the dwarfs of fairy-tale and legend exemplars or typifications? Though the neurophysiology is yet to be discovered, I am confident that the empirical studies and the historical tradition home in on a correlation that may well be 'natural'.

FROM 'PLUMP' TO 'PORKY': THE SOCIAL FATE OF FAT

'Fat' and 'thin' are the poles of a tripolar distinction, including 'just right', which is carved out of a continuum of body forms by reference to sharply polarized social meanings. The polarized distinction has remained fairly constant, though we must allow for the appearance of ever more stringent criteria of 'proper' size, partly as a result of medical studies. The publicizing of the discovery of the involvement of fat in heart disease, both as a dietary item and as a body shape, led to a reaction in favour of fat-free foods and thin bodies. I notice a tendency to return to the median line of late. But the reaction against fat is not just prudential. The evaluation of bodies at each of the extremes has reversed in the course of about a hundred years. Schwartz (1986) dates the emergence of a new vocabulary of pejorative terms for fatness from the second half of the nineteenth century. He cites 'dumpy', 'pudgy', 'tubby', 'porky', 'jumbo' and the specifically American 'sod packer' and 'butter ball' as all originating in that era. Yet the plump and chubby family, with rubicund cheeks and a hearty appetite, enacting successful entrepreneurial energy, had been a commonplace of the early nineteenth century both in the United States and Britain. Dickens is full of such exemplary icons as the embodied Pickwick.

Sometime about mid-century we come across the first hints of the 'paradox of superabundance'. Fatness demonstrates the success of a way of life in producing a wealth of goods. It is the ideal visual metaphor for abundance. But looking at such a society from the consumption end, so to say, one can find the bodily celebration of abundance gross. The good trencherman can easily be seen as a glutton. There is both a moral and an aesthetic response to gluttony and both were evident by the mid-nineteenth century in Britain and in the United States. As Schwartz puts it, 'overnutrition [came to be seen as] . . . an atavistic response to abundance.' A delicate and educated sensibility rejected nutritional excess both as immoral in the light of the ever-present reminders of the starving poor and as crudely unrefined. (This double-sided judgement on the hearty eater is ironically displayed in Huxley's *Chrome Yellow*, when it is revealed that the languid beauties who pick at their food at table enjoy some pretty gross feeding in private.) This reaction, however, is not yet a full-blown culture of slimming. It is some way yet to the lean society.

As fatness became more radically devalued, so the pejorative classifications of fat folk became more derogatory. Criminality came to be associated with overweight – male excess with rape and sexual assault, 'female overweight with cheap promiscuity and infanticide' (Schwartz, 1986: 152). The scales began to be thought of, and even to be used as, a diagnostic tool for discovering the hidden characters of people. Thus somatotyping as characterology began its 'scientific' phase.

According to Schwartz (1986: 95), writing of the United States, the culture of slimming, the lean society, came about through the fusion of several influences.

> On the left, a new kinaesthetic ideal [of lightness and control] promulgated by flyers, dancers, efficiency experts and home economists; on the right a new economic model preoccupied with abundance, consumption and over-nutrition [prompted by the paradox that over-production leads to recession]; at the centre, moving up slowly, a new definition of food units in terms of energy.

Body-kinds as noticeable forms are created by society, but they are also, and therefore, icons of that society, a kind of visual or material metaphor through which one enacts one social attitudes. And as such, the body becomes political. 'Fat' can now take on contrary indications, since in a lean society to be fat is be visibly against the grain. More attention has been paid to politicized plumpness of female bodies than of those of males in recent years. I shall take two examples of the role of body fat as societal icon from the writings of women. Some turned away from the lean to the celebration of bodily abundance, while Fonda (1981), retaining, one might say, the aesthetics of the thin, built it on active body work rather than on a passive resistance to food. The exercise enthusiast has no need to starve. The relish with which those who leave the straight and narrow path invoke the classical aesthetic ideal as a societal icon is palpable.

Running the vocabulary of 'weight' through my mind in imagined conversations suggests to me that the terms for the pole of the trichotomy under discussion are quite strongly evaluative. In contemporary English I would say that 'fat' is prejorative, while 'thin' is neutral. Yet we also have 'plump' which seems to me to express a favourable evaluation, while 'scrawny' is unfavourable. Though both 'underweight' and 'overweight' are used to express unfavourable assessments of degree of body fat in technical/medical contexts, I shall try to neutralize them for expository purposes. If that is acceptable, I can now lay out two mappings:

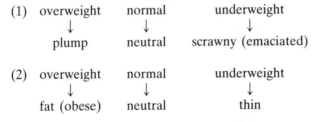

In the first mapping we have a representation of how body fat was evaluated in the nineteenth century, and in the second how it has been evaluated in Western societies recently. Body fat, I suggest, became a metonymic sign for prosperity. Only the poor were thin, and their body form was interpreted as a direct result of under-nourishment. To be seen to be fat, to be bulky, to be plump, was to be perceived as successful, as well enough off to eat more than adequately. It also seems to me that both men's and women's clothes, brightly coloured waistcoats for the one and bustles and hoop skirts for the other, amplified and presented bulk and ought to be seen as part of the metonymic cluster of signs. The visual presentation of people in advertisements of the latter half of the nineteenth century clearly draws on a bulkier model for both men and women than does contemporary advertising.

These brief considerations seem to support the idea that 'fat'/'plump' and 'thin'/'skinny' are treated as body-kinds, in a similar way to that in which man/woman are treated. One difference however, lies in the social scheme of the distinction. Sex differences are salient and liable to be the nub of a mapping because they are relevant to reproduction, without which there can be no human society. What would be the salience of 'fat' and 'thin' body-kinds? I have examined a number of rather superficial mappings onto 'weight' from a variety of social and psychological distinctions. They are obviously historically variable and, despite the authority of Shakespeare, not well grounded in empirical studies of character. However, attempts have been made to give the trichotomy a deeper significance and a greater claim to salience.

It has been argued that there is an important correlation between the contemporary characterology of fatness and gender. Orbach's treatment (1985) is typical of this kind of argument. The tenor of her analysis is that the current pejorative associations of fatness are at bottom sexist, a model of bodily form thrust upon women by the contemporary social order. She claims that the 'fat or thin' issue dominates the thoughts and practices of women more than it does those of men. But this is not just a matter of an aesthetic preference for the thin female body, whether it be in the eyes of men or of women. (In the eyes of men it is surely true that though gross fatness is no longer admired, the kind of shape displayed by Marilyn Monroe has usually been preferred to that of Twiggy.) But the matter is surely more complicated and more interesting. The 'Jane Fonda syndrome' is a new political aesthetic which associates radical rather than feminist politics *per se* with 'thin and fit'. Thus it is more than an aesthetic because the cultivation of the body is made morally mandatory by its being related to a general moral organicism, of which Greenpeace attitudes, macrobiotic foods and 'Save the Whale' campaigns are intrinsic parts. One cannot divorce the attitudes to the body displayed in Jane Fonda's *Workbook* from her attitude to nuclear power stations. These considerations are not overt in Orbach's book, but one can hardly escape them in reflecting on these matters. According to the Jane Fonda model, 'women should invest their time and energy in getting fit and looking good.' Attendance at an aerobics class then is not only prudential, but takes on a high moral tone. According to Orbach, the emancipatory entry into the 'men's world' has led to an increase in involvement of self in body awareness. Women are the majority among the clients of health farms, even though the battle against nature 'always results in [only] transitory gains.' The dark side of this is the prevalence of anorexia nervosa and bulimia which are predominantly women's disorders.

Orbach's commentary upon these matters is not profound. Correctly observing that people generally 'believe that transforming our shape' (and as I pointed out above the same belief animates those who present themselves for sex reassignment surgery) is a solution to a host of other problems, she then goes on to remark that 'women reject food in a symbolic refusal of what the culture has to offer.' This seems to me quite implausible, and Orbach cites no evidence whatever in support of such a daring hypothesis. Most of her observations – and those anyone can make with a sharp eye for social practices – tend to the opposite conclusion, namely that the refusal of food is a prudential adherence to whatever model the culture has to offer, namely the lithe, handsome and ecologically sensitive Jane. Orbach's further prediction that 'until women feel welcome in the world outside the home, their preoccupation with the body will continue' seems to me equally ill grounded. It depends entirely what they find outside the home. If it is a world obsessed with physically demanding sport, men rushing off in the lunch hour to exhaust themselves on the squash court, we can hardly expect ambitious women not to be attracted to the very same way of life. But if the world of commerce were once again to see itself in prosperous paunchiness of Mr Pickwick, the bodies of all concerned will no doubt be turned out in accordance with that ideal.

The complex interplay between environmentalism and the Fonda 'burn', the pleasant pain of muscles hard at work, is tied together through the kind of diet advocated by fibre enthusiasts. Its origins are in anthopological and cross-cultural studies, which show that environmentally balanced lives such as those of the Bushmen involved a high-fibre diet and supported a body free from many of the ailments that cost so much of our time and resources to combat. As Schwartz (1986: 335) remarks, Jane Fonda created a version of the peasant world of physical labour and simple food right within Californian high-style living, radical chic at its apogee.

KRETSCHMERIAN TYPES

Kretschmer's project was located in psychiatry. Was there a correlation between types of mental disorder, as manifested in extremes of temperament, and body types? If I understood him aright, Kretschmer supposed that the secretions of the endocrine glands would be the mediators of any relationships that might be revealed in his studies. The conceptual structure of Kretschmer's thought is similar to that underlying the correlations between the biological body-type dichotomy 'male'/'female' and the social, behavioural 'life-style' dichotomy

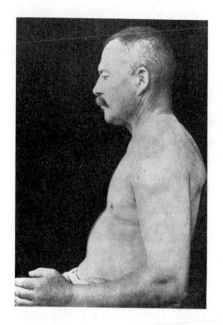
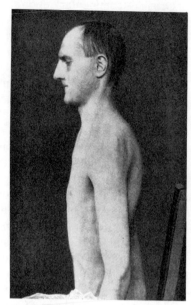
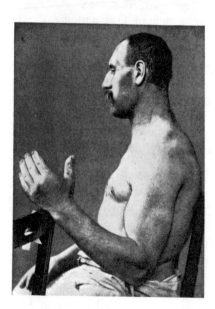

5. Kretschmer types.
(Author.)

'masculine'/'feminine'. Kretschmer's body types are to be laid against the psychiatric (temperament) categories 'cycloid' (manic depressive) and 'schizoid' (schizophrenic). There the resemblance ends. Unlike the way that the gender bimodalities are created by the imposition of the bipolarity of biological sex as an absolute on dimensions of continuously varying characteristics, Kretschmer takes the psychiatric categories to be independently defined by reference to distinctive styles of conduct. Unlike sexual dimorphism, which is given a priori, Kretschmer's three major body types are inductively extracted from a mass of empirical data on skeletal form, musculature, distribution of fat and posture. Furthermore he presents his types as a trimodal distribution of characteristics, with mixed and intermediate forms carefully described.

If the correlation can be established, the conclusion of the work would be a definite proof of a biological basis for some psychiatric problems. Biological dysfunction can be controlled – 'the real conditions of the psychic syndrome may be controlled as regards its somatic basis, while the somatic group of symptoms may be controlled as regards the psychic development which accompanies them' (Kretschmer, 1925: 19).

The three body types are the asthenic, the athletic and the pyknic (see plate 5). According to Kretschmer, they are to be observed in the body forms of both sexes, but are far more readily discerned in the male. The asthenic body is marked by 'a deficiency in thickness combined with an average unlessened length'. An asthenic male appears as 'a lean, narrowly-built man, who looks taller than he is . . . [he] has lean arms with thin muscles . . . a long, narrow, flat chest . . . [he is generally] devoid of fat . . .' (p. 22). People of this build change little as they age. Though some asthenic women are very tall, amongst the Schwabian population they are shorter on average than the population at large.

Kretschmer describes the athletic type as follows:

> a middle-sized to tall man, with particularly wide projecting shoulders, a superb chest, a firm stomach, and a trunk which tapers in its lower region, so that the pelvis, and the magnificent legs, sometimes seem almost graceful compared with the size of the upper limbs and particularly the hypertrophied shoulders. (pp. 25–6)

One can hardly fail to note the aesthetic enthusiasm conveyed by the choice of adjectives. Kretschmer himself comments on the cultural force of aesthetic ideals in influencing 'subjective valuations' of body types. He remarks (p. 29): 'these men at times come quite near to our aesthetic ideal, while our ideal of female beauty is far overstepped by the athletic female.' We shall find this contrast again in the body-building cults, where the male ideal is an exaggerated form of the athletic build, while the female ideal approximates more to the intermediate asthenic-pyknic type.

Finally, the pyknic type is described as of

> middle height, rounded figure, a soft, broad face on a short massive neck, sitting between the shoulders; the magnificent fat paunch protrudes from the deep *vaulted* chest which broadens out towards the lower part of the body. If we look at the limbs we find them soft, rounded, and displaying little muscle-relief... the pyknics tend emphatically to a covering of fat. And besides this the manner in which the fat is disposed is characteristic. (pp. 30, 31)

Having extracted the types with which to build a trimodal distribution and to define mixed and intermediate forms, Kretschmer examined the population of psychiatric cases available to him. These had been classified into two groups, cycloid and schizoid. The upshot was remarkable. Among those classified as cycloid, 58 out of a total group of 81 were of pyknic body type, while 81 out of 175 schizoids were asthenic.

If there is anything of permanent value in Kretschmer's results, then much that passes for mere folk psychology may have a real point. Kretschmer himself remarks (p. 3) that

> in the mind of the man-in-the-street, the devil is usually lean and has a thin beard growing on a narrow chin, while the fat devil has a strain of good-natured stupidity. The intriguer has a hunch-back and slight cough. The old witch shows us a withered hawk-like face. Where there is brightness and jollity we see the fat knight Falstaff – red-nosed and with shining pate. The peasant woman with a sound knowledge of human nature is undersized, tubby, and stands with her arms akimbo. Saints look abnormally lanky, long-limbed, of penetrating vision, pale and godly.

'Of course!' one says. The use of body form as an icon of temperament is a matter of everyday judgement. The body itself is a source of assessments of temperament.

Kretschmer exploits his body-kind taxonomy largely in psychiatric contexts. Correlations are supposed to be found between the cycloid temperament and the pyknic body and the schizoid temperament and the asthenic body. This programme of correlational studies was much elaborated by Sheldon and Stevens (1942). Finding that there were three main somatotypes, endomorphy, mesomorphy and ectomorphy, somewhat similar to the Kretschmerian triad, Sheldon and Stevens looked for an independent typology of temperaments. One feels that despite their disclaimers, it was not quite by chance that they found that there were three. Their temperaments are very somatically defined. This is a point of philosophical interest. According to Sheldon and Stevens, the normal range of lifestyles in which these temperaments are displayed are as follows: the lives of viscerotonic individuals are dominated by the gut; of somatotonic individuals by the voluntary muscles (such a person lives 'primarily for muscular expression'); of cerebrotonic individuals by 'mental intensity and a substitution of cerebration for direct action' (Sheldon and Stevens, 1942: 20). Exaggerated forms of the temperaments can be used to sharpen the concepts of neurosis, giving us the 'viscerotic', 'somatorotic' and 'cerebrotic'.

Sheldon and Stevens built a kind of general psychology of the body on the basis of a statistical study correlating temperament and somatotype. The result are impressive:

Endomorphic with viserotonic   correlation = .79
Mesomorphic with somatotonic   correlation = .82
Ectomorphic with cerebrotonic   correlation = .83

What is the significance of this for one's life? There were well-correlated people in the study and less well-correlated people. Can anything else be correlated with these correlations? Using a rough commonsensical and very North American idea of achievement, doing well in one's life, Sheldon and Stevens found that those who did well in life were preponderantly people whose temperaments and somatotypes were well matched. Can we now introduce the idea of being comfortably settled in one's body? This certainly seems to be one of the implications of Sheldon and Stevens's study. They emphasize that all sorts of mixed temperaments of different strengths occur, but they also assert that 'incompatibilities between morphology and manifest temperament . . . are often encountered in the analysis of personalities having a history of severe internal conflict.' This claim raises some very deep and, so far as I know, unresearched questions and assumptions. If body type and temperament can be 'out of sync' they must have independent origins in each human being. Then the fact that they are often correlated needs explanation. It may be that perceiving one's child as displaying such-and-such a body type is enough to encourage one sort of upbringing rather than another. It may be that body types, like styles of upbringing, run in families. It may be that there is a causal relation, but that it is disturbed in certain cases by accidental external influences. The theme of this chapter has been the idea that body-kinds are carved out of continuously varying bodily characteristics, by a kind of forced mapping of the body's forms onto bipolar and tripolar distinctions which serve a social purpose even though their origins are biological. In applying this principle to the somatic/temperament typologies that I have set out, one is led to wonder whether the salience of the characteristics that serve to identify the tripolar somatic types may not be subtly predetermined by the personal differences displayed as, and taken by the researchers, to be differences in temperament. This would make the need for a causal hypothesis otiose, since the correlations would be semantic and not material. Those who deviate from these norms have simply failed to understand the meaning of their bodies as societal icons.

EVERYDAY BELIEFS ABOUT BODY-KINDS

The body-kind concepts so far analysed have proved to be complex structures, combining social, historical and anatomical criteria in concepts in use amongst us as we look at, judge and interact with each other. But psychologists have found interesting differences in the way we apply body-kind concepts to our assessment of and beliefs about our own bodies.

What concepts of body type enter into our everyday beliefs about our bodies, our attitudes towards them and our practices in relation to them? I know of few people, though there are some, who think of their bodies in terms of Kretschmerian types. The material singularity and spatio-temporal identity of our bodies is integral to the foundation of our sense of ourselves as unique beings. Whatever the more specific body type to which we each believe our bodies belong, this is the most general facet of our physical being. We are materially embodied in a world of other material individuals, some of which are persons and some just things. Whatever else they may be, our bodies are material particulars, and so have shape and size, height and weight.

The question to be addressed in this final section concerns the kind of typological judgements we are inclined to make of our own bodies. In everyday life the more specific body-kind concepts I have already examined are in common use. People believe that as embodied beings they are male or female, short or tall, fat or thin. Only the former is almost always treated as a rigid dichotomy. There is evidence that girls come to a more definite and stable view as to their sexual body identity sooner than do boys. In chapter 1 I introduced the idea of body image in the discussion of the normal way one experiences oneself as embodied. There we were concerned with three aspects of body image: the extent to which awareness of one's body was an important factor in one's sense of one's mode of being; the important matter of 'boundary', the sense of a continuous surface dividing the material universe into that which is one's body and that which is not (Fisher, 1970). (Is one's last meal inside or outside one's body?) Finally we noted the importance of a sense of the spatial location and size of one's body parts. Men, it has been shown, tend to exaggerate the size of theirs, while women tend to minimize theirs. Boundary phenomena include the degree to which one is concerned with the possibility of damaging one's body in everyday contact with the materiality of the ordinary world.

One's idea of one's body as male or female is established very early in life. The transformation of that dichotomy into the socially elaborated and differentiated distinction between masculinity and femininity as dichotomous personal categories is, it seems, proceeding contemporaneously with sex typing, but I have been unable to find much in the way of empirical studies of this phenomenon. Research is usually concerned with parental contributions to the specific form that the masculine/feminine typology takes and to the consequences of its becoming established rather than with the prior question as to the acquisition of the concept of body sex (Lloyd and Archer: 1976). The importance of this belief cannot be exaggerated, since it has been shown that with respect to two central aspects of body image as a material being, namely height and weight, male people and female people have adopted very different attitudes. I cannot discern from the research reports I have read whether this difference should be put down to the fact that males adopt masculinity as their mode of being, while females adopt femininity. It may well be so. Given that both height and weight are continuous variables, mapped onto a bipolar distribution under the influence of dichotomous sex categories, that would not be surprising.

People have quite definite ideas (though not always accurate ones) as to their height and bulk. It is in terms of those ideas that attitudes to the body are conceived. Thirty years ago most American men wanted to be taller than they were, while most American women would have like to be shorter (Calden, Lundy and Schlafer, 1959). More recent studies have shown that people are more inclined to be satisfied with their height than once they were. But bulk is quite another matter. In 1973 *Psychology Today* conducted a large-scale survey of people's attitudes to their bodies. More than two-thirds of both sexes were well satisfied with their height. Only 3 per cent were dissatisfied. But only

43 per cent of men were satisfied with their weight, while the figure of weight satisfaction dropped to 31 per cent for women.

Four ways in which somatic types are generated have emerged from our examples. In the case of the sexes the biological real essence accounts for the historical continuity of the kinds distinction through great changes in social definitions, including the appearance and reappearance of stereotypes of character, behaviour and much else. 'Dwarf' and 'giant' as people types are sustained characterologically. Height and the associated minor clusterings of temperaments around height, despite contradictory locations in the characterological aspects of folklore and fairy-tales, have long served as a peg for social roles. In the third case there seems to be nothing involved in the typing of people by weight but historically ephemeral aesthetic and moral principles, though the very non-somatic character of these criteria makes them formidable. Kretschmer's body types are presented as empirical. He brought them predominantly into relation with typologies of personhood through his studies of the bodily forms of people displaying clear-cut psychopathological symptoms. Sheldon extracted both correlates statistically. I think we can say that much remains to be done before the gap between biometric studies and commonplace readings of character into bodily form is closed.

REFERENCES

Ablon, J. 1984: *Little People of America*. New York: Praeger.

Argyle, M. 1969: *Social Interaction*. London: Methuen.

Calder, G., Lundy, R. M., and Schafer, R. S. 1959: Sex Differences in Body Concepts. *Journal of Consulting Psychology*, 23, 278.

Fisher, S. 1970: *Body Experience in Fantasy and Behaviour*. New York: Appleton-Century-Crofts.

Fonda, J. 1984: *Jane Fonda's Workbook*. Harmondsworth: Penguin.

Hartmann, H. 1950: Comments on the Psychoanalytic Theory of the Ego. *Psychoanalytic Study of the Child*, 5, 74–96.

Hayward, V. J. 1958: *The Dwarfs of Arthurian Romance and Celtic Tradition*. London: Brill.

Keenahan, D. 1990: Disablement and Coping Strategies. Doctoral dissertation, University of Wollongong, New South Wales.

Keyes, R. 1980: *The Height of Your Life*. Boston, Mass.: Little, Brown and Co.

Kretschmer, E. (1925) 1949: *Physique and Character*. London: Routledge and Kegan Paul.

Lloyd, B., and Archer, J. 1976: *Exploring Sex Differences*. London: Academic Press.

Orbach, S. 1985: *Fat is a Feminist Issue*. London: Faber and Faber.

Orbach, S. 1988: *Hunger Strike*. London: Faber and Faber.

Schilder, P. 1950: *The Image and Appearance of the Human Body*. New York: International University Press.

Schwartz, H. 1986: *Never Satisfied: A Cultural History of Diet, Fantasies and Fat*. New York: Free Press.

Sheldon, W., and Stevens, S. S. 1942: *The Varieties of Temperament*. New York: Harper.

Stabler, B., and Underwood, L. E. 1986: *Slow Grows the Child: Psychosocial Aspects of Growth Delay*. Hillsdale, NJ: Erlbaum.

CHAPTER 4

THE EXPERIENCE OF EMBODIMENT I: PARTS AND STATES

I may not be perfect, but parts of me are excellent.
T-shirt motto glimpsed on the campus
of SUNY-Binghamton, 1987

INTRODUCTION: DISMEMBERMENT IN THOUGHT

According to what principles do we anatomize human bodies and differentiate bodily states? In trying to answer this question, both philosophical and anthropological matters will be raised. We shall have to acquaint ourselves with the nature and kinds of classification systems and with the widely different ways other cultures and civilizations than our own have demarcated body parts. Since my main focus of concern is how our bodies enter into our everyday lives and the role that concepts of body, body functions and body parts play in the many ways we think about ourselves, it would be a mistake to set aside all but the classification systems of contemporary human anatomy and physiology. Indeed I am inclined to reject the idea that even these are simple mappings of the way the human body 'really' is, while all other ways of picking out body parts are superstitious or primitive.

In this chapter I shall be concerned with the question of how we experience various kinds of bodily attributes and why we experience them the way we do. I shall distinguish the question of how we experience formal or structural attributes of the body from how we differentiate bodily states, such as hunger. To investigate the former I shall take bodily symmetry and asymmetry as my example. The study of the experience of bodily states will be built around the phenomenon of hysteria. In each case we shall see evidence of the power of social convention in the distinctions available to the members of a culture.

CLASSIFICATION SYSTEMS FOR BODY PARTS

The methods used in biological taxonomy have tended to dominate philosophical discussions of classification systems. Such issues as whether biological classifications pick out 'real' distinctions or are merely conventional ways for putting things into groups dependent entirely on human interests, whether morphological criteria can be linked strongly to phylogenetic relationships and evolutionary histories, have analogues in the case of anatomical classifications. Sapir (1921) pointed out that the ubiquitous tendency to assume that analytic schemes pre-given in a vocabulary are fixed by, and faithfully reflect, a natural order. In fact many such schemes appear arbitrary if compared one with another. Sometimes a social or a theoretical interest can be identified in various ways of dismembering natural beings in thought. I shall try to show that this is the case with the categories used in thinking about the structure of the human body.

The English vocabulary for naming components of the body presents a twofold scheme. There is a structure of parts bounded and articulated by the skeletal joints. And there is a functionally diverse set of organs, the internal relationships between which are not rendered in the common vocabulary. It seems entirely natural that the arm starts at the shoulder, is jointed at the elbow and terminates at the wrist. The chest and belly are less sharply delineated. If they mark a difference between hard and soft parts and take account of the natural constriction of the waist (less marked in men than in women) the diaphragm region is anomalous. The naming of internal parts and organs follows approximately the main features that can be distinguished by overt functions and anatomical prominence. The vocabulary of modern English is influenced here and there by scientific anatomy and physiology so that it takes on the appearance of a mere mirror of the natural bodily order.

Every human being is bilaterally symmetrical (with minor variations in detail) around a vertical plane bisecting the head and terminating between the feet, as if that plane were a mirror and one side a reflection of the other. Surely every culture must take bilateral symmetry as an organizing principle of how body structure is experienced? Hand matches hand, eye matches eye and so on. Those parts of which we each have only one lie in that vertical plane, more or less. Noses, navels and throats are situated in the centre line. But there is another symmetry, which, though less well defined, is of greater importance than the bilateral for some cultures. We could see the body as divided into an upper and a lower half mirrored to the other in a horizontal plane through the waist. As there are legs below, so there are arms above. There are shoulders above and matching hips below, and so on. I shall call this 'bipolar' symmetry. Vocabularies of body parts differ in the extent to which they record bilateral or bipolar symmetry. English favours bilateral symmetry. Hands are bilaterally opposed, while the corresponding bipolar parts are called by the quite different word 'feet'. So we recognize left and right hands and left and right feet rather than upper-hands and lower-hands, the latter being the bipolar concept for those bits we call 'feet'. Fingers are differentiated from toes, arms from legs and so on. There are vocabularies in which bipolar correspondences are reflected in a common register.

For example, in Quechua (Stark, 1969) there is an analytical classification that is based on lower and upper hierarchies of terms as follows:

c-aki	: foot		m-aki	: hand	
c-riru	: toe, c-pampa	: sole	riru	: finger, m-pampa	: palm
silu	: toenail, c-puxyu	: arch	silu	: nail, m-puxyu	: hollow of hand

One is tempted to read 'c-aki', 'm-aki' and so on as constituents of a bipolar structure.

To pursue these matters further we need a technique for hunting down the significance of the major distinctions in body parts and alignments. Ellen (1977) draws a distinction between analytic and synthetic classifications. A synthetic system is based upon the principle that things fall into kinds, according to common properties. First-order kinds can be aggregated into super-kinds and so on. The population of beings so organized remains the same at each phase of the ordering, but the categories become more and more abstract. Thus 'lions' is an organizing category at a lower and more concrete level than 'animal'. If we aggregate all the organisms under an exhaustive list of species names, e.g. 'lion', 'tiger', 'leopard', 'weevil', and these are all the subgroups of 'animal', we shall finish up with the same population of beings as fall under the concept 'animal' itself.

An analytic classification is based on the idea of collecting things into groups as they are articulated in nature. Each member is a member of the group because it is a part of some complex entity of which a member is part. The group name is the name of the complex unity, and is as concrete a being as the parts themselves. Thus the limbs are parts of the human body. In an analytic classification a hand is a body part and is classified with ear and foot etc.; in a synthetic classification a hand is a prehensile organ and is classified with elephant trunk, crab claws, etc.

Each style of classification has its own special problems. In attempting a synthetic classification, we may have to address such questions as whether a hoof is a kind of foot, while in attempting an analytic classification, we may have to address the question of whether a hoof is part of a leg. In Spanish animal feet, *patas*, and human feet, *pies*, do not fall under the same analytical taxon. In English 'leg' usually means 'lower limb minus foot', but in Nailu *ariatua* means the entire lower limb. *Atori* means the lower limb below the knee plus the foot. Thus while in English 'leg' = 'shank' + 'shin' (that is, 'leg' = 'not foot'), in Nuaila *ariatua* means 'shank' + *atori* (that is, it includes the foot). These are differences in analytic classifications.

Both types of classification can be applied to anatomically differentiated body parts. Synthetically 'body' = 'left side' = 'left foot + left shoulder + left ear' and so on, + 'right side'. Analytically the left-side parts aggregate as leftish things whether they are drawn from an articulated whole or not. Whether 'left' is a classifier in a synthetic scheme or an aspect of the elements in an analytic scheme will depend on whether it is or is not a salient category in the metaphysics of the culture. To test for salience we must turn from synthetic to taxomonic classification. In cultures like ours, for which the left/right dichotomy is metaphysically and socially salient, 'left' and 'right' will appear as names of groups of objects, i.e. synthetically. Thus, rather than putting 'left' and 'right leg' under 'leg', and 'leg' and 'arm' under 'limbs', we are inclined to put 'leg' and 'arm' under 'left' and 'right'. Societies for which left and right are significant categories will tend to favour taxonomic over synthetic classifications of the body parts.

LEFT AND RIGHT

Hertz (1973: 5) neatly summarizes the need for a social psychology of the way body parts are gathered under the categories of left and right. 'The vague disposition to right-handedness', he says, 'which seems to be spread throughout the human species, would not be enough to bring about the absolute preponderance of the right hand if this were not reinforced and fixed by influences extraneous to the organism.' This reinforcement leads to a 'physiological mutilation' of the left-handed. Going further, Hertz claims that the social force, a collective representation, is 'an imperative which is half aesthetic and half moral' (1973: 7). This situation has become familiar to us in other case studies. Human biology is responsible for a rather ill-defined tendency towards dichotomy in some distinction or property. This distinction is then mapped onto a rigid, socially determined polarity. This, in its

turn, is mapped back on the original distinction which now is transformed into something more sharp edged than the vague distinction
with which the process of successive mappings began. This is how
secondary and tertiary sexual characteristics are affected by the bipolarity of the rigid distinction between biological male and female when
it is mapped back on the secondary characteristics of men and women.
Women appear less hairy and with a more pronounced hipline than
men. But for the most part the apparent bipolarity of the distinction is
achieved by the use of techniques designed to eliminate borderline
cases. To understand the way left and right are mapped onto human
handedness we must look for the source of the rigid social bipolarity
from which the sharp, unfuzzy distinction with which we are familiar
comes. Many have followed Mary Douglas (1970) in her diagnosis that
there is a fundamental and absolute bipolarity between the sacred and
the profane, the pure and the polluted. Since these are matched pairs
of absolutes, they tend to make the body distinctions upon which they
are mapped appear as absolute as they are. Add to this the further
twist that not only is it the right side that is sacred and the left side that
is profane, but the right pole strengthens the person (or the power of
the ceremony) while the left side weakens both. In this way a small
biological margin in strength becomes a polarized opposition between
the all-powerful right side and the feeble and inept left. What first
exists as a marginal difference, by virtue of the mapping and the
associated practices that favour the use of the right hand, becomes a
real difference in strength and dexterity. At least so it appears. But
in learning to play a musical instrument, drive a car or use a word
processor the seeming difference in the dexterity and strength of the
hands somehow vanishes!

Hertz (1973) suggests that the polluted character of the left hand, for
instance, as this is formalistically incorporated in Indian rules for hand
use (the right is to eat with and the left to wash with) is also manifested
in differences in the rate of turnover of the words for the two poles of
the distinction. Those for the right hand and right body-side remain
fairly stable, while those for the left tend to be ephemeral and liable to
rapid obsolescence. This, if true, would be typical of the fate of any
euphemism. It has a short life in the language because it inevitably
draws our attention to pollution. While etymologically 'right' has its
roots in the concepts of direct or straight, the left 'commands in a dark
and ill-famed region.'

However, so far as I can discern, both the richness of synonyms and
the proliferation of metaphors is about the same for each term.
Admittedly, I can find no term for right-handedness that corresponds
to the colloquial 'cack-handed'. While leftness proliferates into meta-

phors for crippled, defective, clumsy ('two left feet'), inept socially (Fr. *gauche*), remnant ('leftover'), Roman Catholic in Protestant Dundee ('left-footers'), malediction ('left-handed blessing'), abuse ('left-handed compliment') and so on, where it clearly displays its pejorative associations, 'right' proliferates in the same way into metaphors for the good, correct, proper, well made, well chosen and so on. There are some differences. As I remarked, there is no corresponding word for 'cack-handed', nor does 'Righty' have a role to correspond to 'Lefty'. This need present no mystery. The relative scarcity of left-handers, after social pressure has done its work, leaves left-handedness as the more marked of the pair.

The study of ways of classifying body parts brings out much the same factors as we have already seen to be at work in the complex taxonomies of body kinds. I believe that detailed study of other ways of classifying and picking out body parts than by their placement on one side of the body or the other, will show much the same thing. There are cultures that place great stress on differentiating, instead of left parts and right parts, those that belong to the upper half of the body (above the waist) from those that belong below it. Gypsies use this division. Sutherland (1977) shows that the source of the polarity is again a mapping from a good/bad dichotomy, another case in which the poles of purity and pollution play an essential role. He explains the persistence of gypsy clothing styles over millennia as due to the necessity to deal with garments worn above the waist differently from those worn below. So trousers and shirt, skirts and blouse, which we take for granted as traditional gypsy costume, are themselves now signifiers – that is, one-time referents which have become fused with what once signified them – to become signifiers themselves. Sutherland illustrates the depth and persistence of this scheme by pointing out that gypsies need two sets of washing equipment to do the laundry because of fear of cross-pullution. In a similar way traditional Jews need two sets of utensils, one for milk-based dishes and one for those incorporating meat. This gives rise to difficulties when well-meaning civic authorities provide housing for gypsies who might be tempted to leave their itinerant ways for the settled life of cities. Essentially two laundries must be set up for each family.

Not all cultures seem to hold the upper and the lower halves of the body in such a polarized opposition, heavily loaded with moral significance. In some cases each half is seen as the mirror of the other. Thus German for 'glove' is *Handschuh*, the Kewa words for ankle and elbow are the same (Franklin, 1963), while Spaniards use the same word, *dado*, for both fingers and toes. More naïve similarity principles can be seen at work too. For instance, Aleut uses the same word for uvula and for little finger. The point hardly needs further illustration. How body symmetries, reflections and bipolarities are set up is a matter of culture, the imposition on 'plastic' biological entities of distinctions whose origin is to be found in the symbolic and moral orders of this or that culture.

BODY STATES: HYSTERIA AND THE POWER OF THOUGHT

I was tempted to use the term 'subjective' to characterize the way of experiencing body states that I am concerned with in this section. I have in mind the distinction between the way being tired, hungry, deliciously titillated and so on feels to the metaphysical owner of the relevant body, with the way feeling wet, dirty or sun-burned feels. What I am getting at here is the problem of ambiguity and the way that introducing a description may serve to make otherwise ill-focused and inchoate feelings determinate.

We can begin with some rather simple cases and then proceed to the more subtle, which I shall exemplify with the case of hysteria. A feeling that is not accompanied by some obvious physiognomic symptom can sometimes be misidentified, particularly when the classificatory concept is derived from, or even internally related to, the putative cause of the feeling in question. Thus young children (and some adults) have difficulty in telling whether they are ill or tired. Misidentification can lead to inappropriate and ill-judged palliative action. More subtle is the kind of case uncovered by Stanley Schachter (1971) in which the subjective experience of a body state can be known to have arisen from the perception of an environmental symbol for the corrective behaviour that would have been appropriate to the feeling had it arisen from its usual natural causes. Thus some young people in the United States are sometimes inclined to feel hungry when seeing a MacDonalds sign. At these emporia there are offered those things that would have remedied the biological lack that the feeling of hunger is supposed to signal.

These are simple cases. I want to explore in some detail the case of hysteria, where bodily states are clearly apprehended, but in which no source other than cultural convention and life-course strategy can be detected.

The kind of phenomena that we now broadly classify as 'hysterical' have long been recognized and long been puzzled over. Hippocrates identified hysterical mutism and unjustified feelings of suffocation as being of the same type. He also was aware that there are hysterical 'epidemics'. Notoriously he believed that the condition was exclusive to women, brought on by a displacement of the uterus. This was no crazier than the hypothesis of Freud's early collaborator, that it had its seat in the nose! By the eighteenth century it had been realized that both men and women were subject to hysterical attacks, and the existence of hysterical epidemics had been firmly established.

The association of Freud with hysteria in the popular mind does a good deal of violence to history. The modern approach is due to R. B. Carter (1828–1918). He argued that there were three stages in the development of full-blown hysterical symptoms, or perhaps one could say three kinds of 'attacks'. In the primary attack the symptoms are directly caused by the physiological disturbance produced by a profound and intense emotional crisis. In secondary attacks there is an induced or spontaneous return of the emotional state, which once again causes the symptoms. Finally, in the third kind of attack, there are only the hysterical symptoms, which are more or less 'designedly' excited by the patient. Much, of course, depends on how carefully hysteria is distinguished from malingering – that is, from the conscious faking of symptoms. According to Veith (1965: 210), the recognition that in the third stage the patient was, in some sense, in control of the symptoms led to a censorious attitude to hysterics in the nineteenth century and to the development of punitive regimes in search of an effective treatment.

The implication of a non-physical dimension in the production of the symptoms of hysterical attacks opens the question of whether the symptomology is culturally relative and historically changeable. In *Symptoms from Ideas* Reynolds (1869) observed that the number of patients presenting hysterical paralysis was proportional to the number of railway accidents. It would be fascinating to see if the incidence of aircraft accidents played a similar disturbing role among contemporary hysterics. Certainly manifestations are conditioned by social expectancy, taste, religion and so on.

It has been suggested by Veith, among others, that one must know how to 'do' hysteria. And the way one knows this is by having authenticated models to work from. For example, the 'jumping disease of Maine' was clearly modelled on accounts of demonic possession. But perhaps the most striking example of this is the way the prevailing feminine ideal of the nineteenth century became incorporated into hysterical performances. Veith (1965: 209–10) remarks that at that time

young women and girls [of the leisure classes] were expected to be delicate and vulnerable both physically and emotionally, and this image was reflected in their disposition to hysteria and the nature of its symptoms. The delicacy was enhanced by their illness and as a result, the incidence of overt manifestations was further increased.

This is a more subtle observation than just to say that hysteria paid. The hysterical manifestation expressed what it was to be a proper female. This way of looking at hysteria, as a demonstration of adherence to standards of social correctness, runs strongly counter to Freud's general tone in his consideration of hysteria. It has little to do with the complex sexual relationships within the families of those few cases he studied. If the current feminine ideal is implicated in hysteria, we should expect to find the modern counterpart of Victorian hysterics by trying to locate a modern feminine ideal. Is it too far-fetched to suggest that the slim, willowy look favoured by model agencies as a feminine ideal is at the root of anorexia nervosa and its rapid rise to prominence as a female condition? Both nineteenth-century 'delicacy' and twentieth-century aetiolation are available each in their respective historical moments as models for the construction of acts of self-importance.

Orbach (1988) has proposed that the cult of the lean, fit female body, the Fonda ideal, should be analysed in an essentially political way. Intent on explaining the persistence of the intensity of women's interest in their body shape and condition by reference to social exclusion, she argues that anorexia 'is an indicator of how women's troubled relationship to their bodies has shifted focus [from feminization to fitness] rather than lessened.' The anorexic is, according to her analysis, living out a symbolic rejection of society in refusing food. I do not find this analysis convincing. The interesting point is that Orbach should have seen the matter in a political light.

Interestingly, Veith claimed in 1965 that 'the "old fashioned" somatic expressions of hysteria have become suspect among the more sophisticated classes, and hence most physicians observe that obvious conversion symptoms are now rarely encountered.' The term 'conversion symptom' is due to Freud (1959 [1908]: 162). Veith believed that nowadays the symptomology is understood by most people for what it is, namely a non-organic condition. So hysterical displays no longer serve to attract attention. Since this was the primary, though unacknowledged, motivation of those who produced hysterical attacks, the 'disease' has, or should have, nearly disappeared.

Veith (1965: 273–4) is just one amongst many who repeat the claim that hysteria has declined or, it is sometimes said, virtually disappeared. This seems not to be the case. I have heard directly from Keith Oakley that something like the classical symptoms of Freud's

Vienna can still be found in Cairo. But nearer home, psychiatrists tell me that hysteria is still very common, though there are the contemporary symptoms, such as blindness and anaesthesia, which are more common than the sexual disturbances Freud encountered.

I have gained the strong impression that Freud's exclusively sexual theory of the causes of hysteria, be it in its early or its late form, is now not well regarded. In 'The aetiology of hysteria' (1949 [1896]) he proposed that a real infantile sexual experience was implicated in hysteria. The original experience was usually a seduction. It could be rediscovered by tracing back one or more interlinked series of remembered traumas. The seduction 'scene' persisted as an unconscious memory. Having both determining quality and traumatic power, it was the essential component in the causal nexus responsible for the symptoms. Later, for whatever reason, Freud (1959 [1906]: 274) withdrew the 'real seduction' hypothesis in favour of a theory in which 'phantasies of seduction' occurred as 'attempts at fending off memories of the subject's *own* sexual activity'.

REFERENCES

Douglas, M. 1970: *Purity and Danger*. Harmondsworth: Penguin.

Ellen, R. F. 1977: Anatomical Classification and Semiotics of the Body. In J. Blacking (ed.), *The Anthropology of the Body*. London: Academic Press.

Franklin, K. J. 1963: Kewa Ethnolinguistic Concepts of Body Parts. *South Western Journal of Anthropology*, 19, 54–63.

Freud, S. 1955: *The Standard Edition of the Complete Psychological Works of Sigmund Freud* (J. Strachey, ed.), London: Hogarth Press, vol. 2, ch. IV.

Freud, S. 1960: *The Standard Edition of the Complete Psychological Works of Sigmund Freud* (J. Strachey, ed.), London: Hogarth Press, vol. 1, p. 160.

Hertz 1973: The Pre-eminence of the Right Hand: A Study in Polarity. In R. Needham (ed.), *Right and Left: Essays on Dual Symbol Classification*. Chicago: Chicago University Press.

Mahr, A. C. 1960: Anatomical Terminology of the 18C. Delaware Indians: a Study in Semantics. *Anthropological Linguistics*, 2, 1–65.

Orbach, S. 1988: *Hunger Strike*. London: Faber and Faber.

Reynolds, V. 1869: *Symptoms from Ideas*.

Sapir, E. 1921: *Language: an Introduction to the Study of Speech*. New York: Harcourt Brace.

Schachter S. 1971: *Emotion, Obesity and Crime*. New York: Academic Press.

Stark, L. R. 1969: The Lexical Structure of Quechua Body-Parts. *Anthropological Linguistics*, 11, 1–15.

Sutherland, A. 1977: The body as a social symbol among the Rom. In J. Blacking (ed.), *The Anthropology of the Body*. London: Academic Press.

Veith, I. 1965: *Hysteria: The History of a Disease*.

CHAPTER 5

THE EXPERIENCE OF EMBODIMENT II: FEELINGS

. . . the ache changed to the sharp, gripping, radiating cramps in the back and side of 'kidney cholic', a pain that comes and goes in waves so intense that medical textbooks describe it as 'agonizing' and 'unbearable' . . . doctors class kidney cholic as one of three or four most intense pains that a human being can suffer.

R. A. Caro, *New Yorker*

INTRODUCTION: PRIVATE FEELINGS; PUBLIC TALK

The concept of one's 'body' and the contrast with all that is not one's body provides a division in the universe of a quite fundamental character. The realms that a human being experiences seem to fall ever so naturally into the feelings one senses and the things one perceives. It could hardly seem more obvious that there are sensations and there are material things. The itch one feels in one's foot is an entity of the former sort and the football one kicks into the distance an entity of the latter. It seems all too obvious that there are two realms of being that a person can observe.

It also seems entirely obvious that when a person tells another what he or she can observe, they are describing something, whether it be what is felt in the body or seen, heard, touched, etc. in the world. There is a difference though. Material things are public objects of which anyone can be aware and which anyone can describe to anyone else. But sensations are supposedly private objects of which only the person who experiences them can be aware. While people can be mistaken in their beliefs about the material things in the public realm, one cannot be mistaken in one's beliefs about the sensations that occupy one's private realm. The 'public realm'/'private realm' metaphor is often translated into a contrast between an 'external world' known to all and a plethora of 'internal worlds', one for each speaker. Both are known by observation, but the objects of each person's private world must necessarily be non-physical. In Wittgenstein's words (1958: 47)

> ... here we have two kinds of worlds. Worlds built of different materials; a mental world and a physical world. The mental is liable to be imagined as ... aethereal ... we already know the idea of 'aethereal objects' as a subterfuge, when we are embarrassed about the grammar of certain words, and when all we know is that they are not used as names of material objects.

This picture has been the familiar starting-point for philosophical reflection and psychological study for about 400 years. It is the familiar framework in which Cartesian dualism of *the* body and *the* mind has survived unchanged in its essentials. In this chapter I am returning to some of the issues discussed earlier in the book. But now they will be considered in relation to the problem of giving a just account of bodily experience. In the first chapter the focus of reflection was the question of how one's body is experienced as a bounded realm, as just one's own body. In this chapter the nature of that experience itself is to be the topic. Traditionally the agenda for investigations of sensory experience has been set by the picture I have just sketched. I call this a 'picture' as a conscious reference to the way Wittgenstein approached the topic of bodily sensations. I believe his treatment provides just the hint that the fly needs to escape from the fly-bottle. For the classical picture of experience is a fly-bottle. Once one adopts it, the ordinary conversations in which we discuss our bodily feelings one with another seem to be hazardous in the extreme, while the ordinary confidence we have in our ability to work together in a common world of public objects which we all can perceive, each from his or her own point of view, dissolves in a welter of subjectivism. The problem of recovering a public world in the light of the traditional picture is not my concern. But the status of bodily sensations and the conditions for the possibility of conversations about them is a central topic for any student of human embodiment.

Wittgenstein realized that the traditional picture not only led to scepticism about the declarations that other people make about how they feel, but also rendered one's own experience problematic. While I cannot be sure that I know what you are talking about when you tell me of your aches and pains, how I can be sure that what I am feeling today is a sensation of the same kind as I felt yesterday. If the bridge of a common vocabulary from my observations to your consciousness cannot be constructed, neither can there be a vocabulary that bridges two distinct epochs in mine. My past is just as 'other' to me at this moment as is your present. This startling conclusion is forced upon us when we go deeper into the traditional picture. There is a further puzzle about the public discussion of private sensations which I have not yet brought out, namely how sensation words could have public meanings. The problem is generated by adherence to a traditional and persistent account of how a descriptive vocabulary gets its meaning. It is assumed that the words *for* things can be learned only in the *presence* of those things. To learn the meaning of 'horse', a teacher directs a child's attention to one of those noble animals. By parity of reasoning, for a child to learn the word 'tickle' a teacher must direct that child's attention to one of those mildly irritating feelings. The words for the objects of everyone's public world and of those in one's own private world must be learned in essentially the same way, according to tradition. But if that is so, then it is only too obvious that one could never be sure that one's pupil had got the word right, in the sense of attaching it to a feeling of the very same sort as the teacher used it for. Nor could the learner ever be sure that he or she had picked just the right feeling, since neither teacher nor learner has access to the other's realm of private objects. But it was Wittgenstein's genius to see that the combination of the traditional picture of experience with traditional ideas about the meaning of descriptive words must prove equally fatal for the teacher's ability to develop a vocabulary for distinguishing the objects of his or her own private world. Yesterday's exemplar is not available for comparison with today's sensations. So how does the teacher know what 'tickle' means? But this is not the only assumption about the language of sensation talk that is involved in the traditional picture. There is also the idea that just as I observe both public objects and my private sensations, so in telling of what I observe, what I am doing is describing in the same sense in both cases ('Perhaps this word "describe" tricks us here. I say "I describe my state of mind" and "I describe my room". You need to call to mind the differences between the language games' (Wittgenstein, 1953: 290)). The linguistic theses are clearly tied up with one another and with the main features of the traditional picture.

In short, while we can hardly disagree with the observation that 'pain' is a word used to talk about a certain kind of sensation, it does not at all follow that 'pain' is the name of a certain kind of private object. If it were, then pain *talk* would be impossible. Wittgenstein's strategy for resolving this paradox involves two main investigations. He undertakes a detailed study of sensation discourse, and the conditions under which it can be meaningful. In this way he brings out a deep contrast between the 'grammar' of sensation talk and that of reports based on the observation of public objects. Intercalated with this discussion goes a critical analysis of the traditional 'picture' in which it seemed that sensations were just another kind of object, and that coming to know one's own feelings was just another kind of observing.

The criticism of the idea that sensations are private objects is tied in with a criticism of the idea that the teaching of the meaning of sensation words is achieved through pointing to private objects. If the latter is impossible, and sensation words do have meanings in public conversation, then doubt is also cast on its correlative, the idea that sensations are private objects. Remove one brick and the whole edifice collapses. The paradoxical nature of the traditional picture is only too clear. As Wittgenstein says (1953: 293) '... if we construe the grammar of the expression of sensations on the model of "object and designation of object" drops out of consideration as irrelevant [to the meaning of sensation words].'

The positive linguistic theses by means of which Wittgenstein accomplishes his resolution of the paradox are also interlinked. We learn the use of sensation words in gaining a mastery of what the Hintikkas (1986) have aptly called 'physiognomic language games'. We learn to use 'I'm in such pain' as an alternative *expression* of our feelings to those we are provided with by nature, such as groaning, writhing and rubbing the spot. 'Pain' does not denote pain behaviour, but its use in the conversations of everyday life is made possible by the fact that there is pain behaviour. '[Pain] is not a *something*, but not a *nothing* either' (Wittgenstein, 1953: 304). So the problem of how a word like 'tickle' can have a meaning and the problem of properly characterizing utterances like 'That tickles!' are both solved together. Since avowing or expressing one's pains, tickles, and so on are not descriptions, the cognitive act that the use of the appropriate utterances realizes is not observation. My bodily feelings are not to be taken as empirical evidence that can be consulted in support, of or in criticism of, what I say I feel. There is no gap between an expression of a feeling and a feeling to be filled by evidence. Though there is a gap between a report of an observation and what has been observed, which must be filled by whatever evidence one can gather.

The investigations undertaken in this chapter are entirely Wittgensteinian in spirit, in so far as I have succeeded in explicating those parts of his treatment of these matters that bear directly on the topic of felt embodiment.

In this section I propose to explore our understanding of those sensations in which the body itself is revealed. I shall call these 'body-centred feelings'. In most acts of perceiving, sensations, however implicated, are not the focus of our attention as such. Seeing is the seeing of a distant object, hearing is the hearing of a distant reverberation, smelling is the smelling of gaseous effluvia and so on. Of course we do see, hear, taste and smell ourselves, but then it is as if we were other to ourselves. The body-centred feelings are those through which our physical being as embodied selves is most unequivocally experienced. I shall approach the topic by distinguishing between, and dealing separately with, the 'haptic' aspects of body-centred feelings and with the 'hedonic' aspects of those feelings. By 'haptic' aspects I shall mean mostly the phenomena of touch, and by 'hedonic' aspects I shall mean mostly the phenomena of bodily pleasure and bodily pain.

THE 'HAPTIC' FEELINGS

Until very recently psychologist and philosopher alike assumed that the sense of touch could be understood as if it were a matter of the organization and identification of sensations in the very surface of the body. We were supposed to sense whether something was warm or cold, soft or hard, furry or glabrous, rough or smooth. The haptic sense, like the other sensory modalities, was assumed to be passive, a wax tablet upon which the incoming forces of the 'external' world imposed a form. This long-unquestioned assumption has been quite overturned by the new-style studies in perception undertaken or inspired by J. J. Gibson (1968). Gibson found that what is perceived by touch is determined not by the feelings in the skin, but by the higher-order invariants in the environment which are revealed by active exploration. Thus in a famous experiment Gibson showed that when a soft object and a hard object, of the same geometrical form, were pressed with a certain force on the passive body surface, the experimental participants could not distinguish them. However, when these same people were permitted to touch the objects, with the same impinging force, they had no difficulty whatever in making out which was which. Gibson showed that the essential neural element in this kind of haptic perceiving was not the activation of sensors in the skin, but the unsensed 'messages' from proprioceptors in the joints which were sensitive to the movements required in active explorations. It was these unsensed neural inputs that were the basis for a brain-located analysis in which the higher-order invariants in the environment were picked out. And that was what the participants in the experiments perceived.

But in all these discussions the concept of 'touch' has been taken for granted. The most sophisticated and fruitful analysis that I know of is due to Merleau-Ponty (1964). His analysis has just the kind of phenomenological emphasis that I am after in this section. His famous observation, that the human body is unique in its dual role as both the vehicle of perception and the object perceived, is a widely shared commonplace. For instance, it is emphasized by Fisher and Cleveland (1968) in their studies of the relationship between personality and sense of embodiment.[1] Merleau-Ponty uses his analysis of 'touch' as a model for how all sorts of perceiving in other sense modalities is to be understood. Our capacities to experience the world the way we do derive from features of the sense of touch. Be that as it may, the analysis of 'touch' is the centre-piece of Merleau-Ponty's treatment of the senses and of what it is to be embodied.

He begins his analysis by repudiating Sartre's radical distinction between touching and being touched (Sartre: 1957: 402–3). The peculiar qualities of the phenomenon of touching oneself are the key to understanding, not only touch, but the process of perception generally. He points out (p. 93) that when one touches oneself there is only one sensation, not two. The one sensation though has 'ambiguous organization', by which he means that it has a fluctuating intentionality. It can equally be the thumb that is the felt object or it may be the middle finger, when they are rubbed together. There is almost a paradoxical quality about this, since touching and being touched are neither radically disjoint, nor are they simultaneous or coincident.

If there is anything paradoxical about touch, Merleau-Ponty resolves it with the thesis of reversibility. This thesis is discussed in detail in Dillon (1983). 'Reversibility' is a property of a perceptual situation that permits a decentring of the perceiver from his or her usual role as the centre of conscious awareness. The remarkable thing about touch is that when one touches oneself the act of decentring leaves one still within the very same haptic experience. In more familiar terms, decentring is just a shift in the intentionality of the experience. Perhaps one should not say 'just', since the possibility of this shift is taken by Merleau-Ponty to lie behind, and to make possible, perceiving of all kinds. It is the fission that makes perceiving possible. The essential ambiguity in touching is taken by Merleau-Ponty to resolve the threat of solipsism that attends any phenomenological analysis of human

---

[1] I am particularly grateful to M. C. Dillon for directing my 'haptic' studies.

experience. In touching oneself perceiver and perceived are simultaneously given to consciousness.

What about touching the table, or any other inanimate object? An asymmetry is introduced into the reversibility thesis. It is at this point that the phenomenon of touching oneself is proposed as a model to resolve the difficulty, namely that the table is not a sentient being. It is neither part of myself, nor can I analogize to its feelings from my own, as I might if it were appresented as animate. But in touching myself I have set up the outline form of a 'self/other' dialectic, in which, so to say I, have verified or founded my general intentional stance to experience, in particular to sensory experience.

As a model, touch permits the establishment of a distinction between perceiver and perceived that is wholly within the experiential content of one perceiver. In the sense of touch the body is revealed directly as both the object of perception and the means of perception. But this is true only of *la chair*, 'flesh'. 'Flesh' is neither matter nor spirit nor substance, says Merleau-Ponty (1964: 184). The best analogy is with the old concept of 'element', as applied to earth, air, fire and water. In something like that sense *la chair* is an element of Being in general. It is that which makes facts to be facts. It is as if in seeing something, I experience it as if I myself were visible to it (Merleau-Ponty, 1964: 18).

THE 'HEDONIC' FEELINGS

I have called both pleasure and pain 'hedonic' senses, for want of a better collective term. Analysis will show, however, that they are very different from one another, in particular pain is not the 'opposite' of pleasure.

Pain and pleasure seem somehow akin, and yet opposed. There are indeed both pleasures and pains. However, I shall argue that the structures to the relevant concepts are very different, and that they do not stand in a straightforward opposition one to another. Hume (1788) is famous for including both pleasures and pains in the category of sensation. Among the impressions conveyed by the senses there are 'pleasures and pains that arise from the application of objects or some stimulus to our bodies, as the cutting of flesh with steel and the like'. According to Hume, there are also 'internal', endogenous sensations, feelings produced by motions of the animal spirits, some of which are pleasures and pains.

At least one problem with this treatment is that while pleasure and pain are properly opposed, the differences in their respective alliances with sensations are not carefully enough disentangled. But this is not all there is to Hume's account. Hudson (1982: 552) argues that Hume distinguished between pleasures and pains as sensations and pleasures and pains as sentiments. The sentiments arise in the course of reflection on what is agreeable or disagreeable. For Hume the sentiments of pleasure and pain seem to be somatically realized judgements, for example 'disgust' and 'aversion'. The sentiments are felt, but they have quite different relations to their causes from the hedonic feelings, which are related to such material conditions as needle-points in flesh and claret in mouth.

In all these contexts Hume seems to allow, as we would put it, that pleasures and pains are intentional. There is the pleasure of a cool drink and the pain of a cut. But we need to consider much more carefully what this 'of' relation might express in each case. I shall try to show that the relation of pleasures to their intentional objects is quite different from that of pains of theirs. This difference will prove to be highly significant.

Ryle (1947) called 'pleasure' a 'heed' concept. By that he meant that pleasure can be experienced only when one is attending to whatever it is that is giving pleasure, be it bodily activity or bodily sensation. One cannot have the pleasure without attending to the taste of the Black Forest gâteau. But one can attend to the pain without attending to the feeling of the drilling. This is shown by the fact that an analgesic takes away the pain, but in some cases leaves the awareness of the manipulation and dissection of one's flesh. I believe that there are two concepts of pleasure, clearly identifiable in the distinctive ways that the words 'pleasures', 'pleasure' and 'pleasant' (and synonyms like 'nice') are used. Pleasure in one sense is 'adjectival'. The sensation in one's mouth and throat of cool water on a hot day is pleasant. It gives us pleasure. Drinking cool water is one of life's pleasures. We do not mean by this that there are two sensory states occurring. If pleasure were itself a feeling, there would be the sensation of coolness plus another sensation, the pleasure. After a swim one experiences a pleasant lethargy. One is not saying that one is experiencing a particular muscular sensation and another feeling, the pleasure. The lethargy is the only feeling in the complex constellation of the experience. In these cases the words 'pleasant', 'pleasure' and so on could be thought of as classifiers. We use them to bring together under one concept a great variety of bodily experiences all of which are agreeable to, liked by, and appreciated by, those who experience them. In his characteristically blunt way, Ryle (1947) pointed out that taking pleasure in something or experiencing something as pleasant is not like any typical feeling, either of mood (sad), or of emotion (fearful) or of sensation (tingle). A pleasant experience is one I like.

The second main way of using 'pleasure' and related terms highlights and isolates the approval or appreciative aspect in pleasure. The expression of pleasure is an act of appreciation. In the form most distant from the corporeal context the word 'pleasure' can even appear in such expressions as 'I take great pleasure in introducing our guest speaker . . .' In using such a phrase I report no bodily state. I do no more than express a pro-attitude to the visit and the looked-for performance of the visitor.

For my purpose, in the context of a study of human corporeality, it is the first use that is of interest. Given that 'pleasure' is a classifier, is there anything somatic and experiential that all the sensations that it brings together have in common? Is it like 'green' or 'salty'? The answer to this question is already implicit in the above analysis. Ryle's three disclaimers seem to me to be undeniably correct. Once 'pleasure' is seen not to be the name of a feeling that accompanies certain moods, emotions or sensations, all that remains is the thought that whatever feelings are gathered under the category of 'the pleasant' have only this in common, that those who experience them like them, and sometimes may go so far as to approve of them.

The connection between liking something and approving of it is mediated by complex psychological and social concepts and theories and certainly cannot be taken for granted. Austerity and puritanism, even pathological and paradoxical states of mind like masochism, play a role in mediating the transition from the liked to the approved. Hume seems to have thought that the approval itself appeared somatically as a bodily feeling, the felt surge of the animal spirits (Hume, 1788: II. 1. ii).

Pain, unlike pleasure, is a distinctive type of bodily sensation. If pleasure is adjectival, then pain is nominal. While the pleasure is the stroking, or the taste of cold beer on a hot day, the pain is something other than the 'chinese burn'. The way pain is organized and structured as part of human life can be explored by examining pain talk.

Pains are identified, individuated and described by ascribing to a pain:

(a) a location somewhere within the rim of felt embodiment (including ghost limbs);

(b) an intensity, noting that at the weaker end of the spectrum of intensity lie feeling states that may not be painful at all;

(c) a phenomenal quality, in which a culturally characteristic range of metaphors and similes are employed, such as 'a dull pain'. In

English the vocabulary of qualities also involves metonymy in such usages as 'sharp', 'stinging' pain which recall the quality and nature of the instrument causing the pain or the act that produces it ('stabbing'). We learn to use these metaphors even when we have never been stung or stabbed. There are also purely phenomenal expressions such as 'throbbing'. (This might be a metaphor from the vocabulary of the auditory senses, but seems to me to be quite at home in pain contexts.)

(d) a cause or causes. These may be instruments or they may be lesions. This recalls Merleau-Ponty's concept of reversibility, in which the haptic sense is felt by the person both as subject and as object. It can be the stab or it can be the cut that hurts.

As part of human activity in the public domain, the uses of pain words are firmly connected with certain culturally specific physiognomic displays. I. K. Zola (1985) has shown that these displays are, in some cases at least, correlated with distinctive ways of describing pain. Irish people, for example, display pain feelings in a very low-key way, evidently stoical in their attitudes to pain. They describe pains with a rich vocabulary that permits fine discriminations to be made. Italians, on the other hand, indulge in florid public pain displays. These stylistic differences are very clearly evident in international football matches, which television now permits us to watch closely. The Italian pain vocabulary is much looser and less differentiated than that of the Irish and the conventions of pain talk allow of descriptions of much less precision. See also Craig (1986).

Looking at pain talk expressively opens up the possibility of tying it in to pain experience in a non-paradoxical way. People exhibit a wide range of physiognomic behaviours as overt expressions of pain and other bodily feelings. These may even be differentiated in relation to the discriminated type of pain that is privately experienced. One rubs oneself for one sort of pain, writhes and groans for another, and so on. Pain talk appears first as an alternative expression of pain, a substitute for a groan or a rub. Empirical studies have yet to be done on the conditions that make the substitution appropriate, but it is easy to see how social context might be an important factor, in such matters as conventions and manners of appropriate expression. Pears's (1989) aptly named 'reassuring interlocutors' will ensure that pain talk is appropriate to pain expression. 'Come on now, it can't be that bad!' is the kind of linguistic/expressive disciplinary remark with which we have all been kept in line at some time. But we do discriminate with some refinement between types of pains. 'Pain' is a generic discriminator, but it comprehends a wide variety of specific expressions. The ways these have been used is a matter of great importance to clinicians, who are trying to deal with pain along two dimensions: its causes and its management and amelioration. This topic has been rather ineptly called the 'measurement of pain'. I shall focus my remarks on a recent collective work (McArthur, Cohen and Schandler, 1989), which conveniently brings much recent work together.

Many studies billed as 'pain measurement' literature are actually studies of the everyday lexicon of pain talk, and of efforts to recruit that lexicon to clinical practice. The most interesting concern the semantic structures of the discriminatory lexicon and the extent to which different people use more or less the same set of terms similarly related, consistently. Clinicians are interested in the answers to the three questions:

1.   What sort of pain is A suffering?
2.   Is A's pain more or less intense than it was yesterday?
3.   Is A's pain more or less intense than B's? What does A mean by an 'excruciating pain'? How much less is A's pain when he now talks about it as merely 'niggling'? Is an excruciating (niggling) pain for A more (less) painful than such a pain for B?

To make headway in answering these questions one needs a good deal more conceptual sophistication than is displayed by most of the authors in this volume. Hardly anyone makes the basic distinction between pain talk as description and pain talk as expression. Sternbach (1986) realizes that there is no thing that is 'the pain' as a ubiquitous real entity lying behind the various classes of phenomena that are considered relevant to pain studies, such as groaning, neural processing and so on. A point of importance is that while pain talk acquires its meaning as a substitute for, or alternative to, overt forms of expressive behaviour, once it is established it can well be used descriptively. The fact that most of the terms used discriminatively are obvious, and often naïve, metaphors drawn from source contexts in which a pain is caused in some definite and discriminable way, such as by pricking, pounding, stabbing and so on, shows how closely expression and description are bound up. Wittgenstein's point is simply that pain talk could not become established as a public discourse if words, including pain words, could only be made meaningful by public acts of pointing to exemplars.

The pain lexicon of English includes a number of sets of words that can be used to express rank orders of various kinds – for instance, degree of felt intensity ('nagging' to 'excruciating'), duration ('shooting' to 'aching'), specificity of location ('pricking' to 'dull'), continuous discrete ('aching' to 'throbbing'). Sternbach (1986) protests at the way an uncritical metaphysical realism seems to lie behind much of the research into pain measurement. This assumption comes out in the way that many researchers take for granted that there is something, a pain, that is accessed by different techniques, since 'it' is presumed to be causally related to electrophysiological measures, neurochemical indicators, behavioural displays and subjective feelings. Sternbach emphasizes that the 'its' accessed through these 'channels' need not be metaphysically identical. There must be a relatively reliable relationship between the latter two, since it is that relation upon which the possibility of physiognomic language games depends, which thus makes possible the establishment of pain talk in the resources of any individual speaker. In learning discriminatory vocabulary one is learning what discriminations one ought to make as a member of a social group and one whose pain talk is intelligible to the others.

Most of the pain-measurement literature that I have encountered is deeply confused on fundamental philosophical matters. Consider this sentence from Chapman and Loeser (1989: 8) 'Measurable attributes may exist either in nature (manifest variables) or in theory (latent variables).' That something exists 'in theory' means that it might exist in nature. In the above sentence the contrast is presented as an ontological distinction, whereas it is plainly epistemological. Summing up the problems facing the clinician, they remark that the investigator wants to 'score the patient on the basis of pain, but first the patient must score the pain, a private experience, for the investigator.' Chapman describes his own procedure as letting the patient score the pain, an approach consonant with the 'new' psychology, in which subject's accounts are treated as on an equal footing with those of the 'scientist'. The only flaw in his procedure is that he provides the patients with a lexicon, the McGill Pain Questionnaire (the MPQ), instead of drawing on their actual speech resources. But one could imagine his work developing in more sophisticated directions. Clearly it avoids the fallacy of naïve realism to which Sternbach draws attention.

Overtly the MPQ is an arrangement of about 84 words into 21 sets according to three discriminatory dimensions, sensory, affective and evaluative. Covertly it is a semantic theory for the Canadian English pain lexicon. Throughout this work I have followed the Vygotskian principle that acquiring a lexicon is not a matter of getting the resources to describe an already existing set of naturally distinct and discriminable items, but that in getting up the lexicon a large measure of the discriminability is actually brought into being. Applying Vygotskian principles to this topic, we must notice that there has been a double dose of social construction. First the patient has learned the

PRI : S ——— A ——— E ——— M ——— PRI(T) ——— PPI ———
    (1–10)   (11–15)   (16)   (17–20)   (1–20)

1 FLICKERING QUIVERING PULSING THROBBING BEATING POUNDING	11 TIRING EXHAUSTING	BRIEF MOMENTARY TRANSIENT	RHYTHMIC PERIODIC INTERMITTENT	CONTINUOUS STEADY CONSTANT
	12 SICKENING SUFFOCATING			
2 JUMPING FLASHING SHOOTING	13 FEARFUL FRIGHTFUL TERRIFYING			
3 PRICKING BORING DRILLING STABBING LANCINATING	14 PUNISHING GRUELLING CRUEL VICIOUS KILLING			
4 SHARP CUTTING LACERATING	15 WRETCHED BLINDING			
5 PINCHING PRESSING GNAWING CRAMPING CRUSHING	16 ANNOYING TROUBLESOME MISERABLE INTENSE UNBEARABLE			
6 TUGGING PULLING WRENCHING	17 SPREADING RADIATING PENETRATING PIERCING			
7 HOT BURNING SCALDING SEARING	18 TIGHT NUMB DRAWING SQUEEZING TEARING	E = EXTERNAL I = INTERNAL		
8 TINGLING ITCHY SMARTING STINGING	19 COOL COLD FREEZING			
9 DULL SORE HURTING ACHING HEAVY	20 NAGGING NAUSEATING AGONIZING DREADFUL TORTURING	COMMENTS:		
10 TENDER TAUT RASPING SPLITTING	PPI 0 NO PAIN 1 MILD 2 DISCOMFORTING 3 DISTRESSING 4 HORRIBLE 5 EXCRUCIATING			

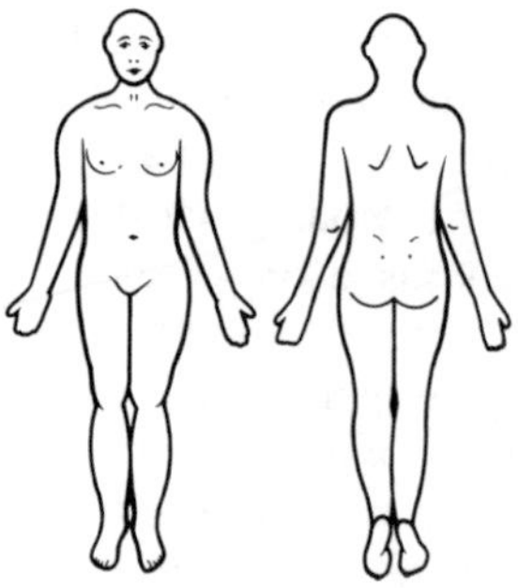

FIGURE 5.1 The MPQ.

lexicon and so has come to have a highly differentiated sensory field. Then, confronted with the clinician and the MPQ, the patient is invited to rediscriminate. Only if the semantic structure of the MPQ matches the structure of the person's native resources do we have an ontologically acceptable procedure. The proposals made by McArthur, Cohen and Schandler (1989) to use partial credit testing to produce a standardized lexicon incorporating the probability that a patient will use words in the same ways as others, leads in precisely the wrong direction, if it is an empirically viable investigative procedure that they are looking for. Their project presupposes a given set of discriminable states of the experienced body, pains. The problem for patient and clinician alike is to find words for them. This is like the idea that used to animate biological taxonomists. It was taken for granted that there existed a given population of animal and plant types. The task of the taxonomist was to construct a terminology for expressing these natural, but humanly discriminable, classes. We now see biological classification as a complex interplay between the discrimination of natural kinds and the creation of specific differences through the very act of classification. In the case of pain one is inclined to say that there are no natural kinds, and that the complex array of discriminable discomforts is a product of the cultural assimilation of a range of legitimated displays and lexical items, united through the Wittgenstein process of the playing of physiognomic language games. To give this bold claim some support I shall briefly examine the MPQ in its role as a semantic theory.

The format of the MPQ is reproduced in figure 5.1. Though the layout of concepts seems random, a semantic structure of trees and oppositions can easily be constructed around a basic distinction between phenomenal attributes of pain and something one might call 'timbre' (see figure 5.2).

This layout could be regarded as a sketch of the semantic field of the word 'pain' for Anglophone Canadians. The qualifications to a pain expression could be drawing attention to the attribute of the pain and/or to its quality or 'timbre'. The latter seems to be achieved by two main tropes. There is a metonymic use of terms for typical external causes and psychological effects of pain. And there is a set of metaphorical expressions (cf. sections 8 and 9 of the figure), such as 'dull' and 'heavy'. The rationale for the way that qualifying terms are collected up in the MPQ itself escapes me. In the tree layout in figure 5.2 reference to the sections is not meant to exemplify all the terms in a box. For instance, in section 10 there are words for literal phenomenal qualities and words for causal metonymies.

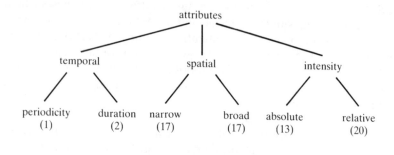

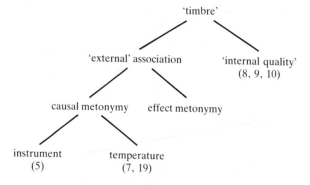

Numbers in brackets refer to instances in numbered sections of the MPQ

FIGURE 5.2

PAINS WITHOUT LESIONS: THE PROBLEM
OF MEANING

Pleasure, pain and touch are, I have argued, the most peremptory and apparently unmistakable ways in which our bodies 'make themselves felt.' The fact that pain can be experienced as an independent sensation leaves open the possibility that there may be pains whose meaning is obscure. How do pains get a meaning for the person who experiences them? The above analysis brings out the extent to which people depend on the identification of external sources of discomfort to give pains meaning. In the absence of such sources problematic internal causes must be imagined (Neal, 1978: 24ff.). There are a myriad cramps, twinges, aches and irritations that need to be assigned an internal cause. At this point medicine begins to play an increasingly important part in the story of pain. In taking a pain to a doctor for diagnosis of its cause, we are in search of its meaning. I suggest that two root ideas are comprehended in the meaning of a pain. There is not only a question of the cause of the discomfort, but also the idea of the pain as a diagnostic sign, pointing into the future. In this second sense it is not just an effect; it is a symptom. Diseases have futures. If the pain is indigestion, then it presages one sort of future, but if it is brought on by a heart condition it presages quite another.

Medical science is baffled, and many people are tormented, by chronic pain. Fibromyalgia is a condition defined wholly in terms of a symptomology of discomforts. There are generalized aches and pains. There is morning stiffness and there are 'tender points', local centres of felt pain. Fibromyalgia is diagnosed when no physical causes can be found. Neither in X-ray investigations, nor in electromyography, nor even in post-mortem examinations do the regions of the body where tender points were picked out show any abnormalities. The history of a century of failures to establish internal bodily causes is reflected in the changing vocabulary of this condition, which has successively been called 'neurasthenia' and 'fibrositis' before settling down in our own time as 'fibromyalgia'. This word simply means 'painful muscle condition' and is about as informative a diagnosis as was 'pyrexia' for the cause of fevers.

There have been two long-standing lines of thought about this condition. The neurophysiological line has centred on the possibility that these are referred pains, deriving from lesions elsewhere in the body, perhaps the spinal cord. Just as indigestion can be felt in the left shoulder, so fibromyalgia is distanced from its physical causes.

Not surprisingly, a second line of thought has developed, expressed in the concept of 'physiogenetic arthritis'. The pain is to be given meaning as a symbolic expression of an emotional problem. However, research into fibromyalgia has shown that the mode of presentation typical of sufferers of this condition does not support the 'expression' hypothesis. These people are rational and non-manipulative. They are quite different in psychological and social style from typical 'sufferers' of 'psychogenic' discomforts. Such people do not give anatomically rational accounts of the symptoms. How is the *meaning gap* closed by those who suffer fibromyalgia and other forms of chronic pain?

Generally speaking, these people feel that they have been deserted by the medical profession. They must do the work of creating meanings for their pain from their own resources, so to say. Kortaba (1983: 22–5) describes how groups of chronic-pain sufferers create meanings for their discomforts in the course of social interactions, particularly in conversations. Borrowing a term from post-structuralism, I shall identify 'pain talk' as one of those discursive practices through which they constitute themselves collectively as persons in good standing. The process is quite complex. Kortaba shows how social ratification of each person's pain experience as genuinely intense confirms its 'reality' and cancels attempts by medical experts discursively to constitute the sufferers as deviant and their pains as psychosomatic – that is, 'non-real'.

The process of reconstitution of persons as non-deviant involves further development of the joint conversation through exchanges of anecdotes concerning the management of pain and techniques for coping. Far from being deviant, those who cope should be esteemed. Thus, via the communal conversation with the afflicted, deviance can be disavowed. Kortaba has shown further that there are formal and informal rules for *displays* of competency in coping with chronic pain – for instance, in how emotional control is displayed. This is a difficult technique, since the emotional possibilities must be indicated while the fact of their suppression can only be shown by their non-display.

Naïvely, and no doubt rightly, one can say that pain and pleasure have their uses. What is biologically necessary or desirable ought to be pleasant to the organism and what is deleterious ought to be painful. Within this simple framework there are many paradoxical bodily phenomena, from the pleasures of consuming *dames blanches* under threat of a *crise de foie* to the pains of effective exercise. I shall return to these matters in chapter 7, where I shall go into the way body-based ascetic cults have tended to reverse the way the common sense of the twentieth century would distribute value to bodily pleasures and pains.

THE FEELING OF DOING

In thinking of how one experiences oneself as embodied, we have moved from the more static aspects of embodiment, the sense of the articulated body structure, through the more momentary and fluid experience of fluxes of bodily feeling. In this section I turn to the sense of embodiment that accompanies the use of one's body and its parts in skilled action. I have in mind such 'practical' activities as using a saw, playing tennis, dancing, playing a musical instrument and so on. Though the libraries and bookshops of the world abound in practical manuals, I have been able to find very little material on the experience of embodiment that our engagement in these activities provides, with the exception of the massive and detailed study by Merleau-Ponty (1948), based on his analysis of the case of Schneider, whose war injuries had affected his manipulative capacities in an instructive way. I hope to offer at least the outline of an explanation of why that must be so. And yet the experience of the rightness of bodily activity is as central to our sense of 'being-in-the-world' as such matters as one's sense of one's location at a certain point of view in space and time, or those matters that have been the focus of this chapter. My discussion then can be little more than a sketch of the main concepts involved, as I see them.

The first step will be to look into the basic structure of a skilled performance. In one of the rare works that discusses these matters at all, Royce (1984) emphasizes the sharp distinction that reigns in both ballet and mime between the merely random and the ordered uses of the body in action. She points to the extraordinary impression made by a drunkard's sway or the agonizing and agonized efforts that a brain-damaged person makes in an effort to act. But how does order reign?

Von Cranach and others (von Cranach and Harré, 1981) have shown how practical action is embedded in a cognitive structure that can be represented as a hierarchy of means/ends pairs. Sometimes such a hierarchy is consciously attended to by an actor, but more often than not it is, as I have remarked in an earlier chapter, inscribed in the body itself. Musicians report 'finding their fingers' going to certain locations, just those locations that will produce the required sound. It seems to me that we should expect the sense of embodiment to be related to means rather than ends; to the *action* of the body parts. The ends towards which the actor is directing his or her actions are properly matters of cognition, of plans, intentions and projects rather than of doings. The focus of the enquiry into felt embodiment ought then to be on means.

What then is skill in performance? Following the hint from Royce, it must surely be sought in some cluster of qualities experienced by the actor in relation to the way the bodily movements that are the means are executed. 'Skilled' is a comparative concept and so its meaning must be sought in relation to its paired opposites such as 'clumsy' or 'inept'. I propose that one's sense of embodiment in action comes only when a kind of random, inept fumbling is gradually succeeded by skilled performance. In an incompetent and bumbling attempt to achieve a practical end one's body hardly seems to be one's own, even though its presence is more emphatically obvious to one's awareness than when one is performing smoothly. What are some of the criteria by which skilled performance can be recognized? At least from the onlookers' point of view, the bodily movements of the skilled actor seem to be characterized by at least three attributes: economy of effort, shortness of executive path and a smooth quality in the action itself. Each of these qualities is comparative and requires some sense in the onlooker of alternative possibilities, ways of acting that are excluded by what is seen to be done. The characteristics of the executive path require something else, namely some idea on the part of the onlooker as to what it is that is being done; what the end is intended to be. We could sum up these characteristics as efficiency in execution.

It is by no means obvious that the actor's sense of embodiment as performer is just a subjective version of the onlooker's sense of the required executive movements. The actor is intent on the end and the more skilled he or she is in the doing, the more the movements themselves have become unattended. Paradoxically, the less well one can carry out some skilled action the more the fact of one's embodiment dominates one's sense of the activity itself. In learning to play the *sarom* in a gamelan, one's sense of one's hand moving almost of its own volition to where, say, the fifth note would be if the numbering were 'rational' is overwhelming. The moment when the order '6, 1, 2, 3, 5, 6, 1' has become second nature is characterized by the disappearance of the body's presence in the action at all. The same 'paradox' plays a central role in Sudnow's (1978) phenomenological ethnomethodology of the jazz piano.

Reflection on this matter seems to leave one with the following: the skilled actor does have a sense of the body's engagement in the action, but it is the very general feeling of an aesthetic 'rightness'. Further analysis of the characteristics of that sense of 'sweetness of movement' takes us away from how embodiment in the action is felt to the onlooker's position, since it is a sense of 'best means'. But 'best means' is a comparative concept which is lost to the skilled actor once skill has been acquired. The unskilled know the contrast between skill and ineptitude in embodied action. I think that the truly skilled performer senses the rightness of the action, not through its fulfilling the onlooker's criteria for rightness, but through the aesthetic delight that a cricketer will report when commenting on a sweet shot through the covers.

The picture that emerges of one's sense of embodied action is emphatically not that of consciously attended movement plans executed through reflexive awareness of the dispositions and motions of the relevant body parts. Merleau-Ponty's Schneider could carry out 'concrete movements', the bodily tasks of everyday life, including those of his trade as a leather worker. However, when called upon to make 'abstract' movements – that is, movements in relation to a conscious attention to his own corporeal frame – he had great difficulty. He seemed to lack the bodily reference system that Schilder called the 'body-image'. Scheider could fulfil the request 'Point to your nose' only by taking hold of it.

Considered with respect to the anatomical displacements required, unthinkingly scratching one's nose and pointing to it on command are more or less identical. The difference lies elsewhere, in that to which one is consciously attending. 'What is pathological about Schneider is the very presence of conscious thought, as a *substitute* for the normal capacity to perform abstract movements without this' (Keat, 1982).

So successful performance of both classes of skilled movement, by a normal person, requires neither a perception of the physical movement of the relevant parts of the body nor a consultation of 'body image'. All skilled action, according to Merleau-Ponty, is characterized by the concentration of attention on that to which it is directed. Schneider cannot make his own body an object of skilled action; not because he cannot think *of* its parts in space. He can. It is because he cannot think spatially *with* it. '... his body is at his disposal as a means of ingress into a familiar surrounding, but not as a means of expression of a gratuitous and free spatial thought' (Merleau-Ponty, 1948: 104).

Merleau-Ponty's conclusion is quite the opposite of current trends in 'cognitive science'. 'Our bodily experience of movement', he claims (p. 140), 'is not a particular case of [theoretical] knowledge; it provides us with a way of access of the world and the object, with a "praktognosia", which has to be recognized as original and perhaps as primary.' This 'bodily practical knowledge' cannot be further analysed by the use of traditional concepts such as 'body = means' and 'mind = plans'. It is in terms of possible practical action that our sense of being-in-the-world is constituted. Thus material objects are conceived first and foremost as *manipulanda*. It is not that people who suffer apraxias are not aware of things. They are paralysed with respect to making use of them. In a fundamental sense manipulable objects do not exist for them.

REFERENCES

Chapman, C. R., and Loeser, J. D. 1989: *Issues in Pain Measurement*. New York: Raven Press.

Craig, K. D. 1986: Social Modelling Influences, in R. A. Sternbach (ed.), *The Psychology of Pain* (pp. 75–7). New York: Raven Press.

Dillon, M. C. 1983: Merleau-Ponty and the Reversibility Thesis, *Man and World*, 16, 365–88.

Douglas, M. 1970: *Purity and Danger*. Harmondsworth: Penguin.

Fisher, S., and Cleveland, S. E. 1968: *Body Image and Personality*. New York: Dover.

Gibson, J. J. 1968: *The Senses Considered as Perceptual Systems*. London: George Allen and Unwin.

Heblen, N. 1985: Towards the Assessment of Clinical Pain. In G. M. Aronoff (ed.), *Clinical Pain* (pp. 455–8). Baltimore–Munich: Urban and Schwarzenberg.

Hintikka, J., and Hintikka, M. 1986: *Investigating Wittgenstein*. Oxford: Basil Blackwell.

Hudson, L. 1982: *Bodies of Knowledge*. London: Weidenfeld and Nicholson.

Hume, D. (1788) (1968): *A Treatise of Human Nature*. London: Oxford University Press.

Keat, R. 1982: Merleau-Ponty and the Phenomenology of the Body. Paper delivered at HRC Seminar, Australian National University, Canberra.

Kortoba, J. A. 1983: *Chronic Pain: Its Social Dimensions*. Beverley Hills, California: Sage.

McArthur, D. L., Cohen, M. J., and Schandler, S. L. 1989: A philosophy for measurement of pain. In Chapman and Loeser (eds.), *op. cit.*

Melzack, R. 1974: *The Puzzle of Pain*. New York: Basic Books.

Merleau-Ponty, M. 1948: *The Phenomenology of Perception*. Evanston: Northwestern University Press.

Merleau-Ponty, M. 1964: *L'Œuil et l'esprit*. Paris: Gallimard.

Neal, H. 1978: *The Politics of Pain*. New York: McGraw-Hill.

Pears, D. 1989: *The False Prison*, Vol. II. Oxford: Oxford University Press.

Ryle, G. 1947: *The Concept of Mind*. London: Hutchinson.

Royce, A. P. 1984: *Movement and Meaning*. Bloomington: Indiana University Press.

Sapir, E. 1921: *Language: on Introduction to the Study of Speech*. New York: Harcourt Brace.

Sartre, J.-P. 1957: *Being and Nothingness*, trans. H. E. Barnes. London: Methuen.

Schachter, S. 1971: *Emotion, Obesity and Crime*. New York: Academic Press.

Sternbach, R. A. 1986: *The Psychology of Pain*. New York: Raven Press.

Sudnow, D. 1978: *Ways of Hand*. London: Routledge and Kegan Paul.

von Cranach, M., and Harré, R. 1981: *The Analysis of Action*. Cambridge: Cambridge University Press.

Wall, P. D., and Melzack, R. 1989: *Textbook of Pain* (p. 273). Edinburgh etc.: Churchill and Livingstone.

Wittgenstein, L. 1953: *Philosophical Investigations*. Oxford: Basil Blackwell.

Wittgenstein, L. 1958: *The Blue and Brown Books*. Oxford: Basil Blackwell.

Zola, I. K., and Kosa, J. 1985. *Poverty and Health*. Cambridge, Mass.: Harvard University Press.

PART II
Evaluations

. . . women who become legendary affect ideas of what feminine beauty is. So that people equate their famed faces with ideal beauty. A flat, gawky lamppost of a woman like Garbo forms a whole generation of clothes and manners not really through classic features or charms at all, but by expressing something archetypal of which both she and her admirers may be quite unconscious. But the type then becomes beauty through her fame.

Sarah Gainham, *Private Worlds*

Human life is a passage through a partially charted archipelago of norms and ideals. Embodiment is a necessary condition for the existence of identifiable persons. People are embodied, physical beings. Many of their actions could have been accomplished only by beings for whom bodies are instruments. Many important human relations are accomplished bodily. Actions and relations are the prime subjects of moral discourse. Inevitably bodies are the focus of all sorts of evaluations. The topic of many of the norms and ideals of human existence is the body and its attributes and powers.

Part of the moral system of every culture involves evaluations of personal actions and attitudes for which the fact of human embodiment is a necessary condition. Human beings reproduce their kind through bodily processes, necessarily requiring the contributions of two embodied beings, related in some human way. So the morality of reproduction is likely to involve all sorts of interpersonal rights and obligations. A major problem to be explored in this part arises from the distinction between the body as simply the locus of moral concern for moral agents and the body itself as an entity of independent moral value. Though there is a good deal of talk that seems to require the body to be taken as an independent moral being, it will prove difficult to pin it down satisfactorily. I owe to Peter Hare a reminder of how much body work involves supererogatory obligations – demands that go 'beyond the call of duty', so to say.

There is another duality in which the body plays an essential part. According to the social-constructionist view, displays of emotion (including those bodily feelings through which one displays one's emotions to oneself) are bodily enactments of moral judgements and appraisals. Some of these judgements concern the body itself. The emotions of embarrassment and shame are as much concerned with the public appearance of the personal body as they are with inappropriate or bad conduct. A person can be, and often is, praised and blamed for their body or matters appertaining to it. By charting the changing scope and nature of the infractions these emotions address, and the shift in the boundaries of the corresponding virtues and vices, a radical change in body morality will be discerned.

Aesthetic and moral norms of bodily behaviour and public appearance are closely bound up with one another. In treating the way people manage disorders of the body it will prove necessary to distinguish between biological states of good and bad functioning and hypotheses about their causes, and the social consequences and aesthetic evaluations of those states as they are assessed and dealt with by people in accordance with local conventions of proper conduct. It is only in the light of such evaluations that the way people deal with disease can be understood. Retreat into illness is a social response to how one's body is feeling and performing. Resort to the gymnasium can be a personal response to how one's body looks and how it seems to be functioning. So can resort to the hairdresser, the paint pot or cosmetic surgery. Much has been written about the historical variability of ideals of personal beauty. Instead of giving a résumé of that mass of material, I have chosen instead to study a strange form of aesthetically motivated body cultivation – the body-building cult. It holds some surprises and offers a good deal of illumination.

In the final investigation in this part I turn to a study of the vulnerable human body as it is the focus of various techniques of social control. Since people are necessarily embodied, perhaps they can be kept in line with the local norms of conduct or even herded into new channels of behaviour by actions directed to their bodies as such. Pleasure and pain are manipulable as rewards and punishments. This is familiar territory. Mutilation is less common in the twentieth century than it was. It can be used to engrave a perpetual reminder of what is right and proper on the body itself. Most fascinating of all is the amplification of the threat of catching a fatal disease to draw a boundary around morally acceptable conduct. The AIDS 'epidemic' is just the latest in a string of such morally and politically 'intensified' infections. Once penicillin had eliminated syphilis, it was only a matter of time before another candidate for sexual policeman appeared. But none has needed such hard work to turn a rare condition into a 'pandemic', as has the HIV infection.

CHAPTER 6

BODILY RIGHTS AND OBLIGATIONS

Ignore the body, lose your soul.

Roger Scruton

INTRODUCTION: BODILY RIGHTS AND OBLIGATIONS
TO THE BODY

Jane Fonda (1981) says: 'I began to realize my body needed to be listened to and strengthened . . . I could create for myself a new approach to health and beauty, an approach which would not only make me look better, but would enable me to handle the intense, multifaceted life I live with more clarity and balance.' This is typical body talk. It presents a mixture of moral, aesthetic and prudential considerations familiar to the contemporary ear. In this passage Jane distinguishes between what her body needed and what she could achieve as a person who is embodied in a well-cared-for organism. Needs belong in the same universe of concepts as rights and obligations. Does Jane have an obligation to her body itself? Do that body's needs engender corresponding rights? Or do this body's needs seem of importance to Jane only in so far as they are involved in the support that her body provides for all the multifaceted activities she is engaged in?

What are we to make of the idea that we may have obligations to our own bodies? Or that our bodies may have rights that we may have a duty to fulfil? Or that the body has intrinsic moral qualities? These queries do pose conceptual problems, since rights, duties and obligations seem typically to be ascribed to, and demanded of, people. Bodies bereft of personhood are not people. But then neither are precious things. Do I have an obligation to help preserve the Mappa Mundi? If I do, does that mean that this precious thing has a right to my support? I think most philosophers would share with lay folk the intuition that these obligations and rights could in the end, by more careful consideration, be shown to devolve on people. My obligation is not to the map as such, but to the people of subsequent generations who would be deprived of an object of wonder and instruction, to the contemplation of which they have a right.

A sensible person aims to be healthy, and so in common prudence takes care of their body. But one comes up against people who seem to consider the cultivation of their bodies as rather more than a step towards the enhancement of individual health and of the chances of personal survival. It is not uncommon to find that such people are also supporters of Greenpeace, ready to assert that the whales have as much right to live on the planet as we ourselves. But when they turn to the plight of the rain forest they tend to argue in terms of person-oriented claims, to mention genetic reserves, the beauty and mystery to be shared by future generations (of people) and so on. The loggers who destroy rain forests are violating the rights of people, not those of trees. Yet one is struck by the way that health enthusiasts tend to talk of their body work and care in ways more reminiscent of debates about whales than of those about trees. One glimpses something of this way of thinking in the way that fitness fanatics are ready to sacrifice some of the rights that belong to the people in their immediate circle to the demands of the body. Some people do spend inordinate amounts of time 'working out', or so it seems to the bystander. Though a superfit mum and dad may be just what a kiddie needs, it is obvious that demands can clash. What is the nature of the clash between obligations to two beings, each of whom has rights – one's child and one's body? Or is the body's cultivation a matter of the moral standing of him or her who is thus embodied? I hope to find some tentative answers to these questions by exploring a number of cases in which in one way or another the body becomes the focus of obligations, rights and duties. In the same vein, but in the opposite direction, Christian ascetics seem to have taken bodily desires and promptings as opposed to the path that must be taken for the salvation of the soul (Rousselle, 1988). Mortifications appear as a kind of inverse cultivation.

OBLIGATION CONCEPTS

A brief sketch of how I am employing the concept of 'obligation' and the distinctions I wish to draw within it will set the scene for the discussion to follow. Though the matter has been much disputed, I shall take it that the concepts of 'obligation' and of 'duty' are synonymous for all practical purposes.

Hare (1981), and many others, distinguish between those acts that are morally required and that it is morally blameworthy to omit and those that one is praised for performing, but not morally blamed for omitting. The latter are acts of supererogation. Hare further distinguishes between a narrow and a broad sense of obligation. In the narrow sense we are obliged to perform the former kind of act, but not the latter. In the broad sense he thinks we have obligations in both cases.

The distinction between special obligations – those owed to particular persons by particular persons, say by one sister to another in just *this* family – and general obligations – those owed to anyone – is due to Hart (1961). It will play an important role in our discussions of the moral obligations that are involved in decisions about surrogate motherhood.

People are frequently faced with moral dilemmas in which obligation are, or seem to be, in conflict. In practice one must prevail over the other so that something does get done. Those that tend to be overridden on occasions of conflict have been called prima-facie obligations (Ross, 1939). It has generally been held that even when overridden, prima-facie obligations still, in a sense, exist and are, so to say, capable of re-emergence when the situation changes.

Obligations and rights are generally reciprocally defined. Hohfeld (1923) distinguished three levels of rights, and I shall draw on this way of identifying rights in what follows. A person has a right-1 to do something (play tennis) or to have something (a second slice of toast) if there is no obligation on that person not to do the relevant action or to take the relevant item. A person has a right-2 (to walk a certain country path) when others have an obligation not to stop the person exercising that right. A yet stronger right-3 belongs to a person to do or to have something if others have an obligation to facilitate the action (save themselves from drowning) or to provide the object (food to the starving).

The idea of a bodily obligation is vague. To sharpen it I shall distinguish between a body-relevant moral action, say killing, in which the body is topic, but the person so embodied the target, and a body-relevant moral target, say a person. There is the question of what kinds of body-relevant actions moral judgements might typically be about. Is stuffing oneself with food such an action? Then there is the question of which beings are properly the targets of moral judgements. Is a foetus a being whose fate attracts moral judgements as such? In this chapter the body will first appear as topic and then, and tentatively, as target. Two kinds of question parallel the topic/target distinction. Do I have rights to a certain kind of treatment by virtue of the fact of embodiment? Does my body as such have rights that engender obligations on myself and others towards it? Recent trends in popular discourse do seem to suggest that bodies have rights in themselves. This thought will be given a detailed exploration. Broadly speaking there are two kinds of acts relevant to bodies. There are those through which a human body is (merely) preserved and maintained. Then there are those by which it is cultivated and its condition enhanced above that needed for mere organic survival or, on the contrary, mortified. Is the latter a work of supererogation?

DISPOSAL AND CONSERVATION

A comparison between the practices of body cultivation and some of our ways of treating things will help to throw light on how the body itself might be a target for obligatory acts. Bodies, like things, can be taken to pieces or dismantled, and parts can be disposed of for use elsewhere. I have in mind not just the modern practice of transplant surgery, but such traditional activities as scalp hunting and the old colonial trade in Maori tattooed heads.

The moral wrongness of certain cases of the dismantling of human bodies is obviously connected with the fact that in extreme cases it leads to the injury, and even death, of a person. Surgeons are increasingly able to dismantle, and painlessly to reassemble, human bodies generally with preservation of the personhood of the person so embodied. The rapidity of advances in medical technology suggests further steps in this direction, adumbrated so far only in science-fiction tales about mind and brain transplants – for instance, Leiber's (1982) fantasy *Beyond Rejection*. Objections to prefrontal lobotomy are couched in terms of loss of personhood rather than as protests on behalf of the body as such.

In exploring the issues involved in considering bodies as topics and as targets of moral consideration, I shall follow the strategy of chapter 1 and work through various comparisons between bodies and things. One can compare the rights of dismemberment and disposal that I have over my things with the rights of dismemberment and disposal, if any, that I have over my body. People sometimes dismantle, and even dispose of, the bodies of others. Rights and obligations are involved there too. Are the moral relations in which I stand to the bodies of others similar to those in which I stand to my own body? One can also compare rights to know about the nature of my things and of the treatment meted out to them (say in the local garage) with the rights I have to know about the nature and attributes of my body and to be told the specific details of treatments to which it might be subjected from time to time. Again the extension of this comparison to the rights of others to know about my things and about my body will add another dimension.

Correlative and contrary to rights of disposal and dismemberment of the bodies of myself and others will be obligations to retain possession of my body and to maintain its integrity and unity. These too are worth comparing with corresponding obligations I may have concerning things. If a person's right of disposal over some bodily part can be shown to fail, it may or may not open up the possibility that he or she has a positive duty to maintain or conserve that part, or even to retain possession of it.

In resolving issues about bodily rights and obligations much will depend on how far and in what form the concept of 'ownership' can be applied to the relation between a person and their own and other people's bodies and body parts. Kant has argued that the concept of ownership could never properly be applied even to the relation between a person and their own most disposable body parts such as teeth, an argument we shall consider in some detail.

An obvious starting-point to a discussion of moral rights and obligations of ownership is to consider legal parallels. Can some bodily obligations be understood in terms of the demands that arise through one's legal ownership of one's body? The notion of a person as the metaphysical owner of their own body is unproblematic. At least a necessary condition for the identity of a person as just this person is to be found in the persistence and integrity of just that body. Both Strawson (1959) and Hampshire (1959) have argued convincingly for this thesis. Is it compatible with some measure of legal ownership that a person might have of their body? In his *Lectures on Ethics* (17**) Kant comes down emphatically against the intelligibility of any relation of ownership, legal or otherwise, between a person and their body.

Man cannot dispose over himself because he is not a thing; he is not his own property; to say that he is would be self-contradictory; for in so far as he is a person he is a Subject in whom the ownership of things can be invested, and if he were his own property, he would be a thing over which he could have ownership. But a person cannot be a property and so cannot be a thing which can be owned, for it is impossible to be a person and a thing, the proprietor and the property.

Accordingly a man is not at his own disposal. He is not entitled to sell a limb, not even one of his teeth. (p. 165)[1]

(One should note that in this passage the masculine grammatical gender of the pronouns is not tied to the presumed biological sex of their referents. It simply agrees with the conventional grammatical gender of the species term 'Man'.)

The last sentence shows us that Kant did not have in mind a purely mentalistic or spiritual concept of a person, but of persons as embodied beings whose limbs are as much a part of them as their memories or their labour power. The idea that there is any comparability between Embodied Person and Thing considered in the context set by the rights and obligations of vendors and purchasers is ruled out a priori. The argument seems to me to beg the question. It assumes that a body and its parts cannot be regarded in a detached fashion by the person thus embodied. But this is just the point at issue.

In general the owner of a thing owns its parts. In the absence of any externally imposed restrictions, an owner can freely dispose of the parts of the things he or she owns by sale, lease or gift. The fact of ownership generally entails rights to transfer ownership to someone else. One can sell bits of one's old car for spares, or even dispose of it for scrap, without a moral qualm. But there are limits. If the car happens to be a Type 33 Bugatti or a Jaguar SS1 there seems to be some sort of obligation not to destroy it. Does this mean that there is a right to protection vested in the machine?

The fact that the scrap merchant will melt the car down does seem to be a relevant consideration. The use to which a new owner might put what he or she has acquired could be one source of a possible restriction on the rights of owners to make unrestricted transfer of ownership. Recall the plot of *Synoidal green*. In that story the central crisis of the film is prompted by the hero's discovery that the bodies people make over to the state are used not to train medical students or for any other socially proper use, but as raw material for the production of food for the lower classes. There are two issues. Can one dismantle the Bugatti with a clear conscience and sell off its parts one by one, knowing that they will be used to repair and restore other Bugattis? Could one countenance as other than an act of vandalism the actions of the scrap merchant in melting down the remains of the car and so destroying it? Or of the greedy property developer in pulling down a listed building?

---

[1]   I am grateful to Judith Hughes for this reference.

The problem raised by the first issue is the moral status of aesthetic value, if any. English law, providing protection for such works of art as listed buildings, seems to recognize that both a moral and an aesthetic wrong would be done by an owner dismantling, and more particularly destroying, the structure. In the case of a work of art, even partial dismantling may amount to aesthetic destruction since, if the work is an integrated whole, the abstraction of any of its parts decreases its aesthetic value and so merits legal sanctions. But how can the law be used to forbid an aesthetic outrage? By recognizing a moral element in the fault. The law regulates relations between persons so that there must be an interpersonal injury in permitting, or assisting at, the irreparable damage to, or destruction of, a work of art. It arises simply enough in the loss to persons of the right to enjoy, and be uplifted by, the thing in question.

There are some dismantlings, say cutting off my hair for sale or giving blood for transfusion, that would not violate a principle of integrity. The fact that the hair will regrow and that the blood is replaced naturally is not the only base for freedom of disposition. Once a kidney has been sacrificed, current medical technology offers no hope of its regrowth. Its disposal is permitted because the remaining kidney takes over the function previously performed by both. That the donor goes on living after the sale or donation of a body part may not be enough to ensure the moral neutrality of the act. It seems to me intuitively clear that the offer of a whole limb for transplant would be morally troublesome and certain to be rejected. This intuition rests, I suggest, on a rather vague, but important, concept of organic well-being, involving such root ideas as good functioning and bodily integrity. Blood, hair, skin, sections of veins and even single kidneys can be disposed of without detriment to general bodily well-being.

The bodies so far considered have been living embodiments of persons. We cannot leave the topic without some discussion of the moral issues surrounding post-mortem donation, or even sale. At first sight it would seem that since one's body, post mortem, is no longer the seat of personhood, it is no longer morally protected. But the matter is not quite so simple. It is tasteless, but hardly immoral, to take money now from some institution for the privilege of making post-mortem use of one's corpse. Many of us offer our corpses quite freely. In the case of the commercial transaction the purchaser has invested in a body future, much as speculators in other commodities may buy up futures, The cocoa crop of 1991 is sold long before it has begun to appear on the trees. Having sold my body future, am I under a novel kind of obligation? Am I morally obliged to maintain the integrity of the merchandise, to avoid those occasions of risk in which it might be totally destroyed, say by fire? I suppose that cocoa farmers, having sold the crop futures, have an obligation to maintain adequate standards of husbandry until it is harvested. I am inclined to think that the vendor of a body future is in much the same case as a cocoa farmer. Once again, however, it is clear that this obligation to body care is rooted in a relation between persons – vendor and purchaser – and that there is no more a moral obligation to the body as such than the farmers have to the cocoa trees as such.

The parallel between rights of disposal that accrue to owners of aesthetically valuable things and those that people have over their bodies seems close enough to cast doubt on Kant's absolute prohibition on admitting the concept of 'ownership' to a place in the discussion and explication of the relation between a person and their body. His refusal to countenance the sale even of a tooth is too absolute. His arguments would seem to rule out gifts of parts of living bodies as well. Kidney transplants and blood transfusions would be not only morally, but logically, prohibited if no shred of the ownership concept survived critical assessment of how persons are related to their bodies.

So far I have discussed the matter of disposal only from the point of view of the donor's rights over his or her body and its parts. But what happens to organic remains more generally has recently become an important public issue. How are donor's moral obligations related to, or affected by, the use to which donated parts are put? The outline of the moral debate is very simple. Human value, the good of persons, provides the moral footing. Spare parts from people will be used for the repair of the bodies of other people – not to feed the piranhas in the local aquarium. The rules for the proper and reverent disposal of detached parts, and even whole bodily remains, are so devised as to honour the personhood of him or her who has been so embodied. Transplant surgery is just a special case of honourable disposal of body parts. Debate has been most heated on the subject of the proper uses and disposal of foetal tissue from abortuses and spare embryos, waste bodies accidentally or deliberately created in the process of human reproduction. I shall return to this issue.

RIGHTS TO KNOWLEDGE OF ONE'S BODY; OBLIGATIONS TO DISCLOSE IT AND RIGHTS TO DEMAND IT

Restrictions on rights to know about material things and substances seem explicable entirely in terms of relevant social goods. Knowledge of the way to make explosives or of how to synthesize certain undesirable drugs may be restricted to those thought responsible enough not to be liable to misuse that knowledge. To lead into the case of knowledge of my body the question about knowledge can be sharpened by restricting the material things and substances at issue to those I do, or might legitimately, own. It seems to me that whatever I do own I have unrestricted rights to obtain knowledge of. These rights seem to me to be those that fit the second level of Hohfeld's triadic distinction. But even if an object is of a socially harmless character, the fact that it is yours rather than mine seems to me to involve a restriction of how much I may know about it. And this is not just because I would have to interfere with it to find out certain things about it, but because knowledge of something is one of the privileges and rights of ownership. I am not sure whence this restriction derives. Only if there is the possibility of you becoming the owner of my house am I obliged to disclose its hidden defects to you. At first sight it looks as if the rights that an owner has to obtain knowledge of whatever he or she owns and to restrict its transmission to others are very nearly absolute.

I own my body in two senses. I have metaphysical ownership via the role it plays in my sense of personal identity, and legal ownership in the rights I have over its dismemberment and disposal. At first sight it would seem that it would follow that my rights to knowledge of my body and its states would be at least as broad as those I have to knowledge of the things I own. Indeed at first sight one would be inclined to say that these rights are at the third level of Hohfeld's scheme. Others are obliged positively to assist their fulfilment. However, English law recognizes two dimensions in which this right to knowledge is restricted. Doctors are not obliged to disclose the state of a patient's body to that patient if in their view the patient's coming to know the relevant facts would jeopardize their chances of recovery. One might argue that this principle, though paternalistic, is so obviously in the best interests of the patient that it can hardly be disputed. But in the Sidaway judgement (1985) the House of Lords broadened the principle of knowledge restrictions for the good of an individual to include the good of people in general. Doctors were confirmed in their rights to keep some fact about a patient's body from that person if knowledge of it would jeoparize the outcome of a clinical experiment deemed to be in the general good. One's body becomes part of the material resources of the collective whose rights to know about it may override those of the person who is thus embodied. In this case, as in the others I have examined, the body as such is not the target or source of rights and obligations, but merely the occasion or locus of their exercise. The body enters the argument only in so far as it is the material vehicle of personhood and the topic of moral judgements.

One sometimes comes across remarks, particularly those of health and diet enthusiasts, that suggest the existence of something like an obligation to learn about one's body and to become acquainted with its current states and conditions. The metaphor of 'listening' to one's body is commonly used. Once again a little reflection suggests that acquiring knowledge of one's body in this context is not a moral obligation so much as a sensible precaution. It is neither a question of a right to obtain knowledge nor a right to be known. One can hardly manage one's body properly if one is ignorant of its state and mode of functioning.

RIGHTS AND OBLIGATIONS WITH RESPECT TO THE USE OF THE HUMAN BODY

A great variety of highly contestable rights and obligations has grown up around the role of human bodies in reproduction, in Western Christian societies. The system that held sway in the nineteenth century is not wholly obsolete and some of the discussions about such topics as abortion and contraception reflect the persistence of remnants of the old ways of thinking about these matters. Much recent discussion of body use has turned particularly on the rights of women – that is, of people embodied in female bodies – to manage the reproductive capacities of those very bodies. Moral problems encountered in reflection on such topics as abortion have been discussed almost *ad nauseam*. I shall turn my attention to the moral problems that seem to arise in the practice of surrogate motherhood. Are there obligations that fall upon women as people embodied in reproductive 'engines' that do not fall upon men? One issue that has persistently surfaced and resurfaced has been whether the rights of use of a certain body for reproductive purposes are wholly invested in the person thus embodied, or whether other people have rights in that person's reproductive body use as well. A similar question has arisen in respect of obligations. Are women, necessarily embodied in female bodies, under any obligations to use those bodies reproductively? If so are these special or general obligations? A medieval or renaissance queen had a special obligation to provide the kingdom with sons. It has been suggested that any woman is under a general obligation to act as a surrogate mother.

There is a traditional moral order within which the age-old form of the human reproductive process is embedded. We seem to be witnessing the emergence of a new moral order in response to the appearance of new forms of the reproductive process. A schematic representation of the variants now possible within the process of human reproduction can make the relevant clusters of moral obligations clear. Three modes of parenting are successively involved in the reproductive process.

1.   There is *genetic parenting* comprising the relevant activities of those involved in the conception of a foetus.

2.   There is *gestatory parenting*, the process of bearing the foetus to term, a process in which a male parent has only a voluntary and supporting role.

3.   Finally there is *social parenting* in which once again both male and female parents play complementary and, it seems, indispensable roles, in the post-natal upbringing of an infant until it reaches relative maturity.

I shall call the people involved at each stage the genetic, the gestatory and the social parents respectively.

The traditional moral order of reproductive obligations, rights and duties is built around the 'canonical' case in which the genetic, gestatory and social parents are the same human pair throughout. In the old order adoption by a pair who are not genetic and gestatory parents, but assume the role of social parenting, is the only variation on this scheme. Genetic fathering by an 'outsider' is immoral in this scheme. It is worth remarking that the outlines of the old order are not only defined by reference to the welfare of the new born, but also by reference to psychological and social relations among the adults involved, such as jealousy and conceptions of honour. The growth of medical technology and the development of welfare services have influenced the relation of the traditional moral order to the canonical form of the process of human reproduction. For instance, genetic counselling may lead people to feel a moral obligation to interfere with the natural modes of sexual intercourse for fear of conceiving a deformed child. Amniocentesis can be used to detect defects in a foetus, and these may lead people to think they have a moral obligation to interfere in the process of gestation for fear of bringing a deformed foetus to term. Emphasis on the moral and physical welfare of a child may lead the state to decide that the biological parents are not fit persons to undertake social parenting, and to take the child into care.

The new scientific-technical order is built around the fact that all possible variants of the reproductive pattern are possible, since it is no longer necessary for the genetic and gestatory parents to be the same pair of people. In particular, the gestatory mother may not be the female person who has contributed the female gamete to the human embryo implanted in the surrogate mother, who will play the role of gestatory parent. A more complex array of personnel is evident where the genetic and gestatory female parent is the same woman, the gestatory and social male parent is the same man (a situation made possible through AID technology), while the social female parent is someone else, the social partner of the male genetic parent.

I shall discuss the moral issues raised by these various possibilities in the light of a treatment suggested by Roger Scruton, sketched in an article in *The Times* (London) (Scruton, 1985). Scruton draws a distinction between a technical and a moral relationship between one being and another. The woman who is merely the gestatory parent, the host mother, takes on obligations only to those with whom she has contracted to carry the alien foetus. Logically she is no more than a glorified baby sitter, with no special 'internal' relationship to the new life. The surrogate mother has rented out her body by selling her gestatory power. The immorality that Scruton sees in the transaction is not Kantian. It is not that the host mother cannot enter into commercial transactions involving her body on the grounds that she does not own it in the sense required for those sorts of use. The moral defect lies in the structure of obligations. The surrogate has acquired a moral obligation only to the genetic parents, and not to the foetus with which she is so intimately involved.

The most troublesome kind of case legally has come from the situation in which a surrogate contributes genetically to the foetus herself. Having borne the foetus to term, the surrogate may refuse to hand over the child, claiming that there now exists not only a natural sentiment uniting her to the child, but natural obligations and rights as well. The traditional moral order of parenting obligations can be invoked to insist on the indissolubility of mothering rights in all three phases of female parenting. In short, if a person, embodied in a female form, is both the genetic and gestatory parent, she has a natural right to be social parent as well.

The aspect of surrogacy that I want to emphasize in this discussion is not so much the rights women have over their own bodies and the bodies of the infants they bear, but what can be said about the reciprocal obligations that people so embodied have to those bodies. Does a woman who enters into a surrogacy contract have a special obligation to care for her own body and that of the implanted foetus by virtue of the contract – that is, an obligation that enjoins a level of care over and above what would be required by prudential considerations alone?

This question cannot be answered in any simple fashion. It exposes an ambiguity at the very foundations of body morality, that between individual and collective obligations.

DUTIES TO THE COLLECTIVE

Even a cursory glance at recent feminist writing on such matters as the rights and duties of women with respect to the process of human reproduction discloses a strand of extreme individualism in the underlying assumptions of many arguments and declarations. It is evident, for instance, in the following manifesto:

> I will choose what enters me, what becomes of my flesh. Without choice no politics, no ethics lives. I am not your cornfield, your uranium mine, nor your calf for fattening, nor your cow for milking. You may not use me as your factory. Priests and legislators do not hold shares in my womb or my mind. This is my body. If I give it to you I want it back. My life is a non-negotiable demand.

Under 'individualism' a person's rights over the disposal of their body, including its reproductive powers, are absolute. Under 'collectivism' a person's individual rights are balanced against duties that one may owe to the relevant collective. Some of these duties may be derived from the kind of body one possesses. There are various possibilities, including the case where the body in question is youthful, where it is healthy, where it is strong, as well the case where it is female. When the survival of a human group depends on the use of a specially endowed body, one might argue that a person, as a member of the group, is under an obligation to use it in the interests of that group. One *should* use one's youthful and powerful body to go for help. Is there an equivalent 'should' that involves the femaleness of one's body? In the individualist moral framework of the above manifesto it is abundantly clear that no such obligation can be derived.

Before I turn to detailed arguments around the issue of surrogacy, I would like to explore the dichotomy between individualist/collectivist moral positions more deeply. I shall trace the influence of an unexamined individualism in a well-known argument put forward by J. J. Thomson (1971). I must confess at the outset that I find Thomson's position morally disturbing – even shocking. In essence her argument builds up a case for a principled way of distinguishing those situations in which abortion is justified and those in which it is not. The key concept is 'right of use' and the key argument questions the extension of right of use to a class of persons one might call 'the uninvited'. Thomson's argument is built around an extremely complex example, involving a continuous and prolonged blood transfusion between one person, *A*, and another, *B*. *A* is recruited without explicit consent, while *B*'s life depends on the hook-up. A simpler example in which the moral structure becomes more transparent could be constructed by comparing the woman who is unwittingly pregnant with the owner of an apartment who finds herself entertaining an uninvited guest, a squatter. According to Thomson, so absolute are the rights of an individual that the owner is morally justified in ejecting the visitor, even though the visitor will be likely to die of exposure. The visitor's right to life is made conditional on the property rights of the owner. So far as I can see, Thomson's case amounts to no more than a simple use of the dubious principle of double effect. Moral considerations apply only to intended actions and hence are individualist in an absolute sense, since only individuals can have or lack intentions. Side effects that are not intended are morally irrelevant, even when they can be rationally anticipated.

Commenting on this argument, Wilcox (1989) points out that in discussions of abortion and surrogacy the use of expressions such as 'loan' and 'ownership' are metaphors. Like all metaphors, they are semantic Trojan horses. The infiltrators in this case are the hosts of individualism. Taken that way, the 'owner' of the apartment has no duty other than the protection of her own property. And this simply excludes without argument the possibility of collective duties to other members of the human race qua human. Once we accept the metaphors of the world of personal property, the argument is preempted and the principle of double effect emerges as the natural defence against an accusation of murder, or at least callous disregard. There are good arguments in favour of the right to abort a foetus, but this is not one of them.

Once again it seems that the discussion has developed in such a way that the heart of the issue of surrogacy seems to involve questions as to duties and rights that derive from the fact of embodiment rather than towards the body as such. The question of whether distinctive kinds of bodies demand certain special treatments as of right is overshadowed by the question of whether the possession of such-and-such a kind of body is a sufficient condition for the ascription to persons so embodied of rights and duties over and above those that they have just by virtue of being human beings. Is accepting the obligation of surrogacy a work of supererogation?

It has been argued that women belong to two collectives, by virtue of embodiment. Along with men they belong to the human collective, the tribe, even the species. But by virtue of being embodied as female, they belong to another collective, the beings charged with the continuous recreation and maintenance of the human race. This is the collective of women. As a human being, no woman has either a right or an obligation to act as a surrogate mother. But as a woman, she has

6. The Australian sisters.
(Courtesy of the AGE (Melbourne).)

both a right to act as a surrogate, and even a duty to do so. Surrogate motherhood, in this setting, is not a vulgar commercial transaction, but the fulfilment of a sacred moral duty. The collectives whose welfare and whose demands are taken to override those of women as individuals are biologically based, but socially empowered. It could be argued that genetic similarity imposes a special obligation on sisters, mothers and daughters and other close relatives to act as surrogates for one another (see plate 6; in particular note the expressions on the faces of the two women.) According to gene-selection theory (Dawkins, 1986), reproductive behaviour, at all three stages of the reproductive process, should favour one's own genes. Close relatives share many of the same genes. Assisting one's genetic kin to reproduce their genes, in this new way, favours the genetic basis of a family and so engenders a special obligation of surrogacy on its female members.

MORALITY AND REPRODUCTIVE TECHNOLOGY

In the discussion so far I have assumed that the shift in reproductive 'technology' is morally neutral in itself. Scruton is the only philosopher, so far as I know, who has challenged that assumption. In the newspaper article to which I have already referred he presents an argument for setting aside the scientific-technical reproductive methods as immoral in themselves. I am somewhat uneasy at ascribing exactly the arguments I shall expound to the real Roger Scruton. The following arguments seem to me to be within the spirit of his article. In summary these arguments run as follows:

1.   Sexual relations are morally tied to parenting – that is, sexual intercourse is good only in so far as it is a step in the production of new persons. I think the implication for Scruton is that, in my terms, the three phases of parenting cannot be separated. It could be argued, for example, that only strongly bonded pairs are likely to make good social parents, and in so far as sexual intercourse is a means of bonding a couple, that activity ties together both conception and subsequent gestation with social parenting. But it could be objected that reproduction may not be the only good that comes from sexual pairing. The Christian marriage service reminds us that marriage is also ordained for the help the one may have of the other.

2.   Scruton also seems to be arguing that engaging in the first two phases of parenting entails an obligation on those taking part to undertake the third phase, the upbringing of their offspring. This may well be true. But it does not follow that a wholesome desire to engage in the third phase requires that one achieve parenthood in the traditional way. It is precisely this option that the scientific-technical order makes possible by the technical separation of the three phases of parenting. Surrogate motherhood does seem to provoke a clash of moral intuitions. The woman who bore the child, regardless of the sources of its genetic endowment, seems to be required by the Scruton principle to undertake its upbringing. Yet we can hardly treat the desire of a couple to bring up a child, whatever its origins, as immoral. The

Scruton principle must be applied, 'other things being equal'. If the biological mother is incapacitated, mentally disturbed and so on, adoption may be the only morally right course. Room is thus made for surrogacy where the quasi-biological mother is deleted by her entering into a self-denying contract. There are all sorts of ways in which we recognize that the third phase of parenting can be separated from the first and second. Surrogacy is just one of them.

3.   In his article Scruton argues against the moral probity of the scientific-technical order itself, within which surrogacy has become a practical possibility. He claims that within this moral order pregnancy is taken to be a misfortune, since the point of sexual relations in the new order is not procreation. But this claim is weak. In the traditional moral order there were plenty of situations in which pregnancy was not so much a misfortune as a disaster. 'Go! Do not darken my doorstep again!' might seem to us to come from the script of a banal melodrama, but it had plenty of exemplifications in real life, not to mention the moment of realization of the imminent arrival of the tenth or more child to add to the blessings of a poor family. Furthermore, it is to the scientific-technical order that many otherwise childless couples owe the joys of parenthood, one means to which is surrogacy.

Though Scruton chose the ephemeral medium of a daily newspaper for the publication of his analysis of bodily obligations, his argument is of profound importance. It succinctly catches the mood of the reactionary aspect of much contemporary discussion of these issues. His first step is to highlight sexual love and the love of children as 'the forces by which we live, and which govern our smaller obligations'. This point is argued even more forcibly in his extended study of sexuality, in which 'normal' (that is, nineteenth-century) sexual attitudes and relations are declared to be definitive of our humanity (Scruton, 1986). These loves occur and have their proper meaning only in the context of incarnation, of human embodiment. Sexual morality, the moral governance of these loves, is the means by which people undertake moral responsibility for their flesh. Setting the reproductive process in a scientific-technical order puts 'the body outside the sphere of moral sentiment' and effectively hands its moral governance over to a set of non-moral principles, part prudential and part commercial. Scruton's final step is to argue that certain uses of the body are sinful just because they 'enable us to escape the obligations which the body itself imposes.' It is wrong to escape one's obligations.

Several radical objections spring to mind, one of which I have already entered in the context of the discussion of surrogacy. It seems to me obvious (as I have argued in detail in *Ways of Being*, vol. 1

Social Being) that sexual and parental love are far from being dominant among the forces by which human beings live. They are subordin-
ate at every stage of history to the search for honour. Brutus, one
remembers, gained enormous credit by an act still being celebrated in
revolutionary France. He sacrificed his monarchist sons to political
principle. His honour, as a republican, required it. The basic forces of
the moral life occur not in the context of incarnation, but in the world
of symbolically mediated social relations.

Secondly the body 'imposes other obligations' than the imperative of
reproduction. It demands care and cultivation, at the very least for
prudential reasons. Personhood, at its highest pitch, can be sustained
only in a well-managed body. Furthermore, the discipline of the management of the body is also a discipline of character. In that thought
the apparently opposing lines of argument of St John of the Cross and
Jane Fonda intersect.

RIGHTS OF, AND OBLIGATIONS TO, THE USE OF THE BODY

The discussion has led through a number of cases in which the concept
of, and reference to, the human body has figured as an essential part
of the content of moral judgements. In each case the role of the body
has been secondary, since the target and the source of the rights and
obligations invoked have turned out to be, in one way or another, a
person or persons. Perhaps in the discourse of health cults we shall find
reference to obligations that have the body itself as the target of moral
concern rather than the person so embodied.

Much recent health and fitness rhetoric seems to suggest that people
are under an obligation to maintain their bodies in good physical
condition. This is not just a matter of looking good and feeling well. A
sense of 'right functioning' seems to be involved, a concept defined
more in bodily terms than by reference to its phenomological accom-
paniments. Sometimes health enthusiasts seem to imply – for instance
in the quotation from Jane Fonda that heads this chapter – that correlative rights to good treatment are invested in the body itself.

I begin by comparing my obligation to care for my body with my
obligation to care for anyone else's. Considerations concerning the
latter seem to centre on two matters. Do my obligations to a body
depend on the status of 'its' person – that is, do they depend on
whether it embodies a potential, an actual or a former person? Obligations of care and maintenance appear rather different in the three
temporal sectors of bodily existence. Prenatally the moral status of the

body in question derives from its role in the future embodiment of a possible person. During the normal course of life a body embodies some definite person, with distinctive rights and duties. The final sector of regard covers the period during which a body is still manifestly the body of a distinguishable former person, dead or alive, corpse or zombie. As we have seen repeatedly in this chapter, in the normal course of life the obligations that someone has to the bodies of others arise through obligations to the persons so embodied. In the case of zombies (the undead of Nosferatu fame as well as the living vegetables maintained on high-tech life-support systems) it seems to be widely agreed that there are no obligations to maintain and care for a body that will never be that person again. Whatever reverence is due to it is identical with that due to a corpse, and derives from the respect we feel for the person once so embodied. This is a protection against social indignities rather than against organic decay.

Again it seems to be widely agreed, and not just on the liberal side of the abortion debate, that there are cases where the obligation to maintain and care for another human body can be overridden. Two clear cases are:

1. When the person-supporting organic lives of others are threatened we can suspend the obligation of care for a human body, and even destroy it. In a manhunt for a mass murderer thought likely to kill again, we tend to think that the police are morally justified in 'gunning him down'.

2. When the body whose existence threatens the actual person-supporting role of another body is only potentially the body of a possible person, the obligations on others to care for and to maintain it are suspended. Arguments for this view are well summarized in Glover (1977). The overriding argument seems to me to be that that there is no absolute guarantee that any potentially person-supporting body will develop so as actually to sustain a person. Nor do we know which person this body will perhaps support. On the balance lies the life and welfare of an actual person, already in existence and located in various moral orders. In all these cases it turns out that it is persons and not bodies as such that are the focus fo moral consideration.

Obligations to maintain and care for my own body are often defined with respect to prudential considerations. Again judgements of whether a self-directed action is right or wrong turn on persons and draw attention away from the body as such. For instance, in discussions on the corporeal vice of smoking it is not the injury to the body as such that is the focus of moral disapproval, but the social costs incurred in putting right this self-inflicted injury (not to mention the bodily harm done to others).

So far the question of the moral relevance of attributes of bodies towards which obligations might arise has persistently reverted to issues that depend on the fact that a human body is the material seat of personhood. But many people have come to regard a flabby, ill-kept body as not only aesthetically, but morally, offensive. (In pursuit of the truly bodily obligation one must set aside the person-relative judgement that a flabby body is a sign of weakness of will and self-indulgence.) One is tempted, on first acquaintance, to treat the advice of health enthusiasts when it is not merely prudential, as pointing to a supererogatory obligation. We may admire the admirable and beautiful Jane Fonda's strength of character and fortitude in enduring 'the burn', but we can hardly be morally obliged to emulate it. Her regime is care beyond the normal call of duty. But that still leaves the question of whether there may not be some residual duty – an obligation on everyone to take care of this wondrous mechanism, the body, outside prudential considerations and beyond issues of social utility, yet falling short of the supererogatory. The trick seems to be to personify the body, thus remaining within the traditional moral framework, but extending the range of beings taken as persons. When Jane advises us to listen to our bodies we are half inclined to hear them as other persons.

What possible sense can be made of this? There is an analogous case in which the vicarious assignment of personhood grounds very important moral judgements, namely the case of the rights of animals. Household pets are most often endowed with personhood. Let us try out the idea that a human body is to be thought of as a pet with a permanent live-in master or mistress.

The idea scores an immediate success with the spare-embryos problem. *In vitro* fertilization procedures usually produce many more embryos than could be implanted in the mother. Should they be used for medical research? Do they have any rights, any moral protection? In the framework of the pet analogy they have the status of strays. Since it is the master or mistress who vicariously personifies their pet, strays are available for medical research in well-run and humane laboratories where the work is of unquestioned human benefit, since they are not even vicariously persons. By the same line of argument, spare embryos can be used for medical research, but since, in a loose sense, they are human, they can be used only for serious purposes. It would be improper, for instance, to enclose one or two in magnifying plastic for table decorations.

The line of argument sketched out above is highly tendentious. To

to look briefly at those arguments
s from considerations independent
ification above. Two main lines of
ts of animals as such. The first is
al similarity is used to extend the
by phylum from human beings to
ove will not help us in our quest
it is rooted in the morality of the
nimals have rights just in so far as
, who have rights because they are
arity is deployed rather differently
o establish qualitative similarity of
ans and other animals. Then one
certain states of consciousness, in
te independently of which kind of
rk (1977) and others have pointed
Without further qualification the
o the central moral position would
human, bodies for food, provided
and the butchery painless. It is not
just a matter of how animals feel that matters morally, but the uses to
which they are put. It is a kind of contempt perhaps that lies at the
root of what makes certain ways treating animals objectionable.

To return to the analogy, its weaknesses are now even more apparent. Neither the avoidance of suffering nor the celebration of respect and reverence for bodies fits well into the whole gamut of human views on embodiment. The morality of the body cults is not averse to suffering as a proof of virtue and commitment, nor has contempt for the body been unknown. Yet the metaphor that invites one to separate one's personal being from one's embodiment does not wholly fail us. There is another dimension in which my body could stand over against *me*. It is nature to my culture, savage to my civilization. It is endowed with powers and potencies that are not wholly within my control. It needs to be tamed, its urges overriden. It stands in need of domestication, of being made an obedient pet. If in the course of this programme of cultivation it is helpful to personify the body, so be it. It has been said that in Mary Shelley's famous tale the monster that Frankenstein creates is *the body itself*. As the source of all sorts of promptings, it is indifferent to morality. For the Frankenstein in each of us the body is like a dangerous animal held in check with a fragile leash. I owe to Amy Morgan a further observation on the analogies through which bodies are made to seem to stand over against the persons so embodied. As she pointed out, these analogies involve a

Physical Being
Rom Harré

Erratum

I am grateful to the editors of the following journals and books for permission to make use of material already published therein:

"Health as an aesthetic concept", *Cogito*, spring 1990, pp. 35–40; "Is the body a thing?", *International Journal of Moral and Social Studies*, 1/3, 1986, pp.189–203; "The cult of body building", *International Journal of Moral and Social Studies*, 1990; "Embarrassment", in Crozier, W. Ray (ed) *Shyness and Embarrassment*, Cambridge tacit and primitive Cartesianism. Cognitive and moral powers are assigned to a part of ourselves that seems to exist independently of the body whose attributes are quite other. The ontological duality of mind and body is tacitly reintroduced in the duality of master or mistress and the independent pet. This runs strongly counter to the general anti-Cartesianism with which this book begins. It is exactly the Cartesian account of how we are embodied that must be repudiated. Personhood is intrinsically tied to embodiment through the conditions of personal identity. The personification of bodies can at best be a metaphor for concepts of self-control and self-management.

In the many cases I have touched on it is the intimate tie between persons and their bodies that secretes all sorts of bodily obligations. In each domain the meaning and defensibility of a bodily obligation has hinged on the fact that it is or was or will be a person who is thus embodied. While a body may seem as chunky and uniquely separable an atom as one may well imagine, once it is thought of as someone's body, collective considerations swarm in around it. In a word, though it may seem that our individual bodies are our private possessions, reflection and analysis show the enormous extent to which they 'belong' to this or that collective and in many interesting cases to more than one collective at once.

This complex of moral attitudes to the body seems to have two main components – one is the idea of the body as a source of temptations to evil doing and the other the idea of its discipline. These are familiar notions. In orthodox Christianity the body takes on an autonomous moral character expressed in body-directed attitudes similar to those of contemporary health cults.

I am particularly grateful to Stephen Hancock for instruction on the matter of Christian attitudes to the body. The following account is largely drawn from his notes (Hancock, 1990). There is a continuous thread of Christian opinion, which with hindsight we can identify as orthodox, in which the human body stands as *totus homo* at the very centre of the concept of Christian personhood. It is through the resurrection of the body that the Christian attains immortality. The pagan dualism of imperishable soul and body husk was repeatedly repudiated by the Christian consensus. A way was always found between the Gnostic and the Manichean heresies. Both characterized the human body as intrinsically evil. Thus the Gnostic Marcion rejected the resurrection of the body, because God would have no interest in reviving an evil thing. The Manicheans believed that the material universe, including the human bodies that peopled it, was created by an evil being coeval with God Himself. By contrast Christian orthodoxy asserted the Divine creation of all material things. 'If anyone says that the creation of all flesh is not the work of God, but belongs to the wicked angels, just as Priscillian has said, let him be anathema' declared the Council of Braga in 561 (Denzinger, 1955). The body was necessary to human existence.

However, a body unanimated by a soul is a mere corpse. According to Aquinas, 'unlike the angels the human soul does not possess enough actuality to attain its perfection in a separated state.' Neither soul nor body is a 'complete' substance and each attains its proper perfection only when united in a living human being, a *totus homo*. Aquinas thought that the cultivation of the body in sports and pastimes was wholly proper.

St John of the Cross, among many, drew on the metaphor of 'captivity' to express the paradoxical role of the body in the Christian life. The soul, captive in the body, is drawn to God, but also drawn towards the things of the material world, including the promptings of the body. Though not intrinsically evil, the latter must be resisted and transcended so that the soul's love is only for God. The means of salvation is bodily discipline. The technique of that discipline is abstinence from bodily pleasures and the embrace of suffering (Fargue, 1927; Brown, 1988).

It is striking that while the metaphysical and theoretical roots of Christian and health-cult body practices are about as diverse as could be, the disciplinary matrices in which their respective moral attitudes to the body are set and the practices therein recommended are remarkably similar.

Obligations to cherish, obligations to punish, obligations to control – the necessary role of embodiment in human existence calls all these moral demands on persons into being. The latter two acknowledge the body as an independent source of promptings. The idea of their control follows naturally. But 'control' is a polar concept. Including it in our moral universe makes space also for the concept of promptings that are 'beyond' or 'out of' control.

THE BODY AS ALIBI

Bodily forces pull us down, according to the Christian tradition. What if we cannot manage them? It is no great step to pick upon bodily states and potentialities as alibis in an account of a losing moral struggle. There have been many references to uncontrollable bodily promptings in the history of explanations of drunkenness, and as many exhortations to resist temptation.

The moral problem of drunkenness can be glimpsed statistically.

In the United States 10 per cent of drinkers consume 50 per cent of all the alcohol sold (Bower, 1988). Some people are consuming a great deal and most people not much. There is, therefore, a background of 'normal' consumption (and its relatively minor consequences for conduct and long-term health) against which the anti-social behaviour and poor bodily health of heavy drinkers stand out. Since the behaviour of drunks is evidently offensive to others and the bodily changes deleterious to health, drunkenness is naturally located as an evil in the moral polarity of human conduct. It is easily tied in with self-indulgence and weakness of will.

When people are accused of moral failings, there are broadly three defences open to them. They may try to justify their actions – that is, try to show that what they are doing is not morally reprehensible. They may try to excuse themselves – that is, try to show that, while acknowledging the wrongness of their actions, they had no real choice in the matter. They may try to neutralize accusations of moral fault, arguing that no moral issue is involved. The invention of 'alcoholism' as a disease is a move of the second kind. The 'official' definition by the American National Council on Alcoholism runs as follows: 'a chronic, progressive and potentially fatal disease'. Do you catch it like typhoid or do you inherit it like spina bifida? These are the only relevant questions once the 'disease' idea has taken root. The complex moral framework traditionally surrounding the consumption of alcohol simply dissolves, taking with it the twin ideas of drinking to escape bad social conditions and overindulgence as moral weakness.

Many social observers have commented on the tendency in the United States to redefine moral issues as technical problems. Currently this tendency is manifest in an enthusiastically promoted programme to fill out the 'disease' concept of alcoholism with a genetic basis. However, a recent survey of the results of this research (Searle, 1988) casts grave doubts on the viability of any of the work, which has mostly been based on studies of the drinking habits of twins and adoptees. The point I want to make is just to highlight the persistence of a kind of muted Manicheanism into the twentieth century. Somehow it is in the body that is the source of the evils of drunkenness must be found.

REFERENCES

Aquinas, Thomas 1964: *Summa Theologicae* II. II, q. 168 a2. Oxford, Blackfriars, and London: Eyre and Spottiswoode.
Bower, B. 1988: Alcoholism's Elusive Genes. *Science News*, 134, 74–9.

Brown, R. 1988: *The Body and Society.* New York: Columbia University Press.

Clark, S. R. L. 1977: *The Moral Status of Animals.* Oxford: Clarendon Press.

Dawkins, R. 1986: *The Blind Watchmaker.* Harlow: Longmans Scientific.

Denzinger, H. 1955: *Enchiridion Symbolorum*, 30th edn, trans. R. J. Deferrari.

Fargue, A. 1927: *The Ordinary Ways of the Spiritual Life.* London: Burns and Oates.

Fonda, J. 1981: *Jane Fonda's Workbook.* Harmondsworth: Penguin.

Fox, M. 1980: *Returning to Eden: Animal Rights and Human Responsibility.* New York: Viking Press.

Glover, J. 1977: *Causing Death and Saving Lives* (ch. 3). Harmondsworth: Penguin.

Hampshire, S. 1959: *Thought and Action.* London: Chatto and Windus.

Hancock, S. 1990: Personal Communication.

Hare, R. M. 1981: *Moral Thinking* (p. 149). Oxford: Clarendon Press.

Hart, H. L. A. 1961: *The Concept of Law.* Oxford: Clarendon Press.

Hohfeld, W. 1923: *Fundamental Legal Conceptions.* Oxford: Oxford University Press.

Kant, I. (1780) (1930): *Lectures on Ethics.* London: Methuen.

Leiber, J. 1982: *Beyond Rejection.*

Levin, D. S. 1985: Thomson and the Current State of the Abortion Controversy. *Journal of Applied Philosophy*, 2, 121–5.

Piercy, M. 1986: from *The Body Politic.*

Ross, Sir W. D. 1939: *Foundations of Ethics.* Oxford: Oxford University Press.

Rousselle, A. 1988: *Porneia: On Desire and the Body in Antiquity*, trans. F. Pheasant. Oxford: Basil Blackwell.

Scruton, P. 1985: Ignore the Body, Lose Your Soul. *The Times* (London), 5 February.

Scruton, P. 1986: *A Moral Philosophy of the Erotic.* New York: Free Press.

Searle, J. S. 1988: 'Body Frames' *Journal of Abnormal Psychology*,

Singer, P. 1985: *In Defence of Animals.* Oxford: Basil Blackwell.

Strawson, P. F. 1959: *Individuals.* London: Methuen.

Thomson, J. J. 1971: A Defence of Abortion. *Philosophy and Public Affairs*, 1, 47–66.

Wilcox, J. T. 1989: Nature as Demonic in Thomson's Defense of Abortion. *New Scholasticism*, LXIII, 463–84.

CHAPTER 7

EMOTIONS OF THE BODY

With respect to blushing from strictly moral causes, we meet with the same fundamental principle as before, namely regard for the opinions of others.

Charles Darwin,
The Expression of Emotion in Man and Animals

INTRODUCTION: THE 'CONSTRUCTIONIST' ACCOUNT OF EMOTIONS

An emotion is a bodily enactment of a moral judgement or attitude in accordance with the conventions of local dramatistic roles (Sarbin, 1986). The body is the 'legible' surface from which the moral judgement can be read. A snarl of anger is both an assessment of another's action as a transgression and a reproach. However, the body and its public appearance and display can also be the topic of moral judgements and attitudes, and so the focus of the enactment of a certain class of emotions. Shame, modesty, shyness and embarrassment are, like all emotions, bodily enacted, but in one of their variants they enact unfavourable assessments of, and failures in, the management of the body itself. This is the 'constructionist' view of the emotions.

To study emotions is to study a certain kind of social act. There is no such thing as 'an emotion'. There are only various ways of acting and feeling emotionally, of displaying one's judgements, attitudes and opinions in an appropriate bodily way. For instance, 'anger' is a noun, but it refers not to what someone is or has, but to what someone does. That doing may take the form of a bodily sensation of which only the socially sophisticated person is aware. We should be studying angry people being cross with one another, denouncing and reprimanding each other. By reifying 'anger', we can be tempted into the mistake of thinking that anger is something inside a person exercising its invisible and inaudible influence on what we do. But to be angry is to have taken on the angry role on a particular occasion as the expression of a moral position. This role may involve the feeling of appropriate feelings as well as indulging in suitable public conduct. The bodily feeling is often the somatic expression to oneself of the taking of a moral standpoint.

I have used Sarbin's term 'dramatistic role' to describe a proper way of doing an emotion. He distinguishes this kind of role from dramaturgical roles such as policeman, secretary or team captain. By dramatistic roles he suggests that we should mean the roles that are required in the living out of certain everyday story lines. The role of mourner at a funeral would be such a dramatistic role. Every funeral has a story line and various dramatistic roles are part of its enactment. One can see how emotional enactments and dramatistic roles are intimately related. One adopts the role of protester for the enactment of an objection to some ecologically damaging project. How? Well one joins a march, displays indignation and outrage by waving banners and shouting slogans. There is a theatrical quality to enactments of emotion. Life is full of such role enactments: avenger, rejected lover, bereaved orphan, loser (and winner) of a World Cup 'shoot out' and so on.

Emotional enactments are normative in two ways. They express moral judgements, and proper persons are called upon to make just this kind of judgement. These dramatistic role performances are socially required. One would be morally at fault not to enact the mourner role at a family funeral, just as one would be morally at fault not at least to look ashamed at being caught out in a lie.

Emotions are, and always have been, the bodily enactments of mainly moral judgements and attitudes. In the genesis of such enacted judgements conscious ratiocination seems to have little part to play. Passions are just those states of the bodily being that come over one in the realization of loss, insult, danger, success and so on. One might say that emotions are judgements without premises. But just what kind of bodily state? Public action or private feeling? There is no doubt that before the invention of sensibility in the second half of the eighteenth century it was mainly enactment in public conduct that was the bodily centre of emotion. Before the separation of psyche and *sōma* in the romantic movement sexual love, for instance, is all action, much of it ritualized. Private feeling played an unattended second fiddle.

Our contemporary 'feminized' conception of affection tells us that love must be expressed through soft words and tender caresses. Love must be an individualized experience, best kept quiet and private if it is to flourish. Nothing could be further from the early modern conception, which refused to separate body and feeling, provided little space for sexual intimacy, and insisted that love, defined as cooperation and sharing, express itself through those prime symbols of mutuality, the body social as well as the body biological. (Gillis, 1988: 96–7)

Stearns and Stearns (1988) have charted this transition of Western emotionology in detail, while Hagstrum (1989) and Schama (1989) have explored the same transition from the point of view of literary history and the social and political background to the French revolution respectively. In the invention of sensibility, feeling replaces ritual and heart replaces head in the folk theory of the emotions. It has become increasingly clear with the proliferation of detailed historical studies that the idea of an emotionology of bodily feelings is a comparatively recent invention. However, the assimilation of emotions to the somatic category of visceral reactions even among Americans (Zajoncs, 1980) is still incomplete. For most human beings the emotional life remains largely part of the local moral universe. Zajoncs has identified certain physiological 'habits', induced by training in the local moral order. As premissless judgements physiological processes could be their only antecedents in individual people. They are cognitive nevertheless in that they are public sense-making enactments and evolve from sense-making enactments. Perhaps under the influence of the sentimentalizing of the emotions a characteristic mistake in emotionology has become prevalent, namely that in the display of an emotion a private feeling is expressed. One can easily slip into thinking that it is the feeling that is the real emotion. And from there into the typical Zajoncs's error of identifying it with the accompanying physiological process, even when it is unfelt. But both the display and the feeling are premissless judgements of situation, action or whatever it is that is the occasion for, and so the topic of the emotional state as expression of a moral assessment. When the display is aborted, the feeling remains as the residual expression of chagrin, triumph and so on.

AN EMOTION OF THE BODY

The study of embarrassment[1] may seem a small and insignificant enterprise, and yet it raises some large philosophical, psychological and moral issues. It turns, in part, on the nature of the human self and its

---

[1]   I am grateful to Jerry Parrott for helpful comments on the original paper from which this version is drawn.

relation to the fact of embodiment. Embarrassment is often a very bodily emotion. This is not only through the emphasis on the body's presence on occasions of embarrassment, but also through the way that my personal presence to others is mediated by my visible, audible, tangible, tastable and smellable body. In our culture smell (and taste) are rarely signs of the tangible presence of bodies. Even so, I can be looked at. The appearance of my body can never be denied when I am in company. I can hardly achieve presence without the vulnerability that comes from the possibility of my body itself being unfavourably assessed by the company. Hence the importance of masks, burkas, cloaks and so on in the achievement of bodily presence without the chances of embarrassment.

But embarrassment is also an emotion characteristic of occasions in which a person comes to believe that their conduct is an object of critical public consideration and unflattering judgement. I hope to be able to show through the study of embarrassment how conduct and personal appearance are linked through the grounding of rules and conventions of bodily propriety in conceptions of personal honour. This should provide a general account of the emotions of corporeal self-attention which transcends the enormous variety of kinds of conduct and bodily exposures that are locally taken to be discrediting.

However, I want to go further, to suggest that in the study of this apparently minor emotion we can find indications of profound and widespread changes in the basis of social order. I believe that shame is everywhere giving place to embarrassment as the major affective instrument of conformity. In the shift from shame to embarrassment we see a sign of the widespread recognition of the conventionality (and hence relativity) of morality and of the triviality of breaches. At the same time, embarrassment is shifting in focus from bodily disclosures to conduct, and this, I hope to show, is indicative of changing social attitudes to the social location of women.

To get clear about the concept of embarrassment will call for a quite modest application of the techniques of philosophical analysis. Apart from the grand themes I have touched on, such studies have a more practical value. Embarrassment can trouble people – indeed it can become destructive and even pathological. Clarity in concepts may have a role to play in the ordinary decent business of improving the quality of human life. There are complexities in the 'logic' of the concept, complexities that illustrate a general point about the nature of emotions, a point of some importance in the practical applications of an analysis such as I propose. Emotions are not just bodily perturbations. Embarrassment is not just blushing and squirming. It is a particular case of the interplay between social conventions, moral judgements and bodily reactions. The analysis will enable us to juxta-pose conventions concerning bodily exposure and those concerning character manifestations within the same conceptual framework, and to see how they are sometimes psychologically equivalent. The dis-tribution of credit, however, follows crooked paths. We are embar-rassed by public attention to those matters that are creditable to us as well as those that are discreditable. It has often been remarked that a display of embarrassment, and of its more potent kin, shame, may itself be creditable, and even be prescribed. It may be necessary to remind someone that one need not always blush for one's blushes.

I want to argue that there has been both a shift away from, and back towards, a Victorian relation between displays of bodily parts and attributes and embarrassment. The characterological importance of the concealment of the sexual parts has declined remarkably (more par-ticularly in Europe than in the United States), while the significance of the signs of careful bodily cultivation for character attributions has been enormously amplified. An excessively flabby and ill-kept body is an object of embarrassment (and it may be of shame) both to its possessor and to those who might be unfortunate enough to catch a glimpse of it. We have come to tie body and character in an almost Victorian way. Though the content is vastly different, the underlying structure is similar to the self-attentive bodily emotions of the Victor-ians. Bodily appearances serve as public indices of character.

SOME CLASSICAL ACCOUNTS OF THE EMOTIONS OF DISCREDIT

Shame has attracted much more attention from philosophers and psychologists than has embarrassment. Both are occasioned by painful public attention to something personal, and are manifested in similar displays. A brief look at some of the treatments of shame will help to clarify the grammar of embarrassment, while leaving open the question as to how those important emotions are to be differentiated.

Aristotle: In the *Nichomachean Ethics* (1128[b]) Aristotle defines 'shame' as a kind of 'fear of disrepute [which] produces an effect similar to that produced by fear of danger; for people who feel dis-graced [that is, think themselves disgraced] blush, and those who fear death turn pale.' It is 'in a sense a bodily condition' and so a passion.

Aristotle remarks on the 'double ought' involved, in that we 'praise young people who are prone to that passion.' His more detailed treat-ment in the *Rhetoric* (II, 1383[b]–1385[a]) lists many bad actions that can be a source of shame, but does not mention immodest appearance. In the *Rhetoric* there are three nice additions to the Nichomachean definition. Aristotle observes that it is the disgrace, and not the consequences of the disgrace, that we shrink from: that the others whose opinion of our actions is germane to our feelings are those whose opinions we respect; and when we are ashamed for others, they are people socially linked to us in some way.

Aristotle mentions two kinds of infraction: serious transgressions, such as fleeing from the battlefield, about which one would be rather more than embarrassed, and the merely socially tiresome, such as boastfulness.

One is tempted to think of shame at one pole of a continuum, with embarrassment at the other. This would imply that embarrassment is just a species of shame, the shame we feel when we notice that some relatively trivial transgression is publicly noted. Though this feature does serve to mark one dimension of difference between them, two other important differences will emerge. Parenthetically it is worth reminding ourselves that in ancient Greek there was no word for our most common sense of embarrassment, namely what the dictionary calls 'constrained feeling or manner arising from bashfulness or timidity'. The ancient Greek *aporein* picks up only that sense of embarrassment that the *OED* defines as 'perplexity or hesitation'. It is as if the gap between morality and nature, which we fill with convention, did not exist for the Greeks.

For the most recent important discussion of shame I turn to Sartre's writings. So far as I know, Sartre nowhere discusses embarrassment (the French *rougissement*). The French language, like Spanish, does not mark a distinction between blushing and embarrassment. Embarrassment as a public display of confusion is a different concept. Ricks (1974) suggests, on the basis of literary evidence, that the concept of embarrassment as such has no application to French life. Be that as it may, Sartre's interest is in shame, particularly in the structure of the interpersonal relations within which shame occurs. He pays no attention to the modes by which shame is displayed.

There are two structural conditions for shame:

(1) '... shame is shame of oneself *before the other*. The structures are inseparable' (Sartre, 1943, p. 303). The inseparable structures are the reflexive and the interpersonal.

(2) The former is modelled on the sufferer's beliefs about the latter. 'The experience of my gesture as vulgar is to borrow the other's judgement of it.'

Sartre is unclear about shame itself. Is the experience referred to in the second condition the expression of shame? Or is the experience made possible by the satisfaction of conditions 1 and 2 the occasion for another experience, the experience of shame? I think it must be the latter.

The ubiquity of the Look, actual or potential, in which I see the Other seeing me as a person, which occurs on every occasion in which I take myself to be in human company, would seem to entail that every encounter is potentially an occasion for shame. Not so – Sartre is at pains to implicate the same socio-psychological *structure* in the genesis of a great many other emotions. The structure *seems* to present me with an opportunity for an intimacy with another, by way of grasping the world, including myself, as part of it, from another's point of view. But the bulk of Sartre's famous text is devoted to showing that all attempts to realize the common structure in this way are doomed to failure. 'I am guilty first when beneath the Other's look I experience my alienation and nakedness.' In a very long subsequent passage this tantalizing combination of the apparent opportunity offered by the realization of the existence of the basic structure and my inevitable failure to make use of it in the way I and every one else wants is argued to be the source of hate.

Sartre's analysis supports a point I was at pains to develop in *Personal being*, that the reflexivity upon which the entire range of self-regarding emotions depends is not an external relation between two ontologically distinct beings – say 'I' and 'me'; it is a bringing together of two points of view, mine and my conception of the points of view of other people. Or to put the matter in Wittgenstein's way, the duality is grammatical, not ontological.

EMBARRASSMENT PROPER

Starting from the blush as an expression common to this cluster of emotions, Darwin seems to be concerned more with embarrassment than shame. In contrast to Aristotle's emphasis on conduct, it is bodily presence and physical appearance that Darwin mostly finds salient in the occasions for blushing. In *The expression of emotion in man and animals* (Darwin, 1872, p. 325) Darwin remarks that 'it is not the simple act of reflecting on our own appearance, but the thinking of what others think of us, which excites the blush' (the Sartrean point). While Aristotle focuses on demeaning actions as the source of shame, Darwin is mostly concerned with demeaning appearances as the source of embarrassment, though he sometimes speaks of 'appearances and conduct' in the same breath. The apparent relative salience of bodily presence and appearance to embarrassment rather than conduct might be thought to give us a second dimension for distinguishing embarrassment from shame. But this observation draws attention to one of the analytical problems with understanding embarrassment. One can see how honour is tied up with the conduct, but how is the *value* of the self tied up with appearance? Darwin does not touch on this question at all. It will only become clear when we see embarrassment in the context of virtue. However, it is not, in Darwin's account, an actual unfavourable assessment of our appearance or conduct that is at the root of embarrassment, but the dread of the possibility of it. An adolescent does not blush because anyone has explicitly remarked on his or her bodily presence, only at the thought that that presence might be unfavourably received.

These considerations suggest that embarrassment and shame are not neatly distinguishable by reference to discreditable bodily appearances on the one hand, and disgraceful actions on the other. Bodily shame, on this view, will occur when a wrong appearance in the eyes of others is so tied to personal moral standing that it casts doubt on the virtues of the person involved – that is, when the others take exposure to be a sign of defective moral character. So if I become aware of (or merely believe in) their taking up such an attitude to my dereliction, shame must follow, if I am of good character. Of course if I am a brazen hussy or an arrogant son-of-a-bitch, it will not. So my lack of shame is a second dereliction.

The tie between appearance and self has to do with intentions and the attribution of fault. In many cases of inadvertent breach, neither the action nor the breaching of the convention is intended. Sometimes we intend an action, but do not realize that it is in breach of a convention. But in cases where the action or disclosure is shameful, the action is deliberate and the breach not accidental. (There are hard cases where the fault is grave, but the breach unintended.) But we can reasonably be expected to realize in the moment of fleeing from the battlefield that our flight is disgraceful.

Errol Bedford (1956) has a nice, sharp example. 'Davies was said to be "to his mild embarrassment" the original of Peter Pan.' He could hardly be said to have been ashamed of this role, whatever his feelings and overt behaviour. The concept of 'shame' includes fault, and it was not his fault that Barrie picked him as a model. And we have also noticed that not to display shame at a fault is also a fault, just as not to be embarrassed at an infraction of convention is also an infraction of conventions.

But there are contexts in which the shame or embarrassment one feels is tied in with the failings of others. Armon-Jones (1986) makes

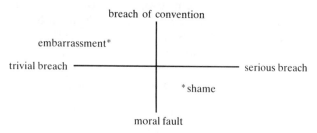

FIGURE 7.1   The 'space' of shame and embarrassment

the point that while she would feel ashamed if she saw a manifest Englishman dead drunk in the streets of Paris, she would only be embarrassed by the similar condition of a Frenchman. One might add that in Peking either situation would be an occasion for shame since the relevant moral community would no doubt be 'European'. The shame arises through the manifest fact that Ms Armon-Jones and the drunk both can be seen to belong to some relevant community. It is as a member of that community that she is shamed, whatever it is. Again, Aristotle clearly anticipated this refinement in his remarks on vicarious shame.

There are some reflexive emotions in other cultures that involve humankind in general. Spaniards place great emphasis on *verguenza ajena*, an intense 'shame/embarrassment' brought on by the foolish or self-demeaning behaviour of a stranger. It is the common membership of the human race that creates the moral community. Translating 'embarrassed' into Spanish is not easy. *Embarazada* means 'pregnant'. The Spanish language tends to favour the flustered behaviour of the embarrassed rather than their blushes as the core semantic concept. For instance, the semantic range covers *desconcertar* ('to be disconcerted'), *aturrullar* ('to be bewildered'), *avergonzar* ('to be ashamed') and *estorbar* ('to be annoying'). In Spain, one might guess, embarrassment is not a separate category from shame since, through *dignidad*, character is always 'on the line'.

We are now in a position to make a tentative distinction between shame and embarrassment. Two axes of difference will be needed and each represents a continuum of distinction. The 'space' of shame/embarrassment might look as is shown in figure 7.1. There are many other locations in the space than those I have singled out, for which we have no specific descriptive terms. Nevertheless I am fairly confident that they represent psychologically real emotional phenomena.

We can relate what is proper more tightly to circumstances by turning to the ever popular dramaturgical model, the analogy of life to the stage. This opens up the idea of seeing a strip of life as a *performance* put on before others. And we can perform well or ill, regardless of what it is we are actually doing. Drawing on Goffman's famous essay 'Face work', Silver, Sabini and Parrott (1987) propose the following definition: 'embarrassment is the flustering caused by the perception that a working consensus disrupted by a botched performance cannot be restored in time.'

Two additions to the Aristotle–Darwin treatment, summarized in the 2-D space in figure 7.1, are implied. Infractions of social conventions cannot, in general, be ignored. They must be remedied. Goffman suggests that remedies are needed to dispel the threat of an inference to the conclusion that the participants (and sometimes even the onlookers) are not committed to the local conventions either through vice or through ignorance. One shows that one is the right sort of person, the kind of person with whom others might wish to consort, by putting right one's own infractions and tactfully assisting others to do the same with theirs. Silver et al. suggest that while the mutual work of face-saving proceeds smoothly, embarrassment does not occur. So it is not the mere fact of failing to maintain the conventions that occasions embarrassment.

Time is required to get remedial work under way. An infraction may be forced into public notice, just because there has not been time to do the remedial work, be it verbal or practical. The 'working consensus' of the above definition must be about the virtues, qualities and characters of the persons involved. Thus what is at issue, because it is what is at risk, is an unfavourable assessment of character. Unless the skirt is pulled down in time or the self-deprecatory remark dropped in fairly soon after the public congratulation, one runs the risk of being taken to be a shameless floozy, a brash oaf and so on, contrary to the working consensus as to the kind of persons we are and consort with. So, in the end, embarrassment has little to do with what has been done or not done, in itself, but in how what is done or not done about what has been done provides evidence for assessments of character.

This point is well taken, but Silver et al. overlook the 'double ought' that governs displays of embarrassment. The display may, *in itself*, be sufficient remedy for the infraction, supplying evidence in default of explicit face-work to support an attribution of good character and virtue. One is not embarrassed because the remedy cannot be carried out in time, being embarrassed *is* the remedy. However, incompetence (the demeaning attribution occasioned by a botched performance) is an example of the kind of milder dereliction that we have been looking for to open up a gap between embarrassment and shame on the dimension of seriousness. One is more than merely embarrassed when caught out in a deliberately intended and morally debased action. Yet one is less than ashamed when one arrives at a formal dinner in T-shirt and jeans.

But the restriction of occasions of embarrassment to noticeably botched performances without public remedy is both too narrow and too vague. Wrong appearances are just as embarrassing as wrong actions and just as much in need of remedy. The embarrassment occasioned by a violation of a local modesty convention is incompletely drawn under the concept of a botched performance. Keeping one's clothing in order is taken for granted as the unintended background to action, hardly a sustained performance. But nevertheless one's honour can be at stake if clothing is ill adjusted. However, if nakedness is the social norm, to be fully dressed can be embarrassing.

Furthermore, Sabini et al. invoke only one aspect of the embarrassment display, fluster (Darwin's 'confusion of thought'). They have nothing to say about blushing. Experience suggests that these modes of display are semantically equivalent, in that either will do as a manifestation of embarrassment. They often occur together, and Darwin gives a physiological account of why that might be, but there are many occasions when disorderly gestures and muddled speech are not accompanied by a blush. And there are other occasions when a blush is all there is to show that someone is embarrassed.

The dramaturgical analysis does bring out the important principle behind the fact that a display of embarrassment is a last-ditch remedy for a breach of conventions. It is better to lose one's reputation for poise than one's character as a modest sort of person.

A still sharper distinction between embarrassment and shame emerges from the apparent anomaly that one can be embarrassed as much by the public attention that is attracted to one's successes as by that attracted by one's failings. One cannot be said to be ashamed at public attention to one's success, unless it had been achieved by discreditable or dishonourable means. Then it is the means, and not the success, that occasions the shame.

A possible explanation of anomalous embarrassement could invoke the virtue of modesty. A display of self-satisfaction in success would breach the modesty conventions. Public attention to oneself in the moment of success opens up the possibility that one's natural pleasure in one's achievement may appear to the others as immodest self-satisfaction. Hence one's successes are occasions of threat to one's character as a proper modest person just in so far as one is the centre of attention. There are cultures in which it would be considered improper not to boast about an achievement or triumph over a defeated rival.

This accounts for the mapping of embarrassment on to the more trivial breaches of the code while shame is mapped on to the more serious. Modesty is a less 'serious' virtue for us nowadays than honesty or integrity. However, this is a recent change in the hierarchy of virtues and I shall come back to reflect more deeply on the nature of bodily modesty below.

OCCASIONS OF, CONDITIONS FOR, AND RESOLUTIONS OF EMBARRASSMENT

A catalogue of some of the conditions under which it seems proper to say that someone was embarrassed can be distilled from these accounts.

a.   One has become the focus of (an apparently excessive) attention from others whose opinion one values with respect to what one has said or done, or how one appears.

b.   One has become aware that others have taken the sayings, doings or appearances in question to be abnormal.

c.   One sees the others as seeing the abnormality of what one has done etc. as an infraction of a rule or convention, adherence to which is a mark of good character and moral virtue.

The question of whether the sufferer's beliefs conforming to a, b and c above are true has only a marginal role to play in our understanding of the significance of embarrassment. So three parallel conditions of merely thinking that the above three objective conditions obtained are also enough for a blush.

d.   One can be just as embarrassed when one is loudly congratulated as one is quietly advised to 'zip up'. There is no paradox in this case since too ready a display of self-satisfaction in one's achievements is in itself a mark of bad character, and public attention of that sort provides room for it. A display of embarrassment immediately cancels that possibility.

There are three socially normative systems of conventions involved. There is the system of conventions concerning appearance and conduct whose violation will draw the attention of onlookers. To the sufferer that degree of attention is itself a violation of the rules of address, and so, even in the absence of any first-order infraction can become embarrassing. Then there is the normative principle that good character is demonstrated in the display of embarrassment. This in turn is relative to either or both of the other two norms, since excessive complacency when the cynosure of all eyes is a display of an unacceptable degree of self-confidence.

People and cultures differ in degrees of embarrassability. In cultures with high embarrassibility, self-confidence, the quality of character that protects against too readily succumbing to embarrassment, is an equivocal virtue. While self-confidence is a quality to be generally admired, it must be displayed with caution since it is perilously close to some generally depreciated attributes such as 'not giving a damn', callousness, arrogance, indifference, contempt and so on. Nevertheless the possibility of a life free from embarrassment particularly attracts the easily embarrassed. Ricks (1974, p. 48) notices that the unembarrassed display 'a self-possession for which the ordinarily embarrassed are grateful to the unembarrassable'.

Surprise

Edelmann and Hampson (1979) placed great weight on the element of surprise in the genesis of embarrassment. It is the sudden exposure that embarrasses. To whom though is the surprise germane? The person embarrassed or the others whose regard and attention actual or potential is the bothersome thing? One way to tackle this is to consider surprise as relative to the degree of expectation of an event. It is the unexpected rather than the merely sudden that occasions surprise. Indeed, something that creeps on the audience quite slowly may be quite surprising. But not all surprises are embarrassing, as has been pointed out in criticism of Edelmann and Hampson. If the others are surprised by what one does or exposes, it is surely because they do not expect it. But what are they not likely to expect? Surely, whatever violates the conventions appropriate to that kind of situation. It is not surprising to see someone take off their trousers in the changing room of a gym, so it is not an occasion for the kind of astonished regard that breeds embarrassment in either actor or audience. A certain famous philosopher was forced to take off his trousers on the shoulder of a large and busy motorway because the pet gerbil he was transporting for one of his children had escaped and run up his leg. He reported this event as highly embarrassing. Surprise then is relevant only as a reflection of the fact that violations of current conventions on which both embarrassment and shame depend are unexpected.

The resolution and escape from embarrassment

I am indebted again to Ricks (1974) for opening up this issue with a brief remark on the complementary role that indignation can play to embarrassment.

The idea seems to be roughly this: a display of embarrassment is, so to say, a mark to be entered in the public record, part of what Goffman called 'character'. It is ambiguous, in that while it serves to display sensitivity, it also contradicts such desirable impressions as that one is cool, sophisticated and experienced. Embarrassment, is not only a sign that one has realized that one has given an impression that is not up to some standard or other, but the embarrassment can itself sometimes be discrediting. Second-order discredit can be cancelled by cancellation of the entry into the public record that one lacks *savoir-faire*. One way of doing that is to display indignation, either on one's own or on someone else's behalf.

Nevertheless, as Aristotle noticed, a display of embarrassment as shame may incur second-order credit, since it shows our awareness of what is proper, if that awareness is a mark of a creditable stage on the way to maturity. As Goffman puts it (1967, p. 108), 'when an individual, receiving a compliment, blushes from modesty, he may lose his reputation for poise but confirm a more important one, that of being modest.' Hence, as Aristotle observes, the young are to be praised for blushing, though a similar blush would be discreditable among the mature. Is this because the blush shows that I know what I should have done or how I should have appeared, but that I have failed to follow the rules and I know it? Or does the blushing of the older person manifest a childish degree of insecurity of social place or a lack of the nonchalance one would expect from a socially experienced person?

There are many face-saving routes out of embarrassment. In one, creditable embarrassment is its own resolution. In another, discreditable embarrassment is displaced by an attack on the Sartrean Other, the self-appropriation of whose assuming judgement led to the blush in the first place – 'How dare you presume to judge me!' 'Take that superior smile off your face!' Most of us just slink away.

Empathy and sympathy

There are marked differences in the degree to which the people of a given culture are embarrassable. We have also noticed the moral ambiguity of immunity to embarrassment. Coolness and ignorance can look much the same. But Ricks (1974) has argued that there are differences in the degree to which cultures admit embarrassment among the stock human reactions. He has suggested that embarrassability is high amongst the English and low among the French, building his case by reference to the moral preoccupations of novelist and poets. I cannot take the intercultural question any further here.

Can personal differences in embarrassability be related to any other psychological traits? Sartre emphasizes that 'assuming the point of view of the other' is an essential condition for the possibility of experiencing a reflexive emotion. But what is the source of my beliefs as to how I look to them, which, against the background of norms of appearance and conduct lead on to embarrassment? Modigliani (1968) explored the idea that capacity for empathy may be the psychological condition for high degrees of embarrassibility. Though his research was methodologically rather slapdash, it did seem to show that degree of empathic sensitivity was not correlated with degree of embarrassability. Modigliani's result is hardly surprising if we reflect on what seems quite obvious: that our beliefs about the opinions of others need not be true to be effective in the genesis of embarrassment.

However, a capacity for sympathy may be behind the degree of embarrassability that some people suffer with respect to the evident embarrassment of others. Burgess is reported as remarking how 'when we see the cheek of an individual suffused with a blush in society, immediately our sympathy is excited towards him; we feel as if we were ourselves concerned, and yet we know not why.' But there are cases where the embarrassment occasioned by the embarrassment of another is not to be explained by reference to fellow feeling. Most embarrassment displays are embarrassing through the threat they pose to yet other people's readings of our characters, as associates of the one whose blushes or flustered behaviour and speech are generally indicative of a lack of maturity and social skill.

DISPLAYING EMBARRASSMENT: THE BLUSH

This fascinating response has not drawn much attention from psychologists in recent years, yet it is the usual sign of embarrassment. It is one of the most striking phenomena of adolescence. It is unknown in infancy. Babies' reactions to being the focus of attention do not include blushing. Infants are also in complete command of the fixed, unwinking stare. Burgess was the first to emphasize that blushing is a physiological response found in all mankind, whether or not a person is dark skinned and the blush invisible.

Darwin remarks that one cannot control blushing. As he says, 'blushing is not only involuntary; but the wish to restrain it, by leading to self-attention, actually increases the tendency' (pp. 310–11). The corollary, that blushing cannot be brought on deliberately, means that embarrassment cannot be feigned. This fact has long been known to actors and actresses, and it has been suggested is the origin of the use of rouge. (The French verb *'rougir'* means both to blush and to apply a cosmetic blush.)

Another curiosity is that blushing is confined to the face and those parts of the upper body that are normally exposed to view without embarrassment. But the hands have never been observed to blush. When suffering from acute embarrassment, some people report tingling and suffusion of warmth over the whole body, but this is not accompanied by any visible blush. Though all people blush, whether their skins are dark or light, it is not known, even to this day, whether in those climes where people go nearly naked blushing is still confined to those areas characteristic of the European blush.

Suggestions as to the evolutionary origins of the phenomenon, if it is indeed biological and not a learned response, have come to grief on the fact that due to its invisibility on the dark skins of the majority of mankind it could not be an ethologically accountable signal of submission, say. Nor for the same reason could it have been sexually selected, though Darwin reports that those Circassian women who blushed the most vividly fetched a higher price in the slave markets of Turkey. Darwin was impressed by the evidence that thinking attentively about some part of the body often led to a dilation of the capillaries in that region. The face, he conjectured, is the usual target of the assessing and critical look, so blushing could be explained as a biologically accidental consequence of the social phenomenon of critical self-attention triggered by the looking of others.

Darwin adds a similar explanation of the confusion of thought and muddle that seems to accompany embarrassment. The blush arises because of a diversion of the blood supply to the face, and *a fortiori* away from the brain, leading to depressed neural functioning. The social basis of the emotion of embarrassment, which is an integral part of this explanation, he supports by citing the fact that people rarely blush when alone, when they are sleeping or dreaming, or even when they are reading about something embarrassing. Without the look from the Sartrean Other, no blush will mantle the damask cheek.

Though Darwin seems to have posed the pure biologists' question (p. 325) 'how it has arisen that the consciousness that others are attending to our personal appearance should have led to the capillaries, especially those of the face, instantly becoming filled with blood?', his answer is an essentially social one.

DISPLAYING EMBARRASSMENT: THE FLUSTER

Disorder in speech and gesture is as much a display of embarrassment as the blush. The behavioural aspects of displays of shame and embarrassment, include squirming, rubbing one foot over the other, casting down the eyes and so on. Bodily awkwardness is both an occasion for, and a manifestation of, embarrassment, feeding on itself. Goffman (1967), following Lord Chesterfield, argues that squirming and casting down of the gaze are best seen as part of the repertoire for concealing emotion, hiding the blush. According to Goffman 'the fixed smile, the nervous hollow laugh, the busy hands, the downward glance that conceals the expression of the eyes, have become famous as signs of the attempt to conceal embarrassment.' In some cultures the whole face may be covered by the hands. And so these acts become as clear a part of the display of embarrassment as the blush itself. Goffman (p. 102) quotes Lord Chesterfield who, icily contemptuous of the middle classes[1] to whom embarrassment is endemic as it is to adolescence, speaks of these actions as 'tricks to keep in countenance' and notice that 'every awkward, ill-bred body' has them.

I owe to S. B. Thomas (personal communication) the idea that the same terminus would be reached from a directly functional analysis of embarrassment displays. In displaying confusion of mind, they make manifest an exculpable lack of poise; in the blush they manifest a recognition of the modesty rules. Content and arousal are 'internally' connected in a Wittgensteinian way.

Modesty and shyness are the character attributes with which embarrassment is typically associated. Shame and chagrin are two emotions whose similarity to and difference from embarrassment I have commented on above. Both shame and embarrassment can occur in cases where my blush is occasioned not by my realization that you are attending to my public gaucheries, immodesty or incompetence, but by my attention to yours. However, I can hardly feel chagrin for your failures, unless we are very closely linked socially.

We tend to associate displays of embarrassment with the virtue of modesty. Many of the expressions from the cluster have two characteristic contexts of use, illustrating the systematic ambiguity of the concept of 'modesty'. There is the context set by the sense of an unwelcome attention being paid by others to some infraction of the local rules of bodily presence and display. But there may also be attention to our reactions to the attention of others of our first-order infractions. We assign the virtue of modesty as follows: a modest young lady would normally pull down her skirt *and* be embarrassed by it riding up, whereas a shameless hussy would let us see her knickers and not give a damn. A modest young man would wrap a towel around

---

[1]   It is well to bear in mind (Grant Webster, personal communication) that modesty conventions have always been class related. Embarrassment is stronger in the middle classes since in terms of character they have more at hazard.

him to change on the beach, whereas an ill-bred lout would merely pull down his shirt tails a fraction. The same duality of context occurs in more abstract matters. A truly modest colleague would keep quiet about his or her receipt of an honorary degree and they would display some measure of embarrassment when others brought it up. An arrogant bitch or self-satisfied oaf would both publicly broadcast the news and show nothing but self-satisfaction in the now reluctant congratulations of his or her peers. However, academic honours are not exactly like underwear. A modest pride is acceptable, but it is a tricky note to strike.

While the study of modesty helps to bring out the 'double ought' in embarrassment, the phenomenon of bodily modesty has further features that are of interest in their own right, as relevant to the larger question of whether the emotions are 'natural' or 'cultural'.

The *OED* (even in the 1989 edition) has amongst the glosses on 'modesty' the following: 'Womanly propriety of behaviour, scrupulous chastity of thought, speech and conduct (in man or woman); reserve or sense of shame proceeding from instinctive aversion to impure or coarse suggestions'. I shall return to the issue raised by the use of 'shame' rather than 'embarrassment' in this definition, and the framing of modesty within the womanly. It is notable that the author of the gloss takes it for granted that modesty arises out of an instinctive aversion, by which I take it is meant something natural. There are two aspects to this: one that a person is naturally put out when others notice something that ought not to be seen; and secondly that there is a common catalogue of bits and pieces of the body that would, if accidentally displayed, lead to embarrassment or perhaps shame.

DISMEMBERING THE CLUSTER OF RELATED CONCEPTS

We rarely find an important concept existing in isolation from others with which it forms a system of terms ordered by similarities and differences. Darwin, for example, ties blushing, and so embarrassment, to modesty, shyness and shame. Chagrin too must be added to this cluster. People who are shy, modest or chagrined tend to be embarrassed when subject to public gaze. Those who are coy may appear embarrassed, but can feign only the superficial squirmings of the embarrassed, and lack the tell-tale blush. While the former are creditable emotions and attributes of character, coyness is discreditable. Shame (a creditable emotion for discreditable acts) and moral character are linked, as I have brought out already, while modesty is a virtue implicated with both. Those who are pert, proud, bold, brassy, shameless and brash earn our disapprobation at least as much for their unrepentant attitude as for what they are unperturbed at displaying.

Embarrassment and its contraries are concepts that necessarily involve an element of display. Their logical grammar excludes their use for hidden feelings and emotions. To be embarrassed is both to blush and to be discombobulated, while to be bold as brass is both to exaggerate your *décolletage* or the shortness of the your 'stubbies' and to seem not to give a damn about anyone taking a longish look. I think the element of display is crucial, since the importance of these styles of behaviour in social life lies not so much in the feelings they betray as in the characters they disclose. Since embarrassment is not a subjective matter, its display is not a sign, or even an expression, of an inner state, the 'real embarrassment'. The concept does not admit of concealed or suppressed embarrassment on the model of concealed or suppressed anger. And this fits with Darwin's important observation that the manifestation of embarrassment, the blush, can be neither inhibited nor feigned.

Many commentators have suggested that modesty is an effect of custom and not its cause. Westermark (1901), for instance, says '... the feeling of shame, far from being the cause of man's [sic] covering his body is, on the contrary, a result of this custom.' Helvétius went so far as to suggest that 'modesty is only the invention of a refined voluptuousness' – that is, that the body is covered to draw attention to it. Mantegazza remarks that 'covering body parts is an (unconscious) way of emphasising or drawing attention to them.' But while this may be true, it is far from explaining why shame and embarrassment attend accidental display. However, these suggestions, if sound, do put paid to the idea that body shame or embarrassment is natural.

It is also worth reminding ourselves of the enormous diversity of parts of the body the display of which is thought to be shameful or immodest. Here is a short list: for Islamic women it is the face and elbow, not the breasts; for traditional Chinese it is the bare feet; for traditional Tahiti clothing is irrelevant, only the untattoed body is immodest; in traditional Alaska (indoors of course) only lip plugs are essential in modesty; in Melanesia clothing is indecent; while in Bali for women to cover the bosom is coquettish at best and a mark of prostitution at worst; Turkish women were required *by law* to cover the back of the hand, while the palm could be displayed, without shame or embarrassment.

Historically our own culture has also shown great diversity. Just one simple contemporary example; many women do not wear anything 'on top' on the beaches or in swimming in Europe, whether it is in municipal baths or at the beach. This change has occurred only in the last fifteen years. The female bosom is now no cause for embarrassment. But not to be properly outfitted in subfusc at an Oxford degree giving would be a cause of the most acute embarrassment.

The realization that the occasions for the display of the virtues of modesty are culturally specific and historically variable is a very modern idea. Readers may enjoy the opinion of Judge Phillips in the judgement he delivered in the case of the US v. Harman (45 Fed. Rep. 423, 1891) which runs as follows:

> There is in the popular conception and heart such a thing as modesty. It was born in the Garden of Eden. After Adam and Eve ate from the fruit of the Tree of Knowledge they passed from that condition of perfectability which some people nowadays aspire to, and, their eyes being opened, they discerned that there was both good and evil. 'and they knew that they were naked, and they sewed figleaves together, and made themselves aprons'. From that day to this, civilised man has carried with him a sense of shame – the feeling that there were some things which the eye – the mind – should not look, and where men and women become so depraved by the use, or so insensate from perverted education, that they will not veil their eyes, nor hold their tongues, the government should perform the office for them in protection of the social compact and the body politic.

As recently as 1935 the following event was reported in Associated News dispatches of 16 and 17 June of that year:

> SHOCKED YONKERS[1] START ROUNDUP OF GIRLS IN SHORTS
> Five young women, handed summonses today for appearing on the streets of Yonkers in shorts, will be treated to the sight of themselves as others see them – and in the movies at that.
>   The women were ordered into court tomorrow on the complaint of Alderman William Slater who said he had been besieged by the objections of citizens at having their Sunday afternoon veranda-gazing monopolized by young women in bare legs sauntering about the streets.

I have several times remarked on the fact that many of the authors I have cited have taken shame rather than embarrassment as the exemplary reflexive emotion. In my general treatment above, I suggested that shame is appropriate in cases of serious derelictions, which would, if publicly noticed, lead to assessments of character so unfavourable as

---

[1] 'Yonkers' is a suburb of New York.

to depreciate one's honour permanently. Embarrassment is the emotion proper to the violation of mere convention, of a code of manners. It would be absurd to say that someone who failed to wear appropriate clothing at an Oxford degree giving was dishonoured by his or her dereliction. Reputation for *savoir-faire* would be lost, but hardly moral character.

Reminding ourselves of this distinction can help to explain why earlier writers tended to discuss bodily exposure and the consequent disturbances in terms of shame rather than embarrassment. Particularly when women's honour was at stake modesty was linked to chastity, in a tight-knit conceptual cluster. Exposure of the female body was treated as dishonourably provocative, and so one was careful to avoid even an accidental exposure of some forbidden part of herself for fear of being mistaken for the kind of slut who deliberately does so. Once the connection between bodily exposure and womanly honour dissolves (or where in many non-Western societies it has never existed) and the conventionality of choice of bits to cover up is recognized, society wide, then only embarrassment can ensue from the violation of some sumptuary role. I remind the reader that in Bali it is immodest for a woman to cover the upper part of her body. This device is a trick of street girls to entice clients.

SHYNESS

So far we have seen the grammar of the word 'embarrassment' to be controlled by the principle that it should be used for disturbances that occur on occasion of sudden and excessive public attention to something personal that society decrees should be kept hidden, or at least unattended and unemphasized, attention to which threatens the self via the possibility that the attention is critical and the regard, in itself, denigratory. We tend to call someone 'shy' when they display some kind of disturbance (something like the marks of embarrassment) on *any* occasion of public attention, and with respect to *any* or *all* personal attributes. Mere bodily presence in the public domain, if noticed, say by address, is enough.

For instance, someone might refuse to appear in the presence of others at all with the claim that 'I'm shy!' or such a refusal might be accounted for by someone else with 'He's shy!' Like any alibi talk, this sort of remark can be studied against the distinction of excuses from justifications. An excuse serves to admit a fault and to give a reason why it was committed, while a justification is a claim that the action was not a fault at all. To shrink from the public gaze is, I think, to be accounted a fault. One has a duty to some measure of sociality. So 'I'm shy' or vicariously 'He's shy' is an excuse and not a justification. It belongs with 'I was too scared' and not with something like 'Don't be so picky: punctuality is neurotic.' Or 'Come on, everyone tries to beat the customs!'

It seems to follow that while 'embarrassment' is a proper emotion and indeed a mark of a certain virtue, shyness is verging on the pathological. Thus with respect to the 'double ought' principle, while embarrassment is a feeling one ought to have, shyness is not.

In the case of shyness, it is both the normality of what is exposed to view (and the whole person is a special case of that normality), that lies at the root of the social disapproval and mildly pathological rating of shyness. Is there anyone who ought to be shy?

I think not, though its polar opposite, 'showing off', is also to be deprecated. It goes something like this: while shyness is something one ought not to feel, and even less display, still it is something that children are expected to exhibit at some passing stage of life. Thus, as in many cases in the moral order, normality and propriety are not in one-to-one correspondence. Notice too that shyness is generally preferred to showing off, in that shyness is excessive modesty, while showing off is tied in with unacceptable character traits like boasting, arrogance and the like. But there are cultures in which boasting is proper, even virtuous. Showing off can reasonably be deprecated in the young, while their shyness is endured with some sympathy. In a way shyness could be thought of as a kind of apprenticeship to proper modesty.

Chagrin is associated with, and typical of, the realization that one has failed in the context of an expectation of success. The worst case occurs when the expectation of success has been publicly declared, and note that that declaration can be retrospectively redefined as boasting if one fails. So failure is deadly for two reasons: one the loss of esteem, honour, etc., consequent on the failure itself, and the other the loss of one's reputation as a modest person, which, as the dictionary says, denotes '... reserve springing from an unexaggerated estimate of one's qualities'. Failure encourages the retrospective redefinition of one's public and optimistic estimate of success as mere boasting. If one brings off a declared project, one could not have been said to have boasted.

In summary the structure of the conceptual system underlying embarrassment seems to be the following:

The virtue involved is modesty, which as having both a characterological and behavioural sense is bimodal. The emotions involved are:

1. Shame – occasioned by the realization that others have become aware of what one has been doing as a moral infraction, a judgement with which I as actor concur.
2. Embarrassment – occasioned by the realization that others have become aware of what one has been doing (in a qualified sense) as a breach of conventions, codes of manners, a judgement with which I, as actor, concur.

We can make sense of this complexity with the thesis that in our culture improper body displays are taken as prima-facie evidence of attributions of bad character.

There is a link between character-modesty and body-modesty, which explains why we have two kinds of modesty. It is the concept of honour, which is tied in with one's reputation in the judgement of others. Violations of the modesty code, the general form of which are failures to adhere to the rule of non-self-emphasis, in either mode, threaten a loss of honour.

This explains the Balinese anomaly, why covering the bosom is immodest; a good woman with her bosom covered would be mistaken for a tart.

It also explains why body-modesty has been a more restrictive code for women than for men in our culture, since, notoriously, there are more good-time girls than gigolos. But more importantly, the old double-standard morality amplified the need to disambiguate accidental disclosures which would have been deliberately provocative if they had been done by a woman of dubious reputation. Accidental disclosure of normally hidden body aspects then can be mistaken for deliberate disclosure with a consequent risk of misattribution of character and the Sartrean realization that has occurred.

COMPLEXITIES OF EMBARRASSMENT

Students of embarrassment, such as Darwin and Goffman, have remarked on how embarrassing it is to be embarrassed, or to watch the embarrassment of others. It seems to me, however, that one cannot be ashamed of one's own shame, though I am not sure about the shame of another. So far as I know, no work has been done on the general question of iterated emotions, in particular the question of why some emotions can be iterated (one can be angry at being angry) and some cannot. Can one be sad at being sad? There are also nested emotions such as being ashamed of being angry, embarrassed at being envious, proud of being sympathetic and so on.

What is the principle behind these cases? The first point to notice is that the embedded emotion is always one in the conditions for which the double-ought principle applies. Being embarrassed at being embarrassed is fairly easily accounted for via the principle that in many cases the infraction that one is embarrassed about is one that someone with more *savoir-faire*, more worldly experience and so on would not find embarrassing. A well-brought-up American lady might feel iterative embarrassment when dressed for the beach European style. An antipodean graduate might be embarrassed that he finds the Oxford ceremonial 'uniform' embarrassing. In the double-ought cases the second ought can be pre- or proscriptive, so the embedding emotion can be a show of consonance of character with the original act (proud of being compassionate) or of dissonance of character with the original act (ashamed of being shy). Once again the issue at issue is the conventional assignments of character and virtue at risk in the event. Thus the embedding emotion may be itself a contribution to facework, a remedy, or in the case of the prescribed embedded emotion, a confirmation.

Embodiment opens up the possibility of being looked at, in person, so to say. The fact that our appearance and our honour are tied up with one another I have treated so far as a source of threat. But every shrinking violet also needs to be noticed, to have his or her existence confirmed. Embarrassment is the adolescent emotion *par excellence*. The predicament of adolescence is precisely the ambiguity of visibility. The enlarged and clumsy body seems only too visible – hence the blush, yet identity as a publicly noticeable being is only confirmed by being seen to have been seen (and in lesser ways heard to have been heard). Is it too indelicate of me to draw your attention to the way that the smell of children changes from babyhood to infancy, from childhood to adolescence? No, because smell too is an occasion for embarrassment. To capture this dark moment of adolescence I borrow a phrase from Ricks (1974: 27) about the ereutophobe 'who yet longs to be stared at, and who plays with her (his) cheeks on fire.'

So far I have drawn attention only to the way that our and others' embarrassment can be itself a source of embarrassment. But the embarrassment of others can also be fun. Perhaps this can throw light on the curious practice of teasing, where the embarrassable and the shy are much at risk, as are the fiery and the feeble. 'Teasing is testing', as someone once remarked. It probes for certain socially undesirable vulnerabilities, such as tendencies to anger and embarrassment, and mercilessly punishes them. Real and (imaginary) shortcomings become the focus of attention of all the world, for that is what the tease is. In teasing, I suggest, we have a coarse-grained model of the general structure of embarrassment. The teaser forces the victim to attend to the demeaning nature of the defect, and not just the defect itself, by forcing attention to the mocking attention that he or she, the teaser, is giving to it. For adolescents the defect can be mere bodily presence. ('Oh that this too too solid flesh would melt', misquotes the embarrassed one in an agony of self-awareness.)

Ricks, again so sure and sharp in his observation (p. 42), remarks: '... an intense self-awareness is both bred from and breeds embarrassment.' And here again is the paradox of adolescence – a proper self-awareness is a prerequisite for the kind of control Goffman called 'impression management'. And the acquisition of it opens up the possibility of a sensitivity to the regard of others that can only too readily invoke the 'critical stare'. I think it is a mistake on the part of some authors to concentrate on the sexuality of adolescence as the focus of self-awareness. The range of that which can be embarrassing is wide, from the new voice of boys to the mere bulky presence of either sex in the physical world.

VICARIOUS EMOTIONS

An important distinction among emotions is whether it makes sense to imagine them as experienced vicariously. Some, such as anger, are readily seen to be possible vicariously; I might well be angry on your behalf, as I sense a transgression against you. But I am quite unable to conceive of vicarious jealousy. The source of this intuition must lie somewhere in the grammar of the concepts. Some light can be thrown on this if we notice that vicarious embarrassment (and perhaps shame) are routine, though a strongly culturally variable in intensity. However, vicarious shyness is, so far as I know, never reported or felt. Why?

Malicious pleasure in your discomfiture is not an unknown emotion. Under what conditions am I likely to experience it? It seems to me that there must already exist some other hostile relationship between us. But if there is no such relationship, then fellow-feeling is, in the absence of any reason to the contrary, taken for granted in our moral system. Our normative expectations assume that within certain bounds my good is your good, and particularly my moral standing is tied in with yours. We have looked at this already in relation to the conditions for face-work, and for the fellowship condition on feeling embarrassed by the behaviour of someone to whom we can be seen to have some social tie. In the case of vicarious embarrassment it is not that I am embarrassed by your behaviour, but that your behaviour might as well have been mine as an occasion for embarrassment.

But we have already seen that shyness is not a proper emotion prescribed for occasions in which I am acutely aware of real or imagined attention being paid to me. Indeed, that emotion is generally proscribed and tolerable only as a stage through which we pass to a proper modesty. It is only as seen on the way to that state that it is tolerable to all. Shyness then cannot be associated with a common set of normative expectations that have been violated accidentally in your case, and so, through fellow-feeling, can be felt as if the violation were relative to me.

Now to take this thought back to the intuition that distinguished anger and jealousy. Anger may, in certain circumstances, be a prescribed emotion. It reflects the sense of proper outrage at an improper infraction of my honour, body space, rights, etc. Jealousy, at least for us, is a proscribed emotion, and so far as my intuition goes, this admits of no exceptions. Envy has varieties – some pro- and some prescribed. It would be too much to say that shyness is prescribed; it is not important enough for that, but it is a mode of display that one generally deprecates while one understands it.

I have already suggested that the fact that embarrassment has appeared only recently as a topic for serious study may have its roots in quite profound social changes of which its current prominence may be an indicator. We may be witnessing a collapse of the distinction between manners and morality. Relativism in matters of ethics is a form of conventionalism, which is as much as to say that a morality is just the manners, custom and conventions of this or that tribe. Bodily modesty then becomes a locally variant set of conventions, and not a virtue deeply embedded in the very quality of manhood or womanhood. The collapse of the distinction between manners and morality would explain the recency of an interest in embarrassment and a decline of attention to shame.

There are cultures that do not make the distinction. Catherine Lutz (1982) tells us that the Ifaluk do not distinguish manners from morality, and that this is reflected in their indigenous emotion clusters. Shame does not exist as a distinctive emotion and whatever we comprehend under the concept is parcelled out into an anger cluster, *song*, and a fear cluster, *metagu*. Jude Dougherty reminded me that classical China was a civilization in which manners rather than morality regulated interpersonal relations under Confucian influence. A study of the self-reflexive emotions of social failures in that culture would be worth making.

By way of final summary, I return to Sartre's way of defining all emotion occasions as deprivations of 'freedom'. The freedom to formulate judgements ad lib gives Sartre a ground for distinguishing shame from hate. In shame I accept the presence of the Other and the restriction on me that imposes, through the Look, on my range of reflexive judgements. In the case of hate, I do not accept the restrictions and long for the destruction of the Other to restore my freedom. It is worth noticing that this is a formal distinction only. No content is involved. But for embarrassment to emerge as a separate emotion there must be a working distinction, so I argue, between manners and morality. It is infractions of the conventions of the former that engender it. Sartre quite fails to pick up the virtue involved. I suggest that in the closed society of French intellectuals the manners–morality distinction is not drawn, and that character in the old-fashioned sense is in jeopardy, even from the unintentional vulgarity of a gesture, to take Sartre's own and telling example. Unlike ordinary men and women whose lives have shifted from the moment-by-moment regulation of a harsh morality to the gentler and culturally malleable influence of a code of manners, the Sartre circle treated manners as a morality. In this respect they regressed, and I suppose regressed gladly, to the moral condition of the women of the Victorian era, where virtue was held to be a stake in the lightest deed. Stephen J. Ross has reminded me that there are no strategies for converting issues of morality into ones of manners. Why not? The answer brings out a paradox. While morality rules character, no such strategies will be wanted, since they would themselves be a sign of a loose character. Once morality has ceased to rule, such strategies will be redundant. What powers the transition from one state of order to the other I leave to historical sociology to discover.

REFERENCES

Aristotle 1954: *Nichomachean Ethics* in *The Works of Aristotle Translated into English*, Vol. IX. Oxford: Clarendon Press.

Aristotle 1931: *Rhetoric* in *The Works of Aristotle Translated into English*, Vol. IX. Oxford: Clarendon Press.

Armon-Jones, C. 1986: The Social Functions of Emotions. In R. Harré (ed.), *The Social Construction of Emotions*. Oxford: Basil Blackwell.

Bedford, E. 1956: Emotions and Statements about them. *Proceedings of the Aristotelian Society*, LVII.

Darwin, C. 1872 (1955): *The Expression of Emotion in Man and Animals*. New York: Philosophical Library.

Edelman, R. J., and Hampson, S. E. 1979: Changes in Non-verbal Behaviour

During Embarrassment. *British Journal of Social and Clinical Psychology*, 18, 385–90a.

Gillis, J. R. 1988: From ritual to romance. In C. Z. Stearns and P. N. Stearns (eds), *Emotion and Social Change*. New York: Holmes and Meier.

Goffman, E. 1967: Face Work. In *Interaction Ritual*. Harmondsworth: Penguin.

Hagstrum, J. 1989: *Eros and Vision*. Evanston, Il.: Northwestern University Press.

Lutz, C. 1982: The Domain of Emotion Words on Ifaluk. *American Ethnologist*, 9, 31–57.

Modigliani, A. 1968: Embarrassment and Embarrassability. *Sociometry*, 31, 313–26.

Ricks, C. 1974: *Keats and Embarrassment*. Oxford: Clarendon Press.

Sarbin, T. 1986: Emotion and Act: Roles and Rhetoric. In R. Harré (ed.), *The Social Construction of Emotions*, 5. Oxford: Basil Blackwell.

Sartre, J.-P. 1943 (1956): *Being and Nothingness*, trans. H. E. Barnes. New York: Pocket Books.

Schama, S. 1989: *Citizens*. London: Penguin.

Silver, M., Sabini J., and Parrot, W. G. 1987: A Dramaturgic Theory of Embarrassment, *Journal for the Theory of Social Behaviour*, 17, 47–61.

Stearns, C. Z. and Stearns, P. N. 1988: *Emotions and Social Change*. New York: Holmes and Meier.

Westermark, E. 1901: *The History of Human Marriage*. London: Longman.

Zajoncs, R. B. 1980: Feeling and Thinking: Preference Needs No Inference. *American Psychologist* 35, 151–75.

CHAPTER 8

DISEASE INTO ILLNESS

The doctor spoke dispassionately, almost brutally, with the relish men of science sometimes have for limiting themselves to inessentials.

Evelyn Waugh, *Brideshead Revisited*

INTRODUCTION: BODILY MALFUNCTION AND ITS SOCIAL ENACTMENT

It hardly needs remarking that the concepts of 'health' and 'illness' are many-faceted. In this chapter I shall explore some of the ways we use them and so some of the ways of 'being healthy' and 'being ill'. They are complex derivations of the simpler biological conditions of bodily health and disease. The main burden of my argument will be to try to demonstrate that the concepts of 'health' and illness' include both aesthetic and social aspects, in short, that they are predominantly evaluative.

The discussion is facilitated by the availability of two terms for the 'negatively' valued conditions. 'Disease' as 'a condition of the body, some part or organ, in which its function is disturbed or deranged' is primarily a biological concept. 'Illness', as a 'bad or unhealthy condition of the body', can be appropriated without too much distortion for the complex social and psychological enactments of 'being ill' that sometimes supervene on the bodily conditions of 'disease'.

I shall be drawing on recent studies of how lay folk use various concepts of health and illness, in particular the work of Claudine Herzlich (1973). It will also emerge that the relation between the concepts of health and 'illness' is not a simple opposition.

SIGNS AND SYMPTOMS

Attention to the state of our own bodies provides each of us with a manifold of potential symptoms or signs. Signs are perceptible manifestations of bodily states and processes. They include both visible and audible states and conditions of the body, as well as all sorts of sensations and feelings, interpreted as perceptions of internal states and processes. I shall say that a sign is a symptom if it is taken by someone as indicative of an imperfect bodily function or abnormal state. The mark that differentiates symptoms from other bodily states and feelings is not generally their unpleasantness, but their meanings. There are disagreeable feelings (for instance, some of the bodily feelings associated with emotions) and unpleasant seen, heard and felt states (for instance, a sweaty skin) that do not usually count as symptoms at all. Pains and aches are disagreeable. Those occurring during, or as the consequence of, 'working out' are not symptoms. There is also an aesthetic element in the concept of 'symptom'. Rashes and dysfunctional processes such as diarrhoea are not only painful, but ugly, though not all aesthetically displeasing body states and conditions count as symptoms. Nor are symptoms to be identified as signs of every kind of abnormal or temporary condition of the body. Injuries are not illnesses, and the signs of broken bones and wounds do not count as symptoms. The importance of the difference between sign and symptom can also be seen in the recent feminist insistence that pregnancy is not an illness, even though it is certainly temporary and in some respects unpleasant. The signs of pregnancy are not symptoms. In this chapter I am not centrally concerned with what the science and profession of medicine makes of poor functioning of a human body, but with how the *concept* of an ill- or well-functioning body and the consequent judgements and assessments of one's own and other people's condition enter into the lives of lay folk. 'Symptom', serving as a technical term in medicine, can be used in commentary on lay concepts, to mark the boundary between illnesses as social and personal enactments of dramatistic sick roles and whatever befalls a human body by way of disease, of biological malfunction. Neither disagreeableness nor abnormality identifies symptoms from the bodily signs. The concept of 'illness' lies at the root of these important practical matters.

THE FORM OF LAY ACCOUNTS

Lay conceptions of disruptions of bodily function make use of a distinction between threats of disorders that arise within the body itself, the endogenous conception of disease, and those that come from an external source, the exogenous conception of disease. Research into lay conceptions of health and illness (e.g. Herzlich, 1973) has shown that people not only think about how illnesses are enacted in the light of the distinction, but differ in the extent to which they tend to think exogenously or endogenously. At the extreme of exogenous thinking are people who put down all their ailments to environmental influence, allergies, 'poisons' and so on. Such people favour 'natural' foods and filter their tap water. A report in *The Times* (London) of 21 June 1990 suggests that about a third of British people have come to regard food materials with suspicion. At the endogenous extreme are those who find a source of bodily maladies in their individual sins. Modern endo-genists are inclined to blame their lack of physical fitness for poor health. Something is awry in them. It is not uncommon to find indivi-duals who enthusiastically adhere to both exogenous and endogenous theories of health. I shall examine this curious conflation of beliefs more closely below.

CONCEPTS OF HEALTH

What is to be healthy? We ask the ritual question 'How are you?' and our acquaintance sincerely replies 'Fine, thanks.' There is one mini-malist concept that could be at work, that of 'health in a vacuum' (Herzlich, 1973: 56). Our interlocutor is not aware of any bodily feelings that could be rated as symptoms. A similar negative concept of health is to be found in Smith's treatment of these matters (Smith, 1983: 32) in what she calls the clinical model of health and illness. In this minimalist sense one is healthy if one does not have a rash or a fever or a pain etc. If symptoms are signs of disease, then in the minimalist sense health is just the absence of disease. But the concept of bodily health is elaborated far beyond the absence of symptoms of disease. There is the idea of health as a physical reservoir that is believed to be a source of resistance to infection and bodily deteriora-tion. And there is the idea of health as a euphoric state defined in an aesthetic of bodily living.

To be healthy, Herzlich found (p. 57), is to be in possession of a 'reservoir of health', which provides a source of resistance to infection. Lay folk think too that there are certain measures by which the reservoir can be augmented. One is advised to 'build oneself up' in readiness for the assault of winter ailments. It is widely held, if prac-tices are anything to go by, that childhood is a particularly apt time to build up the reservoir of resistance. If one has been ill, that reservoir has become depleted and needs to be augmented. Multivitamins will help to do the job. Older traditions among lay folk include hearty eating and putting on weight as part of this reconstructive process. Lay folk use the idea of robust or not so robust constitutions. The 'chronically' healthy, as one might say, have good constitutions and well-filled reservoirs. Their bodies *resist* infection.

Both Smith and Herzlich identify yet another concept of health in lay thought and practice. It is the concept that figures prominently in health cults and health clubs, in healthy-eating advice and so on. I shall call it the eudemonistic concept of health. When one is healthy in this sense, one feels as if one were possessed by a god (cf. Aristotle, *Nichomachean Ethics* 1099^{b}33–1100^{a}5). Smith refers to it as 'exuberance' and Herzlich, less aptly as 'equilibrium'. It is experienced as an autonomous feeling of well-being. Its presence is a positive good and its absence a real lack. It is not just the sense that one is resistant to disease. It is not just a pervasive absence of symptoms. Herzlich (p. 60) catalogues a number of elements within the concept, such as an absence of fatigue, a sense of having ample physical resources for whatever is to hand, a sense of the effectiveness of one's bodily movements and so on. For many people nowadays this concept serves as a norm for how one's body should be. In my view this is plainly an aesthetic concept.

How might the intuition that Herzlich's 'equilibrium' is an aesthetic concept be rationally supported? What sort of argument could be constructed for that interpretation? I shall take it that an aesthetic concept is one that, though applied in the light of certain empirically discernible attributes of some thing or state or process, depends on, and expresses, an evaluation of the subject of prediction according to some locally well-defined, though intrinsically contestable, rank order of those attributes. I may notice the colour tonality of a Picasso clown painting, and through the aesthetic valuation placed on the use of that tonality in that context by that painter, judge the work satisfying. Applying these rather complex considerations to health as well-being clearly shows the concept to be aesthetic. It is not just an empirical claim about the biological functioning of the bodily system. The feelings experienced by someone as healthy as that are valuable in themselves. The ranking of a felt well-being above other somatic experiences is essentially contestable. There are people who prefer the feeling of slouching in an easy chair in front of the telly stuffing themselves with chocolates or soaking up beer. The essential aesthetic aspect of educated taste is clearly involved in valuing the eudemonistic state of health.

We should carefully distinguish this notion of health from the reservoir concept with which it shares some conceptual space. When one feels in good 'shape' one does have a sense of ample physical resources, but this is not the same as the sense of having a well-filled reservoir. It is rather directed towards one's readiness for, and capability of, accomplishing demanding physical or mental tasks. It is, as Smith puts it, one's sense of physical adaptability. One feels ready for anything. In the moment of action one has a sense of effectiveness, of power. Against the background of a eudemonistic sense of well-being, minor disorders, in the sense of clusters of symptoms, do not compromise one's health.

The rhetoric of fitness cults draws on the eudemonistic sense of well-being to define a norm of bodily experience. This is how one *should* feel. Looked at in the light of the project of providing reasons for undertaking programmes of maintenance work on our own bodies, the everyday concepts of health suggest the following: we should build up a reservoir against attack from outside while we should aim at maintaining a sense of bodily well-being against the natural diminution of bodily powers. At this point, aesthetics and prudence overlap since, as Herzlich reports, many people seem to believe that a well-filled reservoir is one of the resources of well-being. The overlap becomes clearer still in the practices of enthusiasts. 'Eating right', adopting a diet of 'good' foods, serves to build up the reservoir. 'Junk food' may even by some be thought as actually depleting that reserve. In some cults the state and quality of consciousness is allied to the kind of food that is eaten, so that too becomes an element in eudemonism. On the other hand, exercise, the eudemonist's main weapon against sloth, not only serves to produce the good feeling of bodily health, but also builds up the reserve.

THE SOCIAL MEDIATION OF SYMPTOMS

The work of Herzlich (1973) clearly demonstrates that, outside the minimalist sense of health as absence of symptoms, lay concepts of illness cannot be defined simply by negating lay concepts of health and vice versa. The relevant lay concepts are not versions of the diagnostic and classificatory concepts of professional medicine. It is customary to distinguish between 'disease' as a medically relevant condition and 'illness' – what ordinary people experience themselves as suffering (Turner, 1984). According to the *OED*, a disease is 'a condition of the body or some part or organ of the body, in which its functions are disturbed or deranged'. This is essentially the medical concept of 'disease'. The lay concept of 'illness' is much more complex.[1]

An illness is a person's response to the recognition of the onset of a disease. A certain cluster of physical conditions is taken up as symptoms. Something is wrong. Then within the conceptual framework invoked by taking up these bodily states as symptoms a certain mode of life is adopted, different from that which the person customarily lives. Declaring oneself ill and taking signs as symptoms are mutually supporting moves. As Herzlich notices (p. 81), 'physical signs acquire meaning according to the limitation of activity they involve.' But what determines whether and how the transition into inactivity is to be made? We are looking here at the conditions under which one makes declarations like 'I can't come in today, I've got a rotten cold', compared with dismissals like 'It's just a snuffle.' It is surely not a simple matter of the severity of the symptoms, even if there were such a thing independently of the 'flight into illness'. We are in familiar territory. The signs of disease reflect and display a biological condition. On the basis of that condition a social construction of something else occurs, a socially legitimated withdrawal from everyday life, within which signs become symptoms. According to Herzlich, 'illness and giving up one's [usual] activities are interchangeable and synonymous in communication.' So 'He's spending a couple of days in bed' and 'He's got a chill' have the same illocutionary force. I must say that my intuitions do not support this claim. Herzlich's studies were done in urban and rural France. I am fairly sure that in English ways of talking that first of the above statements could reasonably be the occasion for asking 'Why?', but not the second. Indeed the second would usually serve as an answer to that very question as posed of the first declaration.

In this respect I differ from Parsons whose analysis requires him to take all forms of illness withdrawal as forms of deviance, which society must control. The adoption of a suitable way of life when one is beset by symptoms is itself a legitimated mode of being and to refuse it would be to become deviant in one's deviance.

It should be clear that whatever illness might be, it is not the negation of health. Both actively being healthy and actively withdrawing into the inactivity that is the proper behaviour for those who are ill are ways of life. Unlike health, illness has two major dimensions in the way people ordinarily view it. There is its temporal span, short or prolonged. And there is its seriousness. Is it life-threatening and is it routinely curable? These are not meant as objective characteristics of some transpersonal condition, but are the ways a person is related to some condition or state of their body. Along both dimensions what someone *does* is the crucial matter. There is a kind of commonality to ways of being ill that has nothing to do with symptoms, but is derived from the common conduct that follows the flight from symptoms into inactivity. To be ill is to be inactive. This 'is' must be taken with care, since we have already seen that Herzlich exaggerates the extent to which illness claims and descriptions of consequential behaviour are 'synonymous in communication'. However, there is no doubt that her observation (p. 81) that 'physical signs acquire meaning [as symptoms] according to the limitation of activity they involve' is sound. But a refinement to Herzlich's case is possible. A distinction could be made between what it is to be ill, in general, namely inactive in relation to the norm of activity required socially from that person at that time of the week in that situation, and the relevant 'mode of illness', say the behaviour proper to someone who has the measles.

Since the transition from experiencing symptoms to withdrawing from active life is socially legitimated, as is also the fact that that withdrawal is what leads to certain physical states counting as symptoms in the first place, the total cluster of symptoms and behaviour is socially defined and as such liable to cultural variation. Herzlich herself discovered that the way the transition to inactivity occurred and the kinds of bodily conditions that were held to require it differed very much between townsfolk and country people. We might also think, just from our ordinary experience of what the people we know do, that those who are generally eudemonistic will be less likely to withdraw into inactivity whatever their bodily condition might be.[2]

On this analysis 'illness' is not an aesthetic concept. It is not a word used to pick out the opposite state to that we have identified in the case of eudemonistic health. The state of someone who is not 'full of beans' for whatever reason is not the basis of an aesthetically dissatisfying experience, so far as our analysis goes. If there is an aesthetic element in the total story of illness, as Herzlich tells it, it must be looked for amongst the symptoms. But not amongst the symptoms as such, since a bodily condition becomes a symptom only if it is interpreted in the light of the illness for which it provides a semantic and empirical support. It must be found amongst bodily conditions whether or not they are drawn into the process of the social construction of an illness. Thus a verruca is an ugly object whether or not it is taken as a ground for a limitation of activity.

If 'illness' is a concept closely tied to inactivity that is itself a condition arrived at by an actor by reference to certain bodily states conceived as symptoms, then surely the conceptual cluster 'fatigue–resting' should be a kind of symptom–illness conceptual nexus. There is no doubt that there is a structural identity between the concepts around tiredness and those of many illnesses, just as there is a structural identity between the clusters of experienced states and bodily behaviour to which these concept clusters enable us to refer. Much will hinge on why one thinks one is tired. Provided that it is possible to locate an exhausting activity in one's immediate past, such as digging the garden in spring, or spending a day word-processing an article for *Cogito*, the 'fatigue–resting' concept cluster is far removed from any thought of illness. But if one's feelings of tiredness cannot so readily be accounted for, then the boundary between fatigue and illness is likely to be fuzzy. One may genuinely be in doubt as to whether one is sickening for something or 'merely' tired. Nervous, intellectual or moral fatigue arising from stressful, but absorbing, activities are, in my experience, more likely to be confused with the onset of illness than those that are the result of bodily work. One becomes exhausted by longstanding apprehension, by intensive mental activity and by working towards a decision in managing some serious moral problem, without paying attention to the activity itself as tiring. The consequent fatigue appears free floating. Fatigue is relevant to the aesthetic element in health concepts by virtue of the fact that, as Herzlich remarks, fatigues of the ambiguous category, whose source is problematic, undermine the eudemonistic sense of well-being through which health appears as an aspect of bodily aesthetics. On the other hand, fatigues that have their origin in well-attended physical and mental efforts may themselves be as aesthetically pleasing as eudemonistic well-being itself. The fatigue one experiences after a day's walking in the hills, followed by a hot bath, is a much sought-after aesthetic experience.[3]

DILEMMATIC ASPECTS OF ILLNESS

Following Herzlich's treatment of illness as a form of action through which one enacts a pattern of proper social behaviour, further refinements can be introduced into the analysis, as we come to recognize different modes of 'illness' conduct. All such modes, we remind ourselves, must be defined relative to the local conception of what are anyone's proper social duties. As Billig (1988: 87) remarks, 'To be healthy is to be fit for social duties – to be ill is to be unable to satisfy them'. Generally speaking, people can choose to be active or inactive in relation to some experienced bodily malfunction, perceived as a symptom. In the inactive mode there are such attitudes as ignoring the symptoms, denying their existence, or simply accepting them passively. There are at least three ways of the taking up of the active stance in relation to perceived symptoms. One can regard the illness as potentially destructive and resist it. We are familiar with the practice of 'fighting a cold' for instance. One takes vitamin C and adopts a generally aggressive attitude to 'it'. But one might regard the symptoms as the occasion for a flight into illness as liberating, as taking one out of the everyday social world for a while. I must confess to finding an occasional bout of mild flu in the middle of the winter term a not unattractive release from duty. But this is far from hankering after a liberating condition, which surely borders on, and sometimes overlaps into, the pathological. There is a third form of the active mode. People can and do turn illnesses into occupations. They accept their bodily withdrawal from normal social duties and construct a new social world around it. This is different from the strategic withdrawals of those who, 'take to their beds' when social difficulties loom; or are struck down by asthma or hay fever just as the demands of the garden become overwhelming. The key notion here is whether or not a person maintains their participation in society. Clearly those who 'fight' illnesses are, in so far as the symptoms permit, full participants in the social order and they are living out narratives that are, as it were, merely enriched forms of those according to which they usually live. But those who adopt either of the other two narrative forms or (in another rhetoric) espouse the corresponding attitudes typical of the other two forms of the active mode, have withdrawn from sociey and no longer participate in everyday activities. Many intermediate cases exist, of course. There are people who continue to take part in everyday life from a 'sick bed' by acting vicariously through those they have appointed as agents. For instance, the cosmologist, Stephen Hawking, by the use of assistants and computing devices continues to function from his wheelchair as both a research worker and a lecturer. He could be described as 'eudemonistically ill'. It seems that the active/inactive contrast is not a simple polarity, but a nesting hierarchy of distinctions amongst attitudes to, and techniques of, actually living out an illness.

The recent studies by Billig (1988) have shown that illness 'occupations' can be interestingly complex. Billig and his co-workers have argued that there are common forms of life where there is more than one narrative form that must be lived out. The simple picture presented by Herzlich assumes that the lived narratives of either of the three forms of the active illness mode are not in competition with an alternative narrative which requires a different action structure to be lived out.

The conceptual structure immanent in all these distinctions and diverse practices could be set out as a contrast between two antitheses.

1. The polar distinction 'Activity/Inactivity' characterizes a way of life and the forms these relations take have to be defined, as we have seen, by reference to the degree to which the ill person participates or does not participate in everyday social life.

2. But there is another polar distinction, which appears in the way people talk about themselves in relation to malfunction – the distinction between a reserve of health that is 'full' and a 'depleted' reserve.

According to where they stand in relation to the first distinction, people will see themselves, and be seen as, defined by reference to some social relation. But according to where someone locates themselves on the 'Full/Depleted' dimension they are reflecting on themselves as individuals. The two major conceptual pairs with which an analyst can characterize the whole process of symptom transformation into social action (of which physical inactivity is only one form) and lived narrative are themselves in a complex interrelation. One's withdrawal into inactivity can be taken as a sign that one's reservoir is depleted and needs to be 'topped up' by rest; while one's sense of a depleted reservoir can be taken as reason for the symptoms that have provided the occasion for the withdrawal. 'I'm ill so I must be worn out' and 'I'm worn out, so that's why I'm ill' express these versions of the relation. While the poles of the antitheses are in conflict, the pair of contrasts are in reciprocal and potentially explanatory relations to one another. I shall call such a structure a 'grammar' for illness narratives, both lived and told.

So far I have been bringing out the social nature of illness against a background of health (that is, of normal social engagement) as if these structures of thought and action were fully internally consistent. To borrow a distinction from linguistics (Billig, 1988: 89) health is the unmarked pole, while illness is the marked pole. Health is assumed unless illness is declared. But individual people exist, as I have remarked throughout this study, in two modes. As embodied beings, they act unthinkingly in the social-material world. But they are also beings who are aware of their bodies as other than themselves. In this mode a person's body is an independent entity to be managed, suffered, worked upon and so on. Our bodies are at once ourselves and they are other than ourselves. Billig and his co-workers have shown how this 'transcendental' fact appears in dilemmatic form in the management of chronic illness and of such standing conditions as 'having a heart problem'. Much of lived illness is, as Billig et al. put it, dilemmatic. Like any other lived narrative, chronic illness has to be carried through within a framework of discursive practices. But these practices, when taken as a whole, are necessarily mutually in conflict. One and the same person has to present themselves in action and talk as one who subscribes to, and indeed actually embodies, the local social norms of health in what they do, while at the same time they must be seen to live within the constraints set by their physical defect. These constraints are in practice collectively imposed on the person by the well-meant reminders of those who form his or her intimate circle. As embodied beings, even the chronically ill must act through their bodies, but as beings concerned to display their adherence to norms of propriety, chronic illness must not only be suffered. It must be done.

NOTES

1 The emphasis in this chapter is on the active participation of the patient in 'declaring oneself ill' and legitimating thereby one's social withdrawal. But the same structure can be deployed in using 'illness' for social control. Victims of disease can be defined as ill and required to withdraw in so far as their symptoms suggest, or can be made to seem to suggest, a physical (cholera) or moral/physical (AIDS) contagion.

2 There is an enormous literature devoted to the concepts of health and illness. I have chosen the works of Herzlich and Smith from among so many partly for their focus on the social processes of the withdrawal into illness and partly for the fact that they are both grounded in detailed studies of how people themselves experience socially what they conceive as bodily malfunction.

REFERENCES

Aristotle 1954: *Nichomachean Ethics*, in *The Works of Aristotle Translated into English*, Vol. IX. Oxford: Oxford University Press.

Billig, M. 1989: *Ideological Dilemmas*. London: Sage.

Herzlich, C. 1973: *Health and Illness*, trans. J. Graham. London and New York: Academic Press.

Payer, L. 1989: *Medicine and Culture*. London: Gollancz.

Smith, J. A. 1983: *The Ideas of Health*. New York: Columbia University Press.

Turner, B. S. 1984: *The Body and Society*. Oxford: Basil Blackwell.

CHAPTER 9

BODY CULTIVATION

Physical strength and size seem to provide influence.
                                    Boethius, *Consolations* III

INTRODUCTION: CHOICE OF BODY FORM

Having dealt at length with the aesthetics of bodily functioning, I turn now to the aesthetics of bodily form. I shall follow the same plan as heretofore, namely to counterpose conceptions of perfection against those of imperfection of form. Conceptions of bodily ideals can be shown to play at least two roles in our patterns of thought and action. They can be involved as concepts in judgements of bodies already given or presented to us, or they can be involved as ideal types guiding remedial or corrective programmes designed to transform a body in the direction of the ideal type. The actual relation between these roles at any moment is dependent on what aspects of bodily form it is within human power to transform. And this dependence is further complicated by the historical variability of ideal body types and by their contemporary variety.

Changes in the aesthetic evaluation of the slim/plump contrast are well documented and are susceptible of a quite plausible socio-economic explanation as visual and symbolic components in self-presentational styles, appropriate to particular forms of the economic organization of society. It would not be an exaggeration to describe the slim/plump distinction as an iconography.

I have already commented in chapter 2 on the relation between available technology and what is taken to be the body essence in

---

[1]   My thanks to Glenda Herrala and Larry Smith for their help in introducing me to the world of body work.

considering the conceptual underpinnings of taxonomies of body kinds. Once again in this context the relationship between exercising body technology and folk practices of bodily transformation (increasingly appropriated by technically qualified 'experts' or at least those presenting themselves as so qualified) and projects for the realization in oneself of a body ideal will become important in explaining how people conceive of their bodies.

The new idea, rampant in our culture, is the 'choice of body form'. I can find little evidence from medieval or renaissance writings of the presence of this concept in everyday thought. One's body *and its general form* were givens. Snub noses, bat's ears, corpulence or emaciation were just *there*. There were a great many aspects of the body that were thought to be under human control. Books of natural 'magick', from the fifteenth century onwards, such as that of Baptista della Porta (1560), list a variety of recipes for achieving changes in complexion, hair colour, and even the colour of the eyes. The lustre of teeth can be improved and the breath sweetened by certain regimes. But so far as I can tell, no attention is given to the question of the transformation of body form. Exercise disciplines and diets for controlling form are noticeable by their absence. When these matters are mentioned, it is in relation to good functioning, not to good form, that they are considered relevant.

In our own times the idea of the controlability of form and techniques for its transformation are very prominent. This takes two modes. In some cases we can choose our form for ourselves. More recently opportunities have arisen for people to choose a bodily form for others, for instance in genetic engineering (Glover, 1984). The choice of sex has been the issue most discussed, but that is only one amongst many possible choices of bodily form that are, at least in principle, now open. Would we wish a child to be of asthenic, pyknic or athletic build? Choice amongst these possibilities, if realizable, would open up some activities to the recipients of our decisions, for instance competitive athletics, and close others, such as the modelling of clothes, and perhaps have an influence on such socially fateful matters as temperament.

The sculptural work of body builders is not the only form that the art of body shaping takes. In discussing 'fat' and 'thin' as body kinds, I showed how attitudes to them were affected by changing aesthetic ideals. Since these are readily transformable kinds, diet can be looked on as a body-shaping technique. In Schwartz (1986) we have a detailed and well-documented account of dieting in this role. Shape, not health, is the aim. Body builders are sculptors. But they are also moralists. Their body work not only shapes flesh, but enhances character. I want to develop that thought a little further in a brief reflection on dieting itself. When the management of one's food intake comes to be seen as itself a virtue, what was a means can become the end. Fatness and gluttony fall apart, the one into an aesthetic universe, the other into morality.

The moral evaluation of eating practices is not new. I owe notice of Plutarch's comments on this matter to Dan Robinson. In his *Moralia*, (sections 7 and 8, 'Odysseus and Gryllus') Plutarch imagines a dialogue between Odysseus and one of his companions, now turned pig by Circe. The man turned pig has found a certain moral superiority in the animal world, including the matter of diet.

> There are the desires for food and drink and here we animals always combine pleasure with utility. You, on the other hand, put pleasure first and the nourishment required by nature second . . . But man's pleasure is so involved with gluttony that everything attracts him . . . He is the only omnivorous creature in the world.
>
> Why, in the first place, does he eat flesh? It is not because of any lack of other food or any inability to procure it. Vegetables and cereals are always available to him in season, one after another . . . But his taste is for luxury; necessary and wholesome food disgusts him; and so he must slaughter animals and take food which is both unnatural and useless.

As Robinson reminded me, the source of Plutarch's moralizing attitude to diet might be found in Plato's comments on diet (*Republic* 7. 559): 'And the desire which goes beyond this, of more delicate food, or other luxuries, which might generally be got rid of, if controlled and trained in youth, and is hurtful to the body, and hurtful to the soul in pursuit of wisdom and virtue, may rightly be called unnecessary.' Gluttony is the exemplary sin of excess.

Schwartz (1986: 334) sees the matter of the moralizing of diet itself as somewhat more complicated. Not only is there an aesthetics of fat and thin body kinds, but there is also a politics of adiposity. Apparently paradoxically certain feminists have seen a moral virtue in not dieting. But choosing that road leaves one open to accusations of the vice of excess. Once again we look to Jane Fonda (1981) for a brilliant solution. Magnify the pain, and so enhance the virtue. Dieting for the sake of a male ideal of feminine slimness is a political error. In emphasizing the painfulness of her diet-plus-exercise regime Jane transformed the moral status of the diet from a rejection of excess to an expression of an even more central Puritan virtue, control. By taking control of one's life through one's diet and one's exercise regime, a woman liberates herself from merely reproducing in her body form the aesthetic standards of others. Though to pursue the matter would take me away from the central focus of this chapter, I cannot forbear to mention a bizarre turn taken by the moralizing of diet. We are all familiar with the moral arguments for vegetarianism in both its modest and its extreme (vegan) form. To use animals for food is argued to be morally wrong by reference to the various claims that those animals might have on our moral sensibilities. One might try to tie in meat-eating with male social and psychological hegemony and so link the rejection of a carnivorous diet with the politics of feminism.

A final theoretical point concerns the biologizing of criteria of perfection. I have presented two sources of such criteria in this introduction, aesthetic and symbolic (socio-economic). However, the biological concept of 'adaptation to an environment' has spawned the idea of species design. The suggestion is that we can ask not only for populational criteria for relative degree of adaptation – that is, the better adapted form is identified by an increase in its proportion in the population over time – but also for absolute criteria. Given the specification of the environmental niche, what would be the optimum characteristics of form and function, say, for a mammal to occupy it? If there has been a serious discussion of the issue of human-species design I do not know of it. In the case studies to follow I shall be exploring conceptual systems that have developed around criteria which have non-biological bases, in particular aesthetic or symbolic origins. Discussions of standards of male and female body ideals, the aesthetics of corporeal beauty and the historical changes to which these are subject are legion. I do not propose to add to them. I turn instead to a study of the living out of an aesthetic ideal of body form in the cult of body-building.

BODY-BUILDING AS SCULPTURE

All sorts of people work out for all sorts of reasons. Body management of one sort or another is implicated in most of them, coupled with a large element of self-presentation. To be seen as, or known to be, one who exercises is a step in the demonstration that one is a person of worth, of virtue and character. Many of us no doubt recall former President Ronald Reagan's claim to be one who 'pumps iron'.

Exercising in this institutionalized way, either by using a machine or by lifting weights, can be done for prudential and/or instrumental reasons. One can exercise to improve one's general health or it can be to 'get in shape' for some other specific bodily activity, say tennis. John McEnroe, a professional tennis player, has talked about weight-lifting as part of his regime of preparation for a tennis tournament. The lifting of weights is not itself a demonstration of Mr McEnroe's virtue. That must be achieved on the tennis court. The case study that forms the focus of this chapter is devoted to an instance of yet another use to which gymnastic equipment is put, namely, 'body building'. In this cult the transformation of the bodily form itself is the aim of those who carry on these activities. The direction of transformation is controlled by certain aesthetic conceptions of ideal bodily form, while the means for achieving it is controlled by certain moral conceptions of virtue.

In discussing their hobby, true body-builders rarely make any reference to prudential (health) or instrumental (sport) motivations. The dominant motives presented in their accounts are aesthetic. However, as we shall see, accounts typically produced by members of the cult also involve subsidiary justificatory themes. Within the overall aesthetic framing of body-building as art work, the body itself is presented in body-builder talk as raw material to be transformed. It is imperfect, but it is perfectible. One contemplates one's body as Michelangelo might have contemplated a block of marble as it lay in the quarry. What can be done with this material? What form can be extracted from it by the technique of the sculptor, guided by his or her vision of a perfection? To its devotees body-building is body sculpture. But it is much more. It is also the theme of a life of virtue. The very 'work out' itself has moral qualities.

THE AESTHETICS OF EXCESS

Art work on the body could be confined to providing a given body with the optimum natural conditions of diet and of exercise proper to humankind, and letting nature take its course. But, as we shall see, the cult of body-building is aimed at the transformation of its practitioners' bodies to match as far as possible an ideal of bodily form that transcends nature. However, in the rhetoric of the cult, references to ancient-Greek ideals are prominent. But these ideals are subject to important and subtle modifications. Here is Joe Weider (1985), a prominent entrepreneur in the cult, enhancing its pedigree by finding its ancestry in a noble forebear. 'Since the dawn of history, strength and physical prowess have been vitally important assets to men and women. The ancient Greeks pitted man against man and sport was born. The classic Greeks developed an admiration for well formed men and women and body building was born.' We need not be too censorious about this bit of flannel. It is the following paragraph that should arrest our attention. Weider goes on to say 'Today's body

7. Greek God.
(Reproduced by kind permission of The Mansell Collection, London.)

builders continue the sacred quest for physical perfection. A way to excel beyond all measure of man, a means of catapulting ordinary performance to the level of the "Gods of Olympus" – this quest is our legacy, left to us by the Ancient Greek athletes.'

One way of getting a grasp of the aesthetics of this cult is to compare the actual ideal forms realized in contemporary body building with their (ostensible) Greek models, plenty of examples of which have

8. Custom car.
(The National Motor Museum, Beaulieu.)

survived in sculpture, either original or in the form of Roman copies. The first historical (and aesthetic) disparity between current body fashions and Greek ideals and practices turns up in the inclusion of references to women in the legitimizing tale. Authorities are unanimously of the opinion that women did not take part in the sacred games or in the military exercises. The inclusion of women is a contemporary phenomenon. According to Weider, '... the Weider Research Clinic realizes, as did the ancient Greek athletes, that physical perfection is the birth-right of every man and woman.' Women are embodied persons, so they too have, like men, a right to seek and find physical perfection – but is there one ideal type for both sexes or does the path to perfection bifurcate?

The answer to this question turns on the way the contemporary aesthetic ideas of the cult differ from those of ancient Greece. Consultation of plates 7 and 9 will show clearly what 'excel beyond all measures of man' means, and how different was the ancient ideal. The

9.   Mr Olympia.
(Reproduced from the *International Journal of Moral and Social Studies*, Volume 4 Number 3, Autumn 1989, page 187.)

aesthetics of contemporary body cults could be defined in terms of the Exaggeration Principle. The principle goes something like this: 'If big is good, huge is better'. Cult fanaticism seems to breed versions of this principle everywhere. The principle reigns among some diet cults, for example. There have been reports of people seriously injuring themselves through foolish application of the principle in versions such as 'Low salt is good, so no salt is better' and 'Some bran is good, so a great quantity of bran is better.' There was a newspaper report of someone needing hospital treatment for the effects of adopting a diet of nothing but bran! I owe to Anthony Winterbourne the observation that the principle also applies to the aesthetics of the custom car cult and to the development of special breeds of dog (see plate 10). The women's body-building cult is schismatic. A minority follow men down the path defined by the Exaggeration Principle, but the majority follow a specifically feminine aesthetics characterized more by a Principle of Refinement. I shall return to the question of the aesthetics of women's body-building later.

SCULPTURAL TECHNIQUE AND LATENT POWER

For men, as for women, the body is raw material. It becomes a psychologically detached art object, already partially, but imperfectly, formed. It needs to be worked on. Aesthetic preferences and the practices of body sculpture are closely interconnected. The musculature of the body is divided into muscle groups, and each group becomes in turn the focus of effort. This effort is directed towards the realization of two qualities – size and definition. The Exaggeration Principle is applied to both these qualities to engender the aesthetic ideal. Muscle groups can be exercised independently, either by skilful use of free weights or by the choice of a Nautilus exercise machine specifically designed for the purpose. A well-equipped gym will have a variety of such machines, one for each muscle group. The ideal of size speaks for itself. The importance of 'definition' to the body-builder can be grasped from the following quotation from a Mr R. Gaspari: 'I'd be sitting in school [university] some days when all I could think about was building pectorals [a muscle group] so striated that they looked like a crazed ocelot had attacked them with razor sharp claws.' The same technique of isolation of parts and individual development is evident in the custom-car cult. Exhaust manifolds and tyres, for instance, are isolated conceptually and then grotesquely exaggerated. This differential emphasis, must of course get its effect by leaving the rest of the machine essentially unchanged. The recent fashions for enormous sun-glasses and portmanteau sized hand bags is reminiscent of this aesthetic too. But why isolate just these muscle groups and just these parts of the car? In both cases we can see that underlying the overt aesthetic preferences lies a symbolism of latent power. It is not the engine that looms so large in the reconstructed vehicle, but the implicit marks of its potency, the exhausts through which the sound of power emerges and the tyres through which that power is transformed into acceleration.

The techniques of achieving size and definition are not irrelevant to understanding the conceptual organization of the aesthetics of the cult. Muscle size, of this extraordinary volume, is achieved by two techniques. The punishing exercise regime damages the muscle body by producing internal lesions. These heal with growth of scar tissue, thus permanently increasing muscle bulk. This is called 'bombing and blitzing', with 'high set' and 'multiple rep'. Volume can also be temporarily increased by the diverting of blood supply to the muscles. Again the right kind of exercise regime can achieve this. The process is graphically described as 'pumping up'. Definition is also a matter of long- and short-term achievements. Well-defined elements in muscle groups can be achieved by exercise programmes. However, a temporary enhancement of definition can be brought about by diet. The favoured regime is tuna fish and water. The aim is to eliminate the layer of subcutaneous fat which tends to soften the muscle outline without any protein loss from the muscle itself. For every dedicated body-builder the purpose of a regime of diet and exercise must be to 'get a good pump and to help chisel a definition'. The sculpturing references are unmistakable. The men's aesthetic criteria then derive from ancient-Greek models, transformed almost out of recognition by the ubiquitous application of the Exaggeration Principle.

The schism among women body-builders has been dramatized in the 'faction' epic *Pumping Iron II: The Women*. The plot centres upon the 1985 competition for the Caesar's Cup, held in Las Vegas. Androgynous women body-builders, followers of the male aesthetic are represented by Bev Francis, while a specific women's aesthetic ideal is represented by Rachel McLish. Arguments about criteria for judging the competition are presented around this clash of aesthetic principles – androgynous or feminine? One judge argues the case for placing no restrictions on the criterion of muscle size for women and for eliminating the criterion of 'femininity'. The film represents reality to the extent that it allows neither Rachel, the protagonist of the feminine ideal, nor Beth, the androgyne, to win. But throughout there was a clear implication that the sorority should reject the Exaggeration Principle and with it the criteria in use in the competitions for men. The final summary is offered in a review of the film in *Muscle and Fitness*, October 1985, in which the reviewer remarks: 'Bev lacked virtually every aesthetic quality that differentiates the body building physique from that of the weight-lifter or somebody else with less muscle. Body building is about the aesthetic development of muscle . . .'

MOTIVATION IN THE BODY CULTS

At this point enough has been explained to enable us to rule out one naïve account of the motivation of body-builders. Body-building is no more than any other body-centred activity, an example of narcissism or self-love. The attention lavished on the body is the same kind of attention that would be lavished on any other art object as one pre-pared it for exhibition at an art show. Marble or flesh – it is all one. The body is an art object to be presented to an audience of *cognoscenti* and a vehicle for a human life, as someone's locus of embodi-ment. In each case we must look for the motivational system that sustains the way the body is presented in daily life. Presentation of a man's built body involves a complex interplay between the hidden and the overt. The musculature of the built body is emblematic of power and strength. But in contrast to the principles governing display of that body in competitions, its appearance in everyday life must be muted. Informants are unanimous in praising modest and covert displays of gross musculature as emblematic of power. Again from *Muscle and Fitness* we have the following:

> When your average pencil-neck on the street sees a body builder walk by, his reaction can range from awe to downright disdain. Whatever the reaction, somewhere in his conscious or subconscious the thought 'That guy is powerful' is sure to exist. Muscles mean power to most folk, and it's part and parcel of the body building mentality to feel powerful with coming of great size.

One should note that feats of strength are not required. The power is latent and resides in the bodily appearance. Discussions with body-builders make it quite clear that the presentation of latent power in everyday life is an end in itself – neither a sexual motivation ('pulling the birds') nor a narcissistic self-love plays much part.

I have already emphasized the fact that the building of muscle size is achieved by encouragement of the growth of scar tissue within the body of the muscle itself. The true body-builder lacks the strength of the genuine athlete. Not only is the power latent (by comparison with the overt demonstrations of body power in competitive weightlifting), but the gross musculature of the built body is merely metonymic or emblematic of strength. Just how far this symbolic quality goes can be judged from the following advertisement text: 'Your accessories can make or break your image. They can enhance your look of power, or make you look sloppy, lackadaisical, unbusinesslike – *weak*.' This aspect throws light on the origins of the aesthetics of the competitive display of built bodies which, we have seen, is in the case of men dominated by the Exaggeration Principle. Muscle *size* symbolizes muscle *strength* by metonymy. Greater volume presents a *visual* sign of latent power. Thus the fact that the competitions are not displays of real power and strength is explicable. The 'power' element is also subtly present in the vocabulary of weight workers. The technical jargon favours a 'tough' phonetics. Thus *p*, *t*, *d* and *b* are favoured over *m*, *n* and *s*, while longer vowels are eschewed for *e* and *i*. So we have 'delts' for 'deltoids', 'abs' for 'abdominals', 'pecs' for 'pectorals' and so on. 'Repetitions' become 'reps'. Thus we are advised to aim for 'dynamic delts by pumping bulk'. You cannot be a soft weakling if you talk like that! So for the proper body-builder accessories and vocabulary conspire to promote the appearance of latent power.

BUILDING CHARACTER AND VIRTUE

Throughout the exercise literature another kind of strength is celebrated – strength of character, moral strength. To persist in one's regime requires not only a huge investment of time (up to two hours per day) but also 'stick-to-it-iveness'. Pain is the measure of the quality of the workout and it must be endured. Not only is 'character' required for the activity, it is conceived to be built by it. Pain (the 'burn') has a dual signifying role. On the one hand it is the physiological sign of the tissue damage without which muscle bulk would not appear. On the other it is the focus of the moral strength through which one carries on the endless cycles of multiple reps.

Are women concerned with these same matters? The schism in female body work suggests that at least some women are. But patently many are not. One way of gauging the motivation behind women's body-building aesthetics is to analyse the autobiographies that regularly appear in men's magazines such as *Muscle and Fitness* and compare them with those in women's body-cult journals such as *Shape*. If men do 'cash in' their bodies, it is usually for the commonplace goods of the bourgeois life. For instance, Mr Olympia 1984 (in real life Mr Lee Haney) tells us that he pursued his competitive career not only as an artist in body work, but to be able to use his winnings in competitions to fund better housing for himself and his family. Women's life stories are quite different. They too are modelled on a traditional bourgeois pattern, but it is that of attracting a man and setting up a family. The story starts with a pen picture of an unattractive, overweight wallflower who, through body work, becomes *svelte* and shapely. In no time she has harvested a husband, a nice house and some regulation kids. This story-line fits in well with my general impression that the women's aesthetics of the body is, with some exceptions, not based on the realization of the conditions for the presentation of latent power. The perfection of a specifically feminine body form is evidently the guiding principle.

A sense of superiority is clearly displayed in the talk of body-builders. In their own eyes they are an elite. However, in studying the cult one soon becomes aware that within that elite there are social divisions. The most important seems to turn on the kind of equipment one uses. Nautilus machines, so named after the cam gear that controls the tension in the pulls, are adapted to each muscle group and one simply moves from one to another in accordance with one's sense of the need to work on this or that group. Free weights, the modern descendents of the old dumb-bells (obtainable with cute pink fluffy covers for 'ladies'), must be manipulated with special skill to work on each muscle system in turn. This is truly 'pumping iron' and those who do it are the aristocrats of the sport. Gyms, at least in the New York area, are ranked socially by the proportion of free weight workers they sustain. When Ronald Reagan confessed to 'pumping iron', the implication that he stood among the 'aristos' was plain to anyone acquainted with the inner structure of the body cult.

RUNNING AS AN ART FORM

The exercise enthusiasts who appear most visibly in daily life are surely the joggers (and their allies, the runners). These activities are persisted in by people long after their injurious effects have become widely known. The ironic, even comic, death of poor Jim Fixx, the great advocate of running who died of its effects, has done little to abate many people's commitment. Jogging finds a place in the body cults largely, I think, because of the complexity of the concept of 'health'. Herzlich (1973) has shown how health is defined both negatively (the absence of symptoms) and positively (a eudemonistic well-being, feeling as if one is possessed by a god). The former falls far short of the latter. Body practices of various kinds fill the gap, including the various forms of running. This location is evident in the writing of Roby and Davis (1970: 3). A close look at the conceptual background to the practices of the cult discloses three main strands, mystical, aesthetic and moral. Some of the content of these strands overlaps with the concepts involved in body-building. First the mystical: a historian of religion would be struck immediately by the Neoplatonic overtones of much of the pseudo-physiology that accompanies the enthusiasm for running. There is frequent reference to a mythic 'centre of health' in the heart. Again from Roby and Davis (ibid.) we have: 'the condition of the heart holds the key to a long and healthy life ...' and 'most significant measure of physical fitness is circulo-respiratory endurance ...' The concept of 'physical fitness' appears in this account. But we must beware of taking this concept prudentially here. If we ask 'fit for what?', the answer can only be 'for running'. The fitness is an end in itself. It is the eudemonistic health of the enthusiast. In just the same way 'aerobic power' is best adapted to more aerobics, though it could be used for all sorts of things. There is a second mystical idea involved, namely 'natural balance'. Imbalances are restored by this kind of exercise (shades of the four humours!). While the devotees of body-building look to Greece, jogging enthusiasts seem to have their eyes on something rather like the Neoplatonic hermetism of the renaissance.

Secondly the aesthetic: in conformity with contemporary fashion, the jogger aims at weight control. The contempt that runners of all kinds feel for those billowing galleons of flesh one sees in the plumper parts of the world is palpable. This contempt has a moral edge to be picked up below. But like body-building, running has its own aesthetics. I quote from Henderson (1985): 'Running is an art form. It fits the broad definition of art as making something where nothing existed before; of making something special and personal from common ingredients available to all ... you're building an ability that didn't exist before you began to run.' It seems that it is not the bodily form one may acquire by the activity, but the running itself (whether or not one aspires to the poetic motion of such as Sebastian Coe) that is aesthetically valuable.

Thirdly the morality: in a way similar to body-building, running is conceived as character building. It gives one 'inner confidence, will power and the ability to resist both mental and physical stress'. How does it do this? By the encouragement of just those qualities needed to persist in the activity, to overcome its inevitable discomforts. There is a further twist to this. Why jog? One can easily adapt one's daily life to a more physical style if one is intent on maintaining good physical health. One can take the stairs rather than the lift, walk to work rather than take the bus. An equal eudemonia might be achieved in this way. But one notices with surprise at first that runners eschew the privacy of running tracks and public parks to jog along the public highway, a danger to themselves and others, not to mention the injury that running on hard surfaces does to knees and hips. The answer is obvious.

In jogging in these public places, one is seen to be virtuous. 'Let your light so shine before men . . .' Character is being built, but it is also being displayed.

BODILY OBLIGATIONS AGAIN

Is there a connection between the aesthetics of a representative sample of the body cults and obligations to the body? The latter concept is one we have been pursuing throughout this book. Why should I keep my body alive? Because it is the seat – that is, the necessary physical grounding – of a person, and persons are morally protected against destruction or dismissal. But why should I follow a regime and *cultivate* my body? Two answers find a source for this obligation in a superior demand. One is prudential. By cultivating my body, I improve the quality of my life directly or indirectly (as in the biographies of body-builders). Direct benefits include greater capacity for valued activities such as mountaineering or sexual intercourse. A cultivated body might also confer a quantitative advantage in the shape of a longer life. However, there is also a social duty to cultivate the body. Unfit and unhealthy people are a burden on social resources and demand the care of others. Anti-smoking campaigns often include this theme. Neither of these answers approaches the moral inwardness of the cults. They seem to demand, as I illustrated with the quotation from Weider, the recognition of an intrinsic duty to one's body. The same tone is evident throughout Jane Fonda's *Workbook* (1981). The moral duty to actualize what is potential seems to be clearly recognized and insisted upon by all. The fact that the aesthetics of body-building and running are distorted by the insertion of the Exaggeration Principle between natural perfection and the cult ideal does not affect this principle. That there is such a *moral* duty was recognized by Aristotle and by Leibniz. It is the positive side of the haunting regret of opportunities wasted. I am unable to think of a way by which this principle can be derived from any of the traditional higher moral imperatives of either a Kantian or a utilitarian cast. It is treated as if it were a categorical imperative, unqualified in its application, but I cannot come up with a transcendental justification for it. As a good it seems to be intrinsic to the activity.

It does have one interesting liason, however. The practices and regimes of body work are not independent of the state of biological science and of the accumulated practical experience of body manage-ment. The general bodily obligation, by itself, yields no casuistry of what one should do by way of daily practices. That can only be derived by embedding the general actualization imperative in a corpus of knowledge and belief as to what is potential in this or that human body* and of what regime would release it.

REFERENCES

Billig, M. 1989: *Ideological Dilemmas*. London: Sage.

Della Porta, B. G. 1560 (1658): *Natural Magick*. London: Young and Speed.

Fonda, J. 1981: *Jane Fonda's Workbook*. Harmondsworth: Penguin.

Glover, J. 1984: *What Sort of People Should There Be?* London: Penguin.

Henderson, J. 1985: Running as an Art Form, *Runners' World*, p. 40. September.

Herzlich, C. 1973: *Health and Illness*, trans. D. Graham. London and New York: Academic Press.

Plato, *Republic*, in *The Dialogues of Plato*, Vol. II, trans. B. Jowett (1953). Oxford: Clarendon Press.

Plutarch 1908: *Moralia*, trans. A. R. Shillito, London: G. Bell and Sons.

Roby, F. B., and Davis, R. P. 1970: *Jogging for Fitness and Weight Control*. Philadelphia: Saunders.

Schwartz, H. 1986: *Never Satisfied*. New York: Free Press.

Weider, J. 1985: Physical Perfectionist: The Eternal Quest. *Muscle and Fitness* (p. 54), October.

---

* 'We can surely do something for you!' A gym manager's comment to the author.

CHAPTER 10

THE BODY AS A LOCUS OF SOCIAL CONTROL

Cornwall: *Lest it see more, prevent it. – Out vile jelly. Where is*
thy lustre now?

King Lear, Act III, Scene vii

A funny thing happened on the way to the Apocalypse.
M. Fumento, *The Myth of Heterosexual AIDS*

INTRODUCTION: EMBODIMENT AND THE MEANS OF COERCION

As used by sociologists, the phrase 'social control' is clearly a
metaphor. In the displacement of the concept of 'control' from its
contexts of lay use the implication of 'intended management of something (or someone) by someone' may not survive the transplantation of
the concept to social theory. In this chapter I shall be exploring several
contexts in which the use of the metaphor of 'social control' is illuminating. With one or two exceptions, which I shall clearly signal, any
implications of control as intentional management that may survive
from common contexts of use are to be ignored. The body itself can be
a locus of social control – that is, it can be the target of practices that
can be seen by the eye of sociology to be effective in the maintenance
of social order. The discussion of these practices will be organized
around four aspects of the fact of personal embodiment. Some bodily
states can be experienced only by the person so embodied. Pain lies
within the rim of felt embodiment. Secondly the body, as Wittgenstein
remarked, is 'the best picture of the human soul'. It is the part of
ourselves that is visible to all others. Thirdly embodiment is among the

necessary conditions for personal identity. Where my body is, there must I be. Finally, the body's condition is often taken as the enactment of a moral position or positions. These four aspects are respectively the roots of the practices of torture, mutilation and branding, imprisonment, and the threat of infection and disease. There is a substantial literature on the first three of these modes of control through the body, and I shall do no more than sketch a brief overview of each of them. The last is very much a live issue and I shall use the alleged epidemic of AIDS to explore it in some detail.

TORTURE AND CORPORAL PUNISHMENT

Torture forms part of a bouquet of bodily practices through which the infliction of pain is used to maintain some social status quo. Torture, however, must be distinguished from other body treatments, such as death, mutilation and the ordeal. In none of the latter is the pain of the subject the prime focus of the treatment. If there is pain, then it is incidental. Torture and corporal punishment generally are defined with respect to the infliction of pain. The UN Declaration against Torture of 1975 defines it thus:

> Torture means any act by which severe pain or suffering, whether physical or mental, is intentionally inflicted by or at the instigation of a public official on a person for such purposes as obtaining from him or a third person information or confession, punishing him for an act he has committed, or intimidating him or other persons.

This definition somewhat broadens the range of the concept as we ordinarily understand it. I shall consider only the torture that is the infliction of physical pain.

Two sorts of question concern me. There are conceptual questions around the concept and its varieties and range of application. Once these are clearly set out and distinguished, empirical questions of efficacy can be asked. Does torture and its little brother corporal punishment actually work as a device by which delinquency and dissent are discouraged or prevented? If not, what explains the widespread use of torture?

Peters (1985) distinguishes three definitions, or perhaps one might say, fields of application of the concept. These are the legal, the moral and the sentimental definitions. He traces the legal concept of torture from its origins in classical Greece to its temporary abolition in the nineteenth-century reforms of the penal systems of Western Europe.

Torture began as part of a legal process for the obtaining of evidence. Citizens in both Greece and Rome were supposed to be people of Ɪnour and thus trustworthy in their depositions. The evidence offered other categories of persons could be trusted only if it had been extracted by force (Peters, 1985: 13). It is not too much to say that in the period of the ancient world slaves and persons of the lower orders were tortured in judicial proceedings as a matter of course.

Peters shows how, in modern times, the role of torture has shifted from an ancillary to the law to the protection of the state. After its abolition in the legal systems of Western Europe torture waited in the wings, so to say, for the political upheavals of the twentieth century. He points to the paradox that as states have become more monolithic, more powerful and more subtly coercive, so has torture reappeared as a means of social control. As such, it now clashes once again with moral sensibility. The moral definition of torture must turn on its evil, and formally upon principles like the golden rule. It may even turn on the idea that suffering is a simple evil and its infliction by someone on another a simple moral fault. The sentimental definition has to do with the revulsion of feeling that follows the contemplation of torture. This revulsion is readily stimulated by our reading accounts of what has been done to people. But that revulsion of feeling may itself be ambiguous. The ubiquity of torture suggests that other forces are at work, particularly the taking of pleasure in the physical sufferings of other people. We can deplore, but can hardly ignore, the fact that suffering both repels and titillates.

I also owe to Peters (1985) the illuminating concept of 'semantic entropy'. The *word* 'torture' has, like many other powerfully evocative words, suffered fatal weakening through a multiplication of contexts of use. Once sharply defined for the infliction of pain in the interests of the extraction of evidence useful to the courts and later to the nation-state, through successive displacements into moral and sentimental contexts, it has come to be used for any form of dissatisfaction. In a world in which all oppressors are said to torture all oppressed, what-ever they do, no one tortures anyone. In these circumstances 'it is as easy to avoid acknowledging its use as it is to accuse another of using it' (Peters, 1985: 155). Just the same devaluations have occurred in the use of words such as 'violence' in the writings of the far left and of words like 'sexism' in the writings of the more extreme feminists.

Torture is resorted to in the interests of the extortion (or sometimes the transformation) of something 'hidden in the mind'. People are tortured to make them reveal their knowledge, or sometimes to reveal their beliefs. But the knowledge must be guilty knowledge and the beliefs forbidden beliefs. Corporal punishment, on the other hand, is aimed at the inculcation of beliefs and habits. Flogging, birching, slapping, tweaking and so on are thought of as means of instruction. If telling someone fails, then the next step is pain.

In both cases, torture and corporal punishment, the pain fills in a gap between behaviour and talk. In putting someone 'to the question' with the help of the rack and the pincers, the ostensible object of the infliction of pain is to move the subject from silence to speech. In caning a schoolboy, the object is to move from exhortation to conforming action. It is the subject's speech that is wanted in the torture case, and it is the instructor's speech that has to be supplemented in the case of punishment. From the standpoint of the thesis of this book, the essential point in all this is that in each case the pain must be given a quite definite meaning. The problem for the inquisitor is more or less the same as that for one suffering from fibromyalgia: to provide a plausible and convincing interpretation of what is suffered within the rim of felt embodiment. In the case of torture, the occurrence of the pain must be understood by the subject to be connected with an essentially negative relation to speech. It occurs because he or she will *not* talk. In the case of pain as instruction, it must be understood by the subject to be connected with an essentially positive relation to action, the doing of what has been forbidden. In the one case you are tortured because you won't talk, in the other because you won't listen. Torture and corporal punishment then must take the form of pain plus exhortation. They are pain contextualized and so made meaningful. As Robespierre put it (Schama, 1989: 828), 'virtue without which terror is harmful, and terror without which virtue is impotent'.

In the above I qualified the project of torture as having as its ostensible object the enforcement of talk on the hitherto silent victim. However as Peters (1985: 162ff.) points out, Orwell's prophetic account of torture identified a somewhat different project. Corporal punishments of all kinds presuppose an anthropology, a general theory of the nature of human beings. Traditionally pain was inflicted on criminals in the belief that they were inherently stubborn, but though capable of supporting great pain, nevertheless always in the end told the truth. At the same time there was an anthropology of childhood encapsulating much the same view. In the twentieth century torture is not primarily aimed at the extraction of information, but at the conversion or destruction of the person. In this it harks back to the anthropology of the Inquisition. The sharp distinction I drew above between extortion and instruction becomes blurred. We could say that in Room 101 Winston Smith learned something. But the general philosophical point is the same – O'Brien makes the meaning of what is required of him quite clear to Smith. As Scarry (1987) points out, somehow the victims must be instructed in the illusion that they themselves ar agents in their own pain.

There remains the question of the efficacy of physical pain in eith of these applications. Does it bring forth hidden information, and dr it facilitate learning? The learning issue is also twofold. There is the learning not to do what it is one wants or is tempted to do, not to believe what one is inclined to believe. Then there is the acquiring of behavioural habits and acceptable beliefs. I would suppose that there would be a considerable literature devoted to the reporting of studies on the absolute and relative effectiveness of various forms of corporal punishment – training by pain. The combined efforts of the Adolescent Psychiatry Unit of the Oxford University Department of Psychiatry and the Educational Studies Department provided me with only one, Hoggart (1985). But it is more an ethnography of punishment than a study of the efficacy of pain.

One can hardly discuss empirical studies of the efficacy of physical punishment without reference to the goals that determine the application of efficacious punishments in the first place. One could sum up the classical 'theories' of punishment as retribution, remedy and reform. It seems to me that empirical studies can be relevant only to the third account of how punishment is justified. It can hardly be an empirical question whether a flogging is a retribution for wrong done or a remedy for a social disorder. In these cases it is the symbolic value of the punishment that is in question.

MUTILATION

The art of the modern torturer is to induce horrific pain in such a way as to leave the body of the victim unmarked. No visible or tangible evidence of the treatment should remain to be used in evidence at some later inquiry. In sharp contrast, mutilation is designed to leave a permanent mark on the body and in many cases to lead to the permanent incapacitation of some natural function or power. In this introductory sketch of the scope of uses of the body in social control I am concerned only to outline a general framework within which varieties of physical coercion can be defined and identified. To this end it will be enough to illustrate the distinctions I want to make with two examples. In certain Islamic countries the punishment for theft is the amputation of the right hand. The pain is, of course, quite incidental to this act of mutilation. It hardly needs remarking that the deprivation of the hand is metonymic. It is the instrument by which theft was committed and its symbolic role is obvious. Just as a person deprived of the right hand in an accident can learn to write with the left, so I have no doubt a thief could as readily pilfer with the hand that remains. Blinding, like clitorectomy, is final and irreversible. Of course vaginal orgasm remains a possibility for such mutilated females. This fact emphasizes the obvious relationship between this form of mutilation and the maintenance of male hegemony even in those societies, such as the Sudan, where the excision is performed by the old women.

There are two main kinds of sexual mutilation practised on women in Muslim Africa (Nordenstam, 1968). Pharaonic female circumscision or infibulation has been outlawed in many places, but is still widely reported (Barclay, 1964). In an operation of almost unimaginable cruelty, the clitoris, labia minora and a substantial part of the labia majora are cut away. The vulva is then sewn up, almost obliterating the vaginal opening. Thus the 'honour' (*ird*) of the family is preserved, since it is virtually impossible for females mutilated in this way to have premarital sexual intercourse. Nordenstam (p. 228) reports that the North Sudanese take it for granted that this barabaric practice does not call for justification, even the crudely utilitarian, since it is just *ada* or custom. Sunna female circumcision is the exact analogue of the male operation, involving simply the excision of the prepuce of the clitoris, and has no discernible physiological or anatomical effect. It is the symbolic force as much as the physical effect of minor mutilations of the sexual organs that is the nub of the matter.

One should include physiological, as well as anatomical, mutilation in any discussion of forced symbolic transformation of the body. (The emphasis throughout this introduction is on forced transformations, so that neither tattooing nor voluntary drug taking, such as drunkenness, counts as mutilation.) I know of a case in Sind in which a child, the heir to a rich estate, was covertly fed with opium by villainous servants and later forced through his addiction to hand over the estate. That is physiological mutilation.

FROM THE LASH TO THE PRISON CELL

In his *Discipline and Punish* of 1979 Michel Foucault laid great emphasis on the role of the body in the kinds of social control that have been exercised through the judicial system. Until the nineteenth century the body was the focus of elaborate, coarse-grained and often spectacular physical punishments. Imprisonment in England was more or less reserved for enemies of the state and for debtors. Other offenders were whipped (birched), humiliated in the stocks, transported to penal colonies, drawn and quartered or, if they were lucky, hanged.

Foucault connects the rise of the prison as a place for the exercise of a new kind of control technique with the transformation of the state from monarchy to emerging bourgeois democracy. In one of his more inspired metaphors he refers to this social arrangement as the condition of capillary power. People are controlled and control others by surveillance. He describes this as 'the moment where it became understood that it was more efficient and profitable in terms of the economy of power to place people under surveillance than to subject them to some exemplary penalty' (Foucault, 1980: 38). Even though it is quite unclear what he means by the 'economy of power', the idea of prison as a place apart in which the abnormal could be segregated from the normal extended the idea of physical or bodily separation from the case of the mad to criminals. Crime was no longer something someone did. A criminal was what someone was. The body was the key.

It was the key in more than one way. Obviously by locking a body in a cell one locked the person in with it. Segregation of bodies ensured the separation of persons. The body now plays a different part in the penal system. Its relevance is no longer by virtue of its capacity to be tortured, mutilated and, as the locus of physical violence, to be the instrument of pain. It is the conceptual fact that people are embodied, more or less one person to each body, that is the salient fact about bodies. Furthermore bodies can be overseen, looked at. They can become objects of 'gaze'. Foucault points out in several places that Bentham's 'Panopticon' was the exemplary invention of the transition to a society managed through surveillance. In the Panopticon the cells, rooms, dormitories or what you will were arranged around a central chamber intended for a supervisor. The interiors of both the central chamber and of the cells were in sight of one another through an ample provision of windows looking both in and out. The inmates were under the gaze of the supervisor and he or she was equally under the gaze of those who inhabited the cells. A perfect prison.

ILLNESS FINDS ITS DISEASE: THE THREAT OF INFECTION

The idea that a bodily malfunction, definable without reference to the social conditions in which it is managed and displayed, could be a stable foundation for a theory of illness is clearly simplistic. The cases examined in chapter 6 involved the transformation of a bodily condition, definable in biological terms, into an illness. This transformation was effected by embedding the symptoms in locally acceptable patterns of social behaviour defined by reference to a set of normative concepts of proper daily living drawn from the local moral order. In a sense, illness behaviour is deviant behaviour and is accountable as such. In the cases now to be considered the deviance is there, so to speak, and the illness is created to realize it in a form that is amenable to social control. The structure is a kind of triangle, with illness and deviance as two of its poles and the third filled in with a biologically definable disease. To fulfil its role in the structure the disease must have certain threatening features.

The illness–deviance–disease conceptual triangle has often served to support programmes of social control and reform. Syphilis warned against sexual misbehaviour, while ringworm and head-lice threatened those who played with the local 'kids'. The most spectacular example in recent years, perhaps in all history, has been the AIDS 'epidemic'. A striking feature of this episode has been the way that while the moral panic was actually under way transforming a rare disease into a species threatening catastrophe, the 'machinery' by which the transformation was being managed was being clearly specified and accurately described by a variety of commentators. So powerful were the forces favouring an AIDS pandemic that the voices of reason were virtually ignored. I shall examine, first of all, the way a rare form of viral infection became the ground for a world-wide media event of great complexity.

The biological basis of the AIDS 'epidemic' is complex. The question of whether there is an identifiable disease to go along with the cluster of symptoms displayed by the victims of AIDS is still at issue. That the human immune system can be infected by a certain family of viruses (nicknamed the 'HIVs') is not in dispute. Nor is it in doubt that in certain cases this infection permits the development of fatal secondary infections and conditions, such as Kaposi's sarcoma. It is in the weakness of the correlations between the infection (or perhaps one should say a positive or negative test result for the infection) and the symptom cluster that doubts are engendered. At the same time a parallel and independent line of research has been showing how sensitive is the human immune system to psychological influences. Depression and social isolation tend to reduce the effectiveness of the body's defensive system, while social and psychological well-being seem to enhance it. The part of the system that seems to be most sensitive to psychological and social conditions are those very T-cells that are the focus of the viral infection. The AIDS epidemic is at the intersection of two kinds of assault on the human immune system, which are intimately interrelated. A diagnosis of AIDS via the detection of antibodies characteristic of an immune reaction to infection, whether or not the person has any symptoms, can socially isolate the person and so induce a lowering of the effectiveness of the immune system, whether or not the system is actually coping with the infection.

To grasp the workings of the social and psychological processes that brought about the 'epidemic', I shall draw on the work of Cohen (1980) and Lemert (1951), as well as the extensive and detailed study recently published by Fumento (1990). Cohen's analytical concepts were developed for his study of another non-existent scourge, witchcraft. It seems now to be beyond dispute that there was no cult of witchcraft in medieval and renaissance Europe. Of course the use of magic was widespread, but there were no covens of devil worshippers and there was no secret religion. The 'epidemic' of witchcraft was real enough in a sense. But it was a social phenomenon, a 'moral panic'. In a moral panic some group of people and the alleged evils they practise are publicly presented as threats to the very existence of the society in which this moral canker occurs. Moral entrepreneurs spring forth to 'man the barricades' against the spread of the insidious and destructive influence that is alleged to be immanent. The media 'might leave behind a diffuse feeling of anxiety about the situation: "Something should be done about it!", "When will it all end?", or "This sort of thing cannot go on for ever", the moral entrepreneurs consciously exploit the moral panic' (Cohen, 1975). Those who are alleged to practise the contaminating activities are not just deviants, but 'folk devils'. They are the source of the contagion. In the case of the AIDS epidemic the moral evil is reified into a physical vector, the virus that passes from person to person. HIV is not just a physical threat, but also morally contaminating. The best remedy against the contagion is to segregate the folk devils who are its source. The quarantine serves the double purpose of halting the spread of the disease and stemming the epidemic of moral contagion. 'Safe sex' is both a repudiation of sexual 'laxity' and a prophylatic against the supposedly life-threatening virus itself.

The story of the AIDS 'epidemic' is wonderfully complex. There were two phases. In the first phase the moral panic was focused on homosexuals, conveniently isolable as the folk devils whose disgusting practices threatened the whole of mankind. The physical and moral contamination coincided. At this point there did indeed exist a medically and biologically real epidemic of some seriousness. In the second phase we find a spectacular amplification of the deviancy. A heterosexual epidemic was promised and sometimes actually announced. Now the folk devils were the sexually promiscuous and the practitioners of 'unsafe' heterosexual sex. I shall look at the deconstruction of the two phases of this event by several authors, with the object of meditating on the ineffectiveness of their interpretations to stem the tide. A cautionary foreword to the analysis is required. In hindsight there is a temptation to accuse the protagonists of the panic of dishonesty. That is very far from my intention. Perhaps the most important and worrying aspect of the whole illusion was the sincerity of those who promoted it. It involves two ways in which sexual practices can be 'wrong'. Homosexuality is one and heterosexual promiscuity is another. Each has figured in the complex moral panic from which the 'epidemic' story emerged, and which is itself maintained by that story.

Lemert (1951) has suggested that new forms of social control 'spring up and crystallize in the interaction between deviants and the rest of society.' Since the interaction in the AIDS case is physically, as well as morally, defined, the new form of social control is readily constructed around the disease entity and its epidemiology. The virus takes on a double role. It is the source of physical contagion and a threat to life, and it has become a metonymic representation of the social deviance of those who reject traditional values in the sexual domain. In practising 'safe sex', one displays one's adherence to the rules of medical good sense and one's adherence to traditional morality. I shall substantiate this suggestion in the detailed analysis to follow.

The use of diseases as agents of social control is not new. AIDS made its appearance in an atmosphere already fraught with a certain measure of medical anxiety. Genital herpes was credited with many of the potent attributes of AIDS. It was said to be incurable. It could be present latent in the body for many years without there being any symptoms to betray its presence. Its consequences were declared to be dire. As an infection of the brainstem, it could lead to madness. It was transmitted mainly through heterosexual relations. It was a promising candidate for a starring role in a moral panic, but it was overtaken by the more spectacular phenomenon of AIDS. However, to ready the latter for a role in the general project of the regulation of sexual behaviour, a heterosexual epidemic had to be announced as immanent or even under way.

One should notice that the bodily conditions that bring on moral panics need not have a sound basis in medical science. For instance, the epidemic of 'hyperactivity' through the treatment for which a programme for the social control of 'spoiled kids' was mounted was an epidemic of diagnoses rather than of disturbed neurophysiologies. I have been told that at the height of that moral panic over 2,000,000 children in the eastern part of the United States had been diagnosed as hyperactive and were being prescribed powerful medicaments! It is not so long ago that the rare disease of mononucleosis 'spread' like wildfire through the universities. A reluctance to attend classes and to get on with one's work could be framed in a disease–illness pattern. A flight into inactivity is legitimated as the illness behaviour appropriate to that disease. Claims to be suffering from very rare allergies, such as an adverse reaction to wheat flour, can be used by individuals to legitimate massive withdrawals from sociality. It is far from my intention to suggest that moral panics and flights into inactivity that are based on mythic diseases are deliberate acts of fraud. On the contrary, they are amongst the uses to which concepts of bodily states and conditions can be put.

DEVIANCY AMPLIFICATION

The first step in our analysis will be to look at the discourse through which the simplistic and disputed correlation 'HIV (virus)–AIDS (syndrome)' is presented as a fatal disease. I shall be citing various claims and pronouncements from a file covering the period of the height of the moral panic, but I shall draw most from a single issue of *Newsweek* (12 August 1985). It is a remarkable document, but typical of the media coverage through which deviancy amplification was achieved. At this point it is the homosexual community that is the main target of moral outrage. Those who have been infected by the virus through transfusions of contaminated blood (whether or not they have developed any aspect of the AIDS syndrome) may be pronounced to be innocent victims, but are treated as sources of contagion. A quotation typical of the era goes as follows: 'More than 6,000 Americans have died as a result of AIDS, giving the disease a frightening mortality rate of 50 per cent. No one has ever been known to recover.' As we shall see below, the tie between signs of infection by the HIV virus and the symptomology of AIDS is so loose that by tying 'recovery' to the symptoms it can be made out that no one with the disease (that is, the virus) *recovers*. Since many people apparently infected with the virus never develop any of the conditions comprised within the loosely drawn boundaries of the AIDS syndrome, it is quite false that no one *infected* recovers. The ambiguity of the phrase 'died as a result of AIDS' opens up just enough space for the thin end of a moral panic to be inserted. The identification of the relevant folk devils is an easy step. It is exemplified in remarks attributed in *Newsweek* to Dr W. H. Heseltine of the Dana-Faber Cancer Institute: 'Once infected, a person is infected for the rest of his life . . . Once infected a person is *infectious*. It is not safe to assume otherwise' (12 Aug. 1985). Anyone from amongst the folk devils can be a carrier, so, it is implied, everyone from that community must be shunned. At this point the 'infectious' population coincided neatly with two overlapping groups of social outcasts, homosexuals and drug abusers. The infected needles of the addicts now carried the dreaded HIV as well as hepatitis.

Phase two was inaugurated with media campaigns of unprecedented starkness. The frantic style of the pronouncements is exemplified by an excerpt from a radio programme broadcast in 1987. The speaker is Oprah Winfrey: 'Listen to me, hard to believe – one in five heterosexuals could be dead from AIDS at the end of the next three years. That's by 1990. One in five. It is no longer just a gay disease. Believe me.' The element of social control was immediately evident. Dr W. R. Dowdle (ibid.: 21) is quoted as saying 'We have to understand that we all have to change our way of living. The message goes out for everybody that the healthy sexual style is the style of the single partner.' In the same number of *Newsweek* Dr D. Francis is quoted as saying 'It will end the sexual revolution. You can take your chances with herpes or hepatitis B, but you can't take your chances with this.' The place once occupied by syphilis is no longer empty. To cap the catalogue of pronouncements I cite from Fumento (1990) a quotation attributed to Otis Brown, the Secretary of Health and Human Services for the US Government: 'If we can't make progress we face a pandemic that will make others, including the black death, seem pale by comparison.' But as Fumento remarks, 'the plague ship would not come in.'

The signs of a return to reason are now everywhere to be seen. *The Times* (London) of 14 January 1990 reported that the official government estimates of AIDS deaths expected in the homosexual and drug-addicted groups in the United Kingdom in the next four years has dropped from 17,000 to 5,000. Fumento, using the latest figures for the United States, suggests an annual death toll among white heterosexuals in that country of about 360. This compares favourably with Oprah Winfrey's prediction of 40,000,000 dead by 1990. It is also about the same as deaths caused by lightning.

RETHINKING THE BIOLOGY OF HIV

The flurry of research into the nature and habits of members of this family of viruses demonstrates very nicely the relation between macro-social phenomena such as the two phases of moral panic I have described – microsocial aspects of the scientific community and biological science. Lots of funding is available for HIV research, thanks to the moral panic. This is not to suggest that medical researchers have in any way nurtured extravagant public responses. But they can hardly regret them! Fumento (1990) attributes a more active role to some members of the homosexual community.

> With the tide of death lapping around them, it has been galling for homosexuals to find that only non-homosexual, non-drug abusing sufferers of AIDS are regarded as innocent victims. More worrying still: if those who get AIDS from donated blood or plasma are victims, then since there must be a culprit; and since the vast majority of tainted blood has undoubtedly been from homosexuals, it is not paranoid for homosexuals to feel themselves blamed.
>
> This is why so many homosexuals have been eager to promote the thesis of a general heterosexual outbreak: the myth of heterosexual AIDS.
>
> In creating this myth homosexuals have been motivated not by malice but by the need to deny responsibility for the disease that was killing them, and for research funds to find a cure for it.

While only a tiny minority of those who have studied the AIDS epidemic go so far as to doubt that HIV has any role in the aetiology of the AIDS syndrome, the looseness of fit between testing positive and displaying AIDS symptoms is worth emphasizing. One must surely ask why it is that Duesberg's carefully argued case for caution (*New Scientist*, 28 April 1988) has been greeted with deafening silence by the AIDS 'establishment'. He pointed out that the claim that the sole cause of the disease is HIV does not satisfy Koch's first postulate. The pathogen is not demonstrably present in all cases of the disease syndrome. Even when 'phantom AIDS', a presentation of symptoms that vanishes when the patient is told of a negative HIV test, are eliminated, there are many cases where symptoms typical of the AIDS syndrome occur in the absence of HIV. Weiss (1990: 279) reports correlational evidence that suggests that 'at least some cases of Kaposi's sarcoma may result from an as-yet-unidentified, sexually transmitted agent.' This condition is virtually unknown in those infected with HIV via blood transfusions, whereas 21 per cent of infected homosexuals develop it. Some homosexuals who display no signs of HIV infection develop Kaposi's sarcoma. (These figures are taken from *US News and World Report*, 9 April 1990: 47.)

These observations have to be set against the background of a very curious phenomenon, the ever-lengthening 'incubation period' specified by some AIDS researchers. One way of explaining away Duesberg's objection is to claim that the apparent exceptions to the principle that HIV causes AIDS are explicable on one of two auxiliary hypotheses. Some exceptions will be the result of some countervailing microbiological agent or process. But others will be registered because the virus has not yet had time to cause its dire consequences. The problem with this line of defence is that as the threat to the population at large has receded, so the latency period has expanded. The figure offered in 1987 was seven years. By 1989 it had increased to ten. But by 1989 the virus had been studied for just ten years. If the link between signs of HIV and symptoms of AIDS is weak, then we would expect the 'incubation' period to expand to keep pace exactly with the length of time that it has been possible to detect the viral infection.

Duesberg has also pointed out that there is another difficulty in the causal hypothesis. A virus harms its victim just in so far as it destroys more cells than the host can 'spare'. HIV infects only a very small proportion of T-cells even in patients with clearly displayed AIDS symptoms. According to Duesberg, the evidence shows that the body produces new T-cells faster than the virus can kill them. His thought goes something like this: collecting up symptoms to create a package, the AIDS syndrome provides medical science with a 'something', though it is plainly an artefact. Assuming the unity and reality of the 'something' leads naturally to the thought that there is another 'something' that is its cause. Looking around among the correlative conditions, we find HIV infection. This is then elevated to the status of a cause. But it was in the very first step that the whole AIDS story was predetermined. It has also been suggested, though I cannot locate the reference, that the virus has 'spread' into populations in perfect synchrony with the spread of testing into those populations. Maybe the virus is widespread in the human population. (It may have been present in Liverpool in the 1950s, for instance.) This observation has the same logical form as the ultimate debunking of the claim that criminal violence was associated with (even caused by) an extra male chromosome. The thesis first emerged from the discovery that tests on prisoners showed an 'abnormal' distribution of the chromosomal anomaly. But when the tests were repeated on a properly constituted sample of the whole male population, it turned out that the 'abnormal' distribution characterized the population at large. The thesis was an artefact of an a-priori assumption of what is to count as normal.

WAS THE AIDS EPIDEMIC EVER REAL?

There is no heterosexual AIDS pandemic, nor is there likely to be. Despite the reservations that the observations of Duesberg and others on the shoddy reasoning behind the epidemiological claims of some HIV virologists should have made salient, there is apparently little room for doubt that there is a complex cluster of disease entities, of pathogens and lethal degenerative processes, rife amongst homosexuals. The intervening 'variable', so to say, is the human immune system. The various lethal conditions get a grip because the immune system is 'down'. But is it down largely because of T-cell infection by HIV? It has been suggested (Schmidt, 1984) that the disease is wholly socially constructed. In chapter 8 we looked at the way that diseases provide the points of departure for the social construction of illnesses. Schmidt has proposed something like the idea that a cluster of illnesses (the AIDS syndrome) has provided the point of departure for the social construction of a disease, HIV infection offering the biological basis.

Schmidt's thesis is simple. The immune system is extraordinarily sensitive to psychological states, particularly depression and contentment. The AIDS epidemic, as a moral panic, is the very stuff of hysteria. Schmidt argues the case for an interplay between hysteria and a lowering of the activity of the immune system in two stages. In the first stage he draws a point-by-point comparison with the famous 'June bug fever' outbreak. One June in the 1930s hundreds of workers in the Ohio textile industry developed a mysterious fever. It was first of all put down to infection from a previously unknown insect, the June bug. The factories involved used cloth imported from England. It was believed that the June bugs came from the bales of imported cotton material. So rapid and apparently serious was the outbreak that alarmed public health officials instigated a vigorous search for the insects with a view to pest control. They were never found and as rapidly as it had erupted the epidemic subsided. The June bug fever was a large-scale example of a familiar hysterical phenomenon. Hysterical epidemics have a characteristic pattern of onset and decline, quite unlike that of mass infections brought on by the spread of a biologically identifiable pathogen. They do not fade away, but disappear with great rapidity. Schmidt suggested that the AIDS epidemic matched the June bug fever scare rather well, so well that hysteria is the best explanation of it.

But Schmidt is a devotee of psycho-history, and that allegiance is evident in the second stage of his analysis. He finds the psychological source of the outbreak in the traumatizing of the general population through the ever-present threat of a nuclear holocaust. Cathexis of the trauma is achieved by the scapegoating of groups of identifiable and deviant outsiders, namely homosexuals and drug-users. Hysterical symptoms appear amongst the victims of this mass resolution. 'The moral backlash has shamed . . . the homosexuals and the drug addicts giving rise to an epidemic of shame-induced depression' (Schmidt, 1984: 51). In the final step he links depression to the AIDS syndrome. 'Epidemics of depression based mostly on shame . . . [give rise to] the reduction of cell-mediated immunity [which] is one of the typical vege-tative signs of severe depression' (p. 39).

There are several points on which one can agree with Schmidt's analysis. Clearly hostile attitudes to homosexuality (unclean) and to recreational sex (sinful indulgence) are an element in the socially amplified aspects of the phenomenon. The disease has been seized on by moral entrepreneurs in a campaign that is part of a larger move-ment towards the re-establishment of a traditional moral order. How-ever, the Freudian undergirding of the psycho-history does not ring true. The tie to the nuclear arms race is thin. The AIDS epidemic does not strike me as plausibly glossed as an unconsciously 'wished for solution to pre-existing conflicts'. Nor do we need so elaborate a hypothesis as the 'guilt about unconscious fantasies stirred up by the sexual resolution' to explain the moral panic. Most people experience some measure of insecurity as the social order loosens and modulates into a new key.

In summary I would present the AIDS epidemic as material for future historians in terms of the public telling of two *stories*. There is a biological story in which a previously unknown virus appears, threaten-ing the whole population. Medical scientists rises to the occasion, fighting a heroic battle of wits. There is also a social story. There is a fatal illness of epidemic proportions which is the result of immoral practices. The threat to mankind can be halted only by a mass return to the strictest sexual morality. Neither of these stories is true. Yet each contains a nugget of fact. Together the stories serve to provide not only an illness, but also the disease to go along with it. It may be that in sober hindsight HIV will fade from a central role in a third story, the story I have been telling, as an interested observer of the social scene.

REFERENCES

Barclay, H. B. 1964: *Buurri al Lemaab*. Ithaca, NY: Cornell University Press.

Cohen, S. 1980: *Folk Devils and Moral Panics*. New York: St Martin's Press.

Duesberg, P. 1978: AIDS and the 'Innocent' Virus, *New Scientist*, 118, 34–5.

Duesberg, P. 1988: HIV is not the cause of AIDS, *Science* 241 (48–68), 514–17.

Foucault, M. 1979: *Discipline and Punish*. Harmondsworth: Penguin.

Foucault, M. 1980: *Power/Knowledge*. Brighton: Harvester.

Fumento, M. 1990: *The Myth of Heterosexual AIDS*. New York. Basic Books.

Hoggart, K. 1985: *To Beat or Not To Beat: Is This a Class Question?* King's College: Occasional papers.

Lemert, E. M. 1951: Is There a Natural History of Social Problems? *American Sociological Review*, 16, 217–23.

Newsweek, 12 August 1985, 20–9.

Nordenstam, 1968: *Sudanese Ethics*. Uppsala: Scandinavian Institute of African Studies.

Peters, E. 1985: *Torture*. Oxford: Basil Blackwell.

Scarry, E. 1987: *The Body in Pain*, ch. 1. New York: Oxford University Press.

Schama, S. 1989: *Citizens*. London: Penguin.

Schmidt, C. G. 1984: The Group Fantasy Origin of AIDS. *Journal of Psychohistory*, 12, 37–78.

Weiss, R. 1990: Critical Kaposis Growth Factor Identified. *Science News*, 137/18, 279.

PART III
Meanings

I did not know that a pattern forms before we are aware of it, and that what we think we make becomes a rigid prison making us.
　　　　　　　　　　　　　　　Margaret Drabble, *The Millstone*

To be used meaningfully, a sign or mark is taken to point beyond itself, to stand for something other than what it is in itself. For something to be able to be made use of this way, to be taken or read in a certain way, that thing must already be differentiated from everything else. It must appear as a figure on a ground. It must be capable of being recognized as a sign, a distinct entity which could be put to significant human use. Of course the sign function is not in the thing. It is only in the context of a fragment of a human form of life that things are signs. The human body is amply provided with differentiable parts, a veritable lexicon of potential signs.

But how do signs signify? By synthesizing the semantic insights of Peirce and Barthes an account of how the body and its parts could be used as signifiers can be developed. In the light of this account an ill-defined and open range of iconic tropes, materially embodied 'figures of speech', can be identified through focusing on some central cases. For instance, it becomes clear on close study that anthropophagi, people eaters, are not, in their own eyes, consuming meat, but powers and sacred substances of many kinds. (The associations of the word 'cannibal' take us far from the anthropology of the consumption of human flesh.)

The body structure offers all sorts of possibilities for finding cosmic and social analogues to this or that piece of human anatomy. But analogy is a two-way relation. Each term in an analogy is a model of the other. The human body has stood in this dual relation to physical things such as the earth and the cosmos, and to abstract entities such as human political associations like the State and the Church.

FIGURE 11.1   Bodily signifiers

Most of this array of once inspiring analogues is of only antiquarian interest. St Hildergard of Bingen was not alone in thinking it possible to read off the wonders of the cosmos from the proportions of the human body. Now we have difficulty in remembering that such commonplace expressions as 'headmaster', 'foothills', 'hand of cards', 'Weirtown, the armpit of the Western world', 'body politic' and the like were once vivid and instructive metaphors. But the body is still capable of engendering a signifier or two (see figure 11.1).

CHAPTER 11

CORPOREAL SEMANTICS

Holst too must have been fat once, but he was thin now. Men like that formed a kind of race apart: you could pick them out the moment you saw them. Hamling, now, was huge, but you could sense that he was hard as well. Holst was even bigger, with shoulders that had probably been wide once, but now his lines had gone soft. And it wasn't only his clothes that were worn out and sagging. His skin had become too big for him, and probably hung in wrinkles. Even the skin of his face was crumpled.

Georges Simenon, *The Stain on the Snow*

INTRODUCTION: SEMANTIC THEORY AND BODILY SIGNIFICATION

A working semantic system is complex and many-layered. At the base are the signs, physically distinguishable entities. Anatomically distinct parts are an (almost) natural repertoire. One must include the qualification 'almost' as a reminder that the way to dismember the human body anatomically is not read directly off the body, but influenced by prior concepts and beliefs; Peirce's categories of Firstness, Secondness and Thirdness can help to distinguish the properties a body part has in itself, independent of any of its uses, from the sense we have of how it might be related to other things, finally distinguished from how it is and has actually been used in concrete contexts. But to explain the last of these aspects in detail, an analysis of signification is required, not least to distinguish signifying relations from other kinds of Thirdness. Barthes's way of using the traditional distinction between the denotation and the connotation of a sign opens up a study of the way local cultural knowledge is involved in any use of distinguishable physical, and particularly anatomical, entities for semantic purposes.

10.   Saint's relics.
(Reproduced by kind permission of The Mansell Collection, London.)

Human bodies can play all sorts of roles in the use of signifying systems. They can be surfaces for the inscription of other signifiers, exerting a subtle influence on how that inscription can be done. But above all they can be signifiers themselves. In a final twist the body and its parts become the thing signified. Signifier and signified collapse into a practical union. In more gradiose manner, in Aztec corporeal cosmology the sacrificial treatment of the bodies of the victims is the cosmic act itself. They become the gods and it as gods too that the people consume their significant parts. The body and blood of Christ are the Church and the Holy Spirit.

RELICS

In the environs of Paris there is said to be a woman of saintly reputation who is providing her followers with relics while she is still alive. The story goes that she is having small pieces of herself cut off (under medical supervision) to give to the faithful. I have been unable to confirm the story, but its very unlikelihood testifies to its truth. I begin this chapter on the body as signified and signifier with some reflections on relics, and other evidences of the widespread view that the body and its parts are, so to say, embodied virtues and vices, material realizations of purity and of defilement, flesh transfigured by meaning.

The body is more than flesh, more than the vehicle for the transport of persons, more than an instrument by means of which human beings act upon and in the material world. Relics are pieces of human bodies, usually recognizable as organs. We can begin our study of corporeal semantics by asking how an organ, preserved as a relic, can have significance. It might be that it *stands for* a virtue by association with the worthy life of the person from whose body it came. But it might be that it is taken as an embodiment of that virtue, a kind of material realization of moral worth. In learning why people preserved all those bodily fragments of saintly persons, we shall get a preliminary glimpse of the semiotics of body. For they can be found in their thousands throughout the Catholic part of Europe. One can wander through cathedral treasuries in which shelf by shelf the silver-mounted glassware of reliquaries displays the shrivelled parts of our virtuous predecessors (see plate 10). The good and evil that men (and women) do lives after them, embodied not only in their carefully preserved organs, but also in the instruments and accoutrements of life. We can glimpse the authentic suit worn by Neville Heath when on the look-out for another bride for his acid bath. Is the way social and moral meaning attaches to bodies and body parts different from the way it attaches to personal possessions which have never been parts of bodies? Is the meaning of one of Muhammad's many surviving turbans, say that in the gatehouse of the Bahd Shahi mosque in Lahore, fundamentally different from the meaning the faithful attach to the shrivelled heart of St Theresa of Avila? Thus my questions are: How are the body and its parts meaningful? And is the manner of their meaning different in kind from the meaningfulness of mere things, even things of use? In chapter 1 we came to see that artefacts and bodies are not so clearly demarcated as one might expect, particularly when questions of moral protection are at issue. The study of the semiotics of relics will help to attain a clear view of the corresponding problem of meaning.

Relics have played a role in the religious and moral life of many communities. In the Catholic doctrine of relics a careful distinction is drawn between acceptable Christian uses of sanctified objects and their role in pagan superstitions. A relic in Catholic canon law can be 'the whole body or parts of it, or the remains of the body after death' (Dooley, 1931: 3). But there are also second- and third-class relics, objects used by, or associated with, a saint. Relics differ in importance. Many first-class relics are 'notable' (*insignis*). In Catholic doctrine body parts and material possessions can both have moral significance.

Relics seem to have come into prominence in the early Christian Church through their role in the setting up of altars. Mass was often celebrated on the gravestone of a saint. It soon became almost mandatory to include a relic in the construction of an altar. Indeed, according to the Fifth Council of Carthage, the presence of a relic could be used as a test of the genuineness of the monument altar. There were obvious 'commercial' advantages in the possession of notable relics. So scandalous did the trade in relics become that in 432 the Code of Justinian explicitly forbade the dividing and selling of the remains of martyrs. The importance of relics also led to the devising of tests for authenticity, including trial by ordeal, efficacy and provenance, the last giving rise to the splendidly named speciality 'lipsanography'.

Official support for the use of relics was from time to time an important source of contention between the Catholic Church and several of its famous apostates. Opponents denounced the cult of relics as superstition. Responses included both a psychological theory to account for the origin of relic cults and a theological doctrine that distinguished Christian from pagan usage. St Augustine (*De civitate Dei* 1) expressed the matter thus: 'If a father's coat or ring, or anything else of that kind, is so much more cherished by his children as love for one's parents is greater, in no way are the bodies themselves to be despised, which are more intimately united to us than any garment; for they belong to man's very nature.' St Thomas Aquinas, basing himself on this remark, argues that 'in memory of them [saints] we ought to honour any relic of theirs in a fitting manner; principally their bodies which were temples and organs of the Holy Ghost...' (*Summa Theologica* III, Q. 25, a.6). The body is not worshipped for its own sake, but for the sake of the soul, related to the body in life as its identical matter. This psychological theory suggests, as Dooley says, an 'instinct of the human heart' or natural tendency to venerate the memory of friend or someone of importance which extends to the relics of such a person. This theory is explicit in canon law (canons 1276 and 1255).

But how is the whole or part of a body efficacious in bringing about miracles, in cures, in answering prayers? The Church explicitly disavowed a causal theory of the power of relics. It is not the relic itself that has the power or virtue of the person from whose remains it has been taken. A relic is, or should be thought to be, the occasion for, rather than a cause of, miraculous events. One might say that in official Catholic teaching relics were taken to have a psychological role. They were not to be adored as actual miracle working or divine entities, but venerated as, so to say, potent reminders of the 'virtues that made men saints'. Here we have a simple, but powerful, semiotics of bodies and body parts. A body or its parts have significance just in so far as they are known to be the remains of someone whose virtue or value they represent. This is indeed a semiotics of body parts as relics. A pagan view which credits relics with the actual power to cure illness or to be the source of virtue merely by touch is not a semiotics at all. The official Catholic doctrine is daily interwoven with paganism, as one can easily observe in famous shrines. I have been advised, when in Santiago de Compostella, to rub my forehead against the forehead of the self-portrait head of Maestro Mateu, in the hope of acquiring some of his legendary power to shape stone.

A GENERAL THEORY OF SIGNS: PEIRCE, BARTHES AND SAUSSURE

The human body is such that its states, conditions, parts and postures serve as signs. It is both a semiotic system in itself and made meaningful by a semiotic system. The human body gives meaning and has meaning. In the official theory of relics we have come across what one might call the zero semiotics – the simplest and most naive account of how a body or part of a body can have meaning. There is an instinct to venerate, or even to be morbidly fascinated by, remains. The semiotic theory, namely how it is that something can have such a meaning, is simple association. I venerated him; this is his turban; I venerate the turban as associated with him. To go further I shall draw upon Peirce's theory of signs, and the semiotics of Barthe.

Peirce used threefold distinctions in his classification schemes, almost throughout his exposition of his theory of signs. The first triad concerns the mode of signification. Any theory of signs must be built around the basic idea of a sign, something that has an intentional aspect for its human users – i.e. that points beyond itself. The system of signs binds together signifiers and signified. There are iconic signs that point beyond themselves by virtue of their similarity to something else – that is, they point by imitation. At the centre of a no-smoking sign there is a picture of a cigarette. Then there are indexical signs, objects that point towards what they signify, such as the finger posts that fascinated Wittgenstein. (This way to the lake →.) Finally Peirce adds symbolic signs. These are signifiers which are conventionally associated with what they mean. For instance, the circle and diagonal bar over an iconic sign expresses a prohibition.

But signs rarely appear singly. Though the primarily application is to verbal-sign usage, Peirce's threefold distinction between rhemes, dicents and arguments could, it seems to me, apply to non-verbal signs as well. A rheme is a single meaningful item, a dicent a cluster that, if properly assembled creates a new level of meaning, and an argument is a cluster of such clusters. In the verbal system these sign categories correspond to words, sentences and thematically coherent paragraphs.

But something more is needed to understand how a mere thing, serving as an indexical rheme, say, can function as a sign. Anachronistically one might cite Wittgenstein's realization that what makes a thing a sign is not what it denotes, but how we use it, for instance, for the *purpose* of denoting something. It is shared understandings of purpose that make joint use possible, and it is the custom of joint use that facilitates shared understandings. But how does this 'get started', so to say? Every meaningful sign use involves an 'interpretant'. To the threefold classifications of signs must be added the threefold Peircian classifications of interpretants. As Short puts it (1986: 98), an interpretant is not an interpreter. Instead it is a particular thought, action or feeling which interprets the sign. Interpreters are formations of interpretants and may, though need not always, be people.

The first triad to consider are immediate, dynamic and final interpretants. As an immediate interpretant, one is considering a sign in its *capacity* to transmit information, induce action, etc. As a dynamic interpretant, one is considering a sign in its capacity as *actually* semiotically effective. As a final interpretant one is considering a sign in the light of 'what *would be* the best interpretant, given a goal of interpretation' (Short, 1986: 107).

According to the second triadic set of distinctions, each interpretant can be considered as it is 'emotional' – that is, as there is a certain felt quality that interprets the sign, such as the peremptory force of the red stop light; as it is 'energetic', that is as there is an action that interprets the sign, such as the stopping of the car at the stop light; and as the sign is experienced as an expression of a rule, the red traffic light is seen as a stop sign – that is, it is seen as an expression of the general requirement that one must stop one's car here and in like situations. This set of distinctions would have been very deep for Peirce himself, since they tie in neatly to his distinction between Firstness, a single intrinsic aspect of something, having reference to nothing else; Secondness, a dyadic property of that which has Firstness as a term; and finally Thirdness, where Secondness is mediated by an actual relation.

I shall call this the 'first' semiotics. As a sign system the human body and its parts and functions requires a 'second' semiotics, through which the way the bodily signifiers have specific content (signifieds) can be understood. I shall draw on the semiotics of Roland Barthes to supply this level of analysis. Barthes's analysis is directed to understanding how icons such as movie stills, pictorial advertisements, etc. are signifiers. The body and its parts, whether in the flesh or in some representation, is surely an iconic signifier.

According to Barthes (1985) there are three kinds of 'messages', linguistic, coded iconic and non-coded iconic. The basic structure that is semiotically 'effective' is *signifier* and *signified*, where the latter is roughly the meaning of the former. So whatever messages there are must lie in the possibilities of the signified. Consider the well-known Dürer engraving of 'praying hands'. There is a literal or coded 'message': the sign, the engraving, which denotes (Barthes's term) human hands. But the iconic message is double. There is a non-coded symbolic message, let us say 'piety'. At the 'symbolic', cultural or connoted message level the signs are discontinuous. It is the composition of the signs that signifies piety. This signified is discontinuous because it is separable from just the drawing of the hands.

Commenting on these two 'levels' of message, Barthes points out that the literal message is, to use my own terminology, open – that is, every image implies a 'floating chain of signifieds' (p. 25). But no other knowledge is required to get this level of message but what is 'involved' in our perception. Anyone can see that it is a pair of hands. But the title, let us say, 'praying hands' helps to 'anchor' the perception. A title, an associated linguistic message, also guides the taking up of the symbolic message – that the icon, in denoting praying hands, connotes piety. Barthes calls this 'selective elucidation' (p. 29). People necessarily vary in their apprehension of the third message, just because their cultural knowledge varies. Those unfamiliar with the conventions of prayer could, for example, take the hands to be just held up to a hot air-drier in an airport loo. Drawing on a linguistic metaphor, Barthes says: 'the image, in its connotation, would thus be constituted by an architecture drawn from a variable depth of lexicons (of idiolects)' (p. 36), by which he means individual cultural knowledge. Signifieds like 'piety' are connotations, the totality of which is to be called a 'rhetoric'. Connotations can be classified according to the standard schema for tropes. So there is metonymy (the case of the hands), asyndeton (juxtaposition without an explicit connection) and so on.

The grasping of a message at the second level, denotation, is a necessary condition for the possibility of the grasping of a message at the third level, connotation. As Barthes puts it, 'the syntagm [i.e. orderly structured presentation] of the denoted message "naturalizes" the system of the connoted message' (p. 39). There are some qualifications I would like to make to the Barthean scheme. In the contexts that I shall be exploring the concept of 'message' must be taken as a metaphor unless we have reason not to do so. Taken literally, it implies an intention on the part of someone to use the icon in question to convey or to express something. Sometimes the body and its parts are indeed the vehicles of just such messages. But oft-times not. Yet even when a body is not being *used* as an icon, nevertheless, as I shall argue, it always *is* one, unless work has been done to deprive it of its iconicity for some practical purpose. In this way a human body is unlike anything else in the universe. Barthes's semiotics recommends itself by reason of its common sense and generally straightforward character. Occasionally there are lapses into a pretentious absurdity, in which analogy and metaphor clog his metalanguage to the point of unintelligibility. For instance, on p. 28 he says: 'polysemy questions meaning, and this question always appears as a dysfunction, even if the disfunction is recuperated by society as a tragic act . . . or a poetic one.' Of course a word or an image that could have a great many meanings is dysfunctional – but spare me the 'tragic recuperation' or the 'terror of uncertain signs'!

In a later essay Barthes (1985) adds a further semiotic level to his account of signs, a level that I shall also take account of in this section of the study. The analysis just set out discloses readily identified signifiers, at each level. There are hands (the informational level) and among the signifieds is piety. Dürer might have intended that reading, though that intention is not necessary to the connotative meaning. It is an 'obvious' meaning, selected from a lexicon of signifiers, common to the inhabitants of Christendom. In the later essay Barthes adds a further element to this level of meaning, namely the sense one has of the signifier as embedded in a story-line. Those hands are the hands of someone who has gone to mass etc. But in reflecting on some stills from Eisenstein's *Ivan the Terrible*, Barthes points to another level or kind of meaning. An icon can also have an 'obtuse' meaning. It is a kind of seen qualification of the iconography through which an image achieves its obvious meanings. It displays the obvious meaning as a kind of make-up, a disguise, to use Barthes's own metaphor. It ironizes the image, imparting a distance from the image-as-if-reality. It forces us to see the image as an image. Barthes calls this a transition from language to signifying (*signifiance*), but it would be better to see it as an invitation (not necessarily issued by the image maker) to an ironic reading. In setting out a version of Barthe's semiotics of the icon, the image, I have been elaborating Peircian 'Thirdness'. These are the conventions, cultural knowledge, etc. by which the image, distinct and individual as a First, and as seen by someone, so a Second, is mediated as a meaningful and significant sign, a Third.

Our semiotics still needs an account of Firstness, of how a thing can be a sign. To give an account of this Hudson (1982) makes use of the most basic idea of all in semiotics, namely that of an excluding contrast. As Barthes puts it (1985: 249), 'the sign is based on an oscillation, that of the *marked* and the *non-marked*, which we call a paradigm.' I want to take up this Saussurean hint. I shall work with the idea that a thing becomes a sign when it is experienced as having a place in a system of signs. This location is its *valeur*. A linguistic sign object has a place in a (linear) sequence of sign objects (syntagm or sequence of syntagms). For instance a word, say 'lock', has various definite locations in a set of sentences. But at each of its locations a linguistic sign object is also experienced as an object 'selected' (and here 'selection' is a metaphor) from a set of alternatives that might have occupied just that place in that syntagm. So in hearing 'lock' as a device for keeping doors inviolate, I do not hear 'catch', 'bolt' and so on. The set of alternatives that constitute the source of *valeur* is the paradigm. When 'lock' is being used to refer to a device for lifting boats up and down a river or canal, not only are its signifieds different from those of the word '[door] lock', but so is its *valeur*, those items with which it stands in contrast. In Hudson's analysis of the semiotics of the human body, the *valeur* of bodily parts and functions is the leitmotif. My analysis will be more complex. Grounded in a variety of contrasts, the human body, its parts and its functions, will appear as iconic signs. The Peircian categories will provide the first level of elaboration which will be further displayed as the cultural artefacts that they are by reference to Barthian 'message' levels.

From these three perspectives on signs and their meanings I propose to extract a methodology. A sign exists as such only by reference to a paradigm – that is, a set of significant, but exclusive, possibilities. A thing, its properties or relations become signs only when they can be seen to be members of a set of other signs of the same ontological category, thing to thing, state to state, event to event, any one of which could have been chosen rather than the one that actually is used as the sign. The first task in a semiotic analysis is to *construct the paradigm*.

The body and its parts rarely appear in the company of words, so the search for the signifieds of a bodily presence as a sign begins, in general, with the application of the Barthian denotative/connotative distinction at Peirce's 'energetic' and 'rule' levels – that is, to the Secondness and Thirdness of sign objects. The second stage of a semiotic study will then be to *describe the signifieds*. This will be undertaken in the medium of ordinary English. I hope that an ideal of the 'ordinary' will be achieved. I believe I am not alone in finding the preciousness of imagery and the unnecessary technical jargon in semiotic writings irritating. Why, for instance, must Barthes (or his translator) use 'diegetic' when they could as easily have said 'pertaining to narrative'?

THE HUMAN BODY AS A SIGNIFIER AND SIGNIFIED

In Barthian terms the human body figures both as a sign system and as that which sign systems signify. The heart, or a conventional heart image, signifies 'love'. A monumental tower can in its turn be taken as a signifier of maleness. In the former a bodily organ is a signifier, in the latter the concrete form of a signified. It is important to grasp that the phallus implicit in the latter case is a signified in the Barthian sense. It is not a referent, but a corporeal concept.

According to the general theory of signs, the possibility of signification begins in the existence of oppositions. I shall explore two oppositional pairings in this section, to illustrate how the full panoply of the corporeal semantics sketched above is needed to gain a proper perspective on the body as a sign system. I shall call these 'structural oppositions'. Male/female and left/right are based on discernible and iconic structural features of the human body taken just as a thing. semantics still leaves a very rich seam of symbols to be mined. Hudson introduces another set of oppositions different from the paired inscriptions of bodily movement. He calls these 'ambivalences'. Again we can see in these oppositions the paradigm sets necessary to the existence his oppositions 'qualitative ambiguities'. For example, he draws on the opposition between the body as a source of disgust and an occasion for delight to construct a semiotic field of signifiers.

We have encountered the male/female dualism in the chapter on body types. There it served to introduce the idea of the social construction of corporeal categories. I showed how the opposition man/woman was built up on, but radically transformed, the biological opposition between male and female. In this section I return to the basic biological opposition to examine how it is recruited and transformed into a sign system, a semiotic field.

The male/female opposition constitutes a simple paradigm. Maleness and femaleness are available as sign objects. From a Peircean point of view the primary and secondary sexual characteristics are the 'emotional' level of relevant attributes. As characterized by Firstness, they can be described independently of one another. Their mutual dependence, or Secondness, appears only when they are considered as the complementary components of a whole reproductive system. As signifiers at this level their signifieds are not specifically human, merely biological. So far maleness and femaleness constitute a paradigm which has no social (e.g. moral) or psychological (e.g. emotional) significance. But at the level of Thirdness the complex web of relations that tie human maleness and femaleness together into a sign system of enormous complexity calls for a subtle and highly elaborated set of signifieds erected on the basis of this very simple paradigm.

In setting out the structure of the semiotics of the sexually dimorphous body I have taken the male/female opposition as a simple biological given. The question of the independence, stability and depth of this opposition has been much questioned. By that I mean asking whether the opposition of two bodily forms with exclusive sets of attributes, as we currently experience it, is not in part a product of the role these distinctions play as signifiers and so a function, in part, of whatever are their signifieds. We have already come across this thought in another context. The projection of the bimodal distribution of secondary sexual characteristics, like the projection of the continuity between youth and age, on to a bipolarity of male or female could only be understood when the oppositions were seen as part of a social system, a system called into being by such matters as the ever-present danger that the tribe become extinct, the social structure of the productive processes and other extrabiological matters.

In yet another metaphor in this trope-littered discourse, we shall call the organic transformations of the given body into the signifying body an 'inscription'. The image is simple. The given body, defined let us say, by its genetic code, is imagined to be a writing surface on which marks could be inscribed. These marks might be the signs of a certain cultural code. Girls might be trained to adopt a certain bodily posture. This becomes 'second nature' and will or could serve as a signifier within the paradigm of femaleness/maleness if boys have been trained into another and complementary posture. In this chapter and in this book generally our topic is a body code, and its signifieds. So we are not interested in complementarities of character or of behaviour except in so far as these are prefigured in the signifieds of maleness and femaleness as signifiers. That girls favour social networks and boys favour social hierarchies is relevant to the studies here reported only in so far as the opposition 'rough and tough':'sweet and neat' appears in the corporeal semantics.

An interesting example of inscription comes from Australia (Grosz, 1987 following Young, 1980). It is tied in with the semiotics of maleness/femaleness where the signifieds are just those opposed character attributes sketched above as 'rough and tough' against 'sweet and neat'. Grosz's suggestion, entangled, I have to say, in some daunting prose, is that at least one pair of corporeal signifiers of these meanings are inscribed. Bodily movements differ between the sexes, according to Grosz. Boys have an 'aggressive', 'carry it through' style of movement, while girls are more tentative in bodily action. This can be seen, so it is said, in the ways boys and girls throw. According to Grosz, the movements made by girls are characterized by 'inhibited intentionality'. Girlish throwing (now appearing as an opposition in a two-member paradigm to boyish throwing) can take on a role as a signifier. The signified might be, for example, something from the 'sweet and neat' Barthian 'cultural lexicon' – say gentleness. Through the inscription process the signifieds of the culture become instrumental in the fashioning of the signifiers. Thirdness infects Secondness, which infects Firstness.

Groszian inscription is a relatively simple process. It could be traced in differential ways of training the physical capabilities of girls and boys. I must confess to some doubts about the ubiquity of the inscription process. In my experience female musicians show none of the alleged womanly 'inhibited intentionality' in the way they use their instruments or their voices when performing. But there are much more complex semiotically significant oppositions to be found in the cluster of paradigm sets built up from the biological opposition male/female. For the next level of complexity I turn to Hudson's study of the sexual body as a repertoire of signifiers.

According to Hudson (1982), 'the body gives us an alphabet of images in terms of which most of our imagining occurs.' Discounting Hudson's overly enthusiastic claim for the generality of corporeal Martians will be able to spot these differences, though they will not be able to grasp their significance as a signifiers. Both structural oppositions are themselves opposed to the oppositional qualities that Hudson has taken as the basic signifiers in his corporeal semantics. I shall call of a system of signs. And by the attachment of signifieds Hudson's 'ambivalences' become significant, bearers of meaning.

The oppositional character of Hudson's ambivalences occurs in the way some feature or aspect or function of the body is capable of being construed in the opposed terms of contrary evaluations. Among the evaluative oppositions he draws on are 'purity/defilement', 'respect/contempt' and a contrast I can sum up as 'nice/nasty'. Since the sexual organs are also closely related to, and indeed function also as, organs of excretion, they are essentially ambivalent – as Hudson puts it there is the 'risk of confusing desire with disgust'. This is not the paradigm of male/female, but cuts across that semiotic opposition with a paradigm built of various versions of the concept pair 'purity/impurity'. This complex of oppositions has been studied in detail by Mary Douglas (1970). Thus both 'male' and 'female' are conceived as merely organ systems, and appear not as paradigm oppositions, but at a generic level of description. At that level each may, as signifier, partake of the ambivalence of the same duality of the signifieds upon which Mary Douglas built her semiotic system. As a vehicle and source of both desire and disgust, the female body is no different from that of the male. Perhaps this accounts for the extraordinary usage, common among speakers of English, for referring to photographs of beautiful, but naked, young women as 'filthy pictures'.

Bodies develop, mature and age along a continuous trajectory. But it is characteristic of human thinking to map such continuities on to polar oppositions. Bodies appear classified according to a cluster of polar oppositions such as 'child/adult', 'young/old' and so on. Indeterminate Peircian Firstness is quickly overlaid with a determinate Secondness achieved by mapping sections carved out of the continuum of bodily change on to sharply etched polarities. So much for the construction of the paradigm sets. Hudson's analysis shows how the signifieds are constructed. In this case, we have need of the whole Barthian scheme. There are clear physical signs of age. In this code white hair *denotes* age. Smooth and supple skin *denotes* youth. But the connotation of 'age' and 'youth' is shot through with ambivalence. Age is a time of disease and delapidation, but it is also a time of authority, experience and wisdom. Age attracts both respect and contempt. In just the same way, considered semiotically, the sexual organs attract both desire and disgust. Hudson also points out that there is another ambivalence, though rather different in structure to the two I have described. While the outside surface of the human body is generally something to which we have positive feelings (though there are complex ambiguities involved in attitudes to, and feelings aroused by, touch, particularly with respect to one's own and the opposite sex), there is no ambiguity about our feelings of revulsion, and even horror, when confronted with the inside of a human body. Underlining this, Hudson remarks that we have a clearer idea about how our livers would taste than we have of how they would look.

According to Hudson, it is these ambivalences that give the human body its unique power as a symbol or public image. In these analyses I have had the naked human body in mind, Kenneth Clarke's 'nude' (Clarke, 1956). Dressed in the accoutrements of this or that milieu and historical epoch, the semiotics of the human form become complex indeed. Fortunately it is not part of my self-imposed remit in this study to engage that complexity.

THE MEANING OF FLESH

Why do some people sometimes eat people and some do not? And why do those who do eat people eat them only on certain occasions? The answer, so it seems, is not a matter of whether the cannibal folk are hungry, or even whether there is a shortage of protein in the natural or cultivated resources available to them. Arens (1987) has argued that cannibalism is a xenophobic fantasy and that people never actually eat people (see plate 11 for a fanciful representation). While there is certainly some truth in his analyses, the authenticated instances are so well established that it would be perverse to deny their existence. So we are back to the original question, why some people sometimes eat people. The answer is to be found in the semiotics of the fleshly body. The body as a sign system has a definite interpretation as a Barthian object and so has a place in the total cultural matrix of any society. In some cases this interpretation and its associated cultural matrix demands that the body be eaten. But it would be a mistake to see human flesh as just another kind of meat. I shall approach the semiotics of flesh through two well-established cases. Among the Hua of New Guinea the eating of certain human flesh, that of the corpses of tribal members, is an essential act for the maintenance of the physical being of the tribe. Among the Aztecs human flesh was eaten as an integral part of a very complex ceremonial programme of human sacrifice essential to the maintenance of the social being of the people and of the physical being of the very universe itself.

Kannibalen auf der Hereforkarte
aus dem 13. Jahrhundert

11. Cannibal feast.
(Reproduced by kind permission of The Mansell Collection, London.)

The Hua practise 'mortuary cannibalism' (Sanday, 1986). It is part of a very complex process of personal maintenance, in which men and women construct and maintain themselves as gendered beings (Meigs, 1984). 'Individual and social identity is [brought into being] by removing negatively [valued] physical substances [from the body] and consuming positively [valued] substances, including the vital essence, *nu*, carried by the corpse of the newly dead' (Sanday, 1986: 46). Food is viewed by the Hua 'as an effusion of the body, particularly of its labour . . .' It is like blood, footprints, etc., 'significantly embued with, both the contaminatory and the engendering power of its producer'.

'Human *nu* is not a renewable resource' (Sanday, 1986: 69). It cannot be produced or regenerated by the efforts of human beings. Since the Hua identify the human body with the source of *nu*, it can only be obtained from the bodies of others, in particular the dead. Losses in one's own or one's generation's *nu* 'must be made up in gains from others.' No lesser good than survival is at stake. The rules of *nu* maintenance provide for a closed system of *nu* transfer. It must flow from the senior to the junior generation. To feed off the *nu* of one's juniors is 'morally contemptible and [physically] dangerous' (Sanday, 1986: 68). One must be careful not to eat food grown by one's eldest son, for instance. Since it is women who produce the new generation, it is to them that mortuary *nu* must pass. They seize the body of the dead and after extravagant displays of grief set about consuming it, and thus they acquire the precious essence, *nu*, essential to the continued life of the tribe. The practices that have grown up around flesh and bodily exudants as signifiers are very complex, since not all *nu* is appropriate for all classes of people. The *nu* rituals serve for category maintenance between the genders. Some female *nu* exudations are contaminants for those men who are in a close social relation to particular women. Wives can pose a threat to the well-being of their husbands through the contaminations of *nu*.

In Barthian/Piercian terms the concept of *nu* creates a Thirdness, and is the main connotative signified of flesh, which, as a natural sign, so to say denotes itself. There is no cosmic reference in the practice of mortuary cannibalism. There is no use for a microcosmic–macrocosmic isomorphism, for instance.

My second case is Aztec cannibalism, which has famously been the subject of a very enlightening debate between M. Harris (1977) and M. Sahlins (1978, 1983). In Hunt's (1977) evocative phrase, the universe of the Aztecs formed a 'phagohierarchy', arranged in an order of consumption, so that the people who ate animals were themselves eaten by gods. But since the teeth and jaws of the divine people-eaters were, at least to all outward appearances, also the teeth and jaws of people, their godliness had to be symbolically achieved. This was done by wearing the skin of the victim. But for the skin to have this symbolic value, the victim also had to be transformed, deified. As Sanday puts it (1986: 172), 'Humans [the captors] ate parts of the offered victims (the rest being reserved for Monteczuma) and donned their skins in order to become the god represented by the victim, for in these sacrifices only gods could be offered to gods.'

The sacrificial rites of the spring calendar in particular were directed to the maintenance of the universe itself. For human sacrifice to be meaningful in that context it is not surprising that a set of macro-microcosmic correspondences were invoked. These linked the three most important bodily organs to aspects of the cosmos. Thus while the signifiers were the organs head, heart and liver, the signified were the cosmic entities heaven, sun and earth respectively. In Barthian terms these were the denotations of the signs. The connotations were social and hierarchical status rankings of warriors, celebrated in the sacrificial ceremonials as the social consequences of personal victories in war. The micro- to macrocosm transfer of power was mediated by blood which 'carried the vital force that conferred divine life' and nourished the gods. So the victims whose hearts were torn out on the high altars were at once prisoners and honoured incarnations of gods. It was only as the latter that they were eaten in the ritual meal that followed the great public sacrifices. The victim/god's body, after the heart (the 'precious eagle-cactus fruit') had been taken, was thrown down the steps of the temple pyramid to be removed by the captor to be flayed and consumed.

THE BODY AS A MEDIUM FOR INSCRIPTION

The corporeal semiotics I have described so far is based upon the 'natural' body and its organic parts as signifiers. The salience of a body part as a sign has turned out to be not just as matter of its standing in some discernible difference relation to other parts. The way certain parts and organs are individuated to be picked out as signifier/signified pairs is influenced by what they signify. That left parts and right parts are selected as salient signifiers is partly a matter of the contrast in what they signify, namely purity and pollution. In this section I turn to a way that the human body is semiotically salient by virtue of what is inscribed on or in it. 'Inscription' can be taken literally in such examples as tattooing and body painting. But the term has been used metaphorically to describe the process by which in certain cultures boys and girls learn the appropriate styles of gender and specific bodily movements and stances (Grosz, 1987).

There are a huge variety of examples of forms of body inscription (Polhemus, 1978). For my purposes two examples will suffice to illustrate the semiotics of this kind of body decoration. In a book on the body itself the semiotics of clothes, jewelry and even personal luggage – that is, of signifying items that are added to the human body – is not to the point. It is to the semiotics of the marking of the body itself that my analysis is directed. Nuba body painting has been very thoroughly investigated by Faris (1972). The process by which the Nubian body is decorated is generally painless and, as Faris notes, something these people evidently greatly enjoy. The bodies of both men and women serve as 'canvasses' for the painter. The painted bodies as signifiers have their own immediate sensory attributes, the Firstness of the very sign itself. Colour and design are the features of the painted body as signifier that serve the general semiotic purpose (see plate 13). What is signified falls into two sets of Barthian connotations. For both sexes the decorative possibilities are related to stages in the life cycle which are jointly defined by biological and cultural categories. But the painted body also signifies as artwork – that is, it has significance according to aesthetic criteria, the connotations of which are complex.

For boys and men the colours and designs of body paint and decorative coiffure are related to position in a ladder of age grades. Unique as far as I know amongst human societies, the age grades of the Nuba are not primarily a matter of differentiated economic activities in the life of the tribe, but are the steps in an expressive order defined by prowess in sport. 'The initial grade, *loer*, is characterized by wrestling; the middle grade, *kadundor*, by bracelet and stick fighting; and the final grade, *kadonga*, by retirement from active tribal sports' (Faris, 1972: 38). These are age grades, so that *loer* are aged from eight to seventeen years, *kadundor* from seventeen to thirty-one, and *kadonga* the oldest. These broad grades are marked by permitted background colours, red, yellow and black respectively. Within the grades ages are more finely distinguished by hair styles which serve as markers of stages in the sporting hierarchies.

The signifiers for girls and women are drawn from a more complex sign system than those in use by men. Patterns of body scarrings are used to signify stages in the reproductive cycle, from menarchy to menopause. In addition to the practices of whole body colour painting and oiling, differentiated coiffures are as elaborate among Nuba women as amongst men.

Nuba body painting and scarring is not just a matter of a system of signs to signify grades in the life cycle. It also involves an aesthetic which is effective in the public display of 'good embodiment', of beautiful and effective bodies. The Nuba resort to clothes only if their body hair is inadequately shaved or if they are conscious of the ageing, and thus of an aesthetic decline, of their bodies. For women pregnancy is an occasion for adopting skirts. Decorating 'ceases when men enter the elder *kadonga* grade. This is because their bodies are no longer considered firm, young and attractive to look at, and in fact they normally begin to wear clothing at this time. This attitude towards the exposure of the attractive body pervades the whole society [women as well as men]' (Faris, 1972: 54). The point of personal art is not representational even when natural forms are the inspiration for designs. It is not a symbolic art in that sense. The aesthetics is concerned with 'projecting the body to the viewer'. It is an aesthetics of emphasis, enlargement and projection.

Faris notes another aspect of Nuba semiotics. It might be located in the dimension of Barthian denotation. Failure to adhere to the rules of the differentiated colour code and age-appropriate hair-styles can threaten disease. Right coloration is a protection against various impending and penetrating influences, including the evil eye. Hair is the body attribute most vulnerable to witchcraft, external and malevolent control of one's person. 'Grooming', remarks Faris, 'is *control* of this material', exerted by oneself or those benevolent towards one.

Lyman and Scott have remarked (1968: 97) that amongst the people of the Western world tattooing is a form of decoration that involves the body surface as a kind of last resort, the only territory one can call one's own. Whatever the force of this thought for understanding tattooing in the West, it would be far from the mark for an analysis of Polynesian body art. Tattooing differs from body painting in several ways, germane to tattoo marks as signifiers. The motifs, so to say, amongst the Maoris, are common both to tattoo as artwork and to other decorative practices, such as wood-carving. The patterns in use have their source in conventional and abstract versions of natural objects. The range of the signified achieved by these blue-dyed spirals, circles, lines and dots can only be understood in relation to the import- ance of the concept of *mana*, the physical embodiment of Maori honour and prestige.

A man rich in *mana* was thereby an object of awe in his actual embodiment. His body and what it touched was impregnated with a power. This was not the abstract symbolic power of status, but real physical potency, liable to injure those who inadvertently came into contact with it. Tattoing was in itself a route to *mana*. When a man or a woman was being decorated they were *tapu*, untouchable, and were obliged to live apart for the duration of the process. Tattooing had its *mana*-enhancing character partly because it was an exceedingly painful process; mere stoical endurance of it enhanced one's status in a culture where prowess in warfare was the supreme social good. However, stoical endurance was not the only connotation of tattoo as signifier. It also signified a certain style, a kind of dandyism (Reeves, 1898: 56). Moreover, this display of high style was not frivolous. Each *moko*, or unique tattoo pattern, was an object to be aesthetically assessed. One displayed one's taste as a patron of the arts on one's very face. A scar is metonymic for the pain endured and thus displays character. But a tattoo is displayed twice over, so as to say; once in relation to the culture of prowess in war and once in relation to personal qualities of cultivated taste. Seen thus, Maori tattooing has much in common as a signifying system with Nuba body art. Both involve a duality of signifieds, the first member of which is to do with the physical force or power of the body itself in sport or in war; the second is to do with aesthetic sensibility.

As a kind of footnote to the latter, Reeves (1898: 89) describes the trade in tattooed heads that followed the first European presence in Polynesia. The Maoris had hung the heads of vanquished, but famous, enemies in their villages as trophies of war and, given the semiotics we have uncovered, as works of art. As such, heads became the material of commercial ventures in art commodities. Not only did existing heads sell for large sums of money, but entrepreneurs began actively to hunt for wonderful specimens, still attached to their living owners. There are even stories of slaves agreeing to be tattooed and to sacrifice their heads (and thus their lives) for money.

Examples of this mode of inscription involve the ways in which male and female human bodies are visibly differentiated. It has been argued by for example Young (1980), that the visible differences between male and female bodies include not only biological, genetically pro- grammed anatomical and physiological properties, but also ways of moving, standing, sitting and so on. The metaphor of 'inscription' has been used to express the thesis that these aspects of embodied mas- culinity and feminity are acquired as cultural artefacts imposed on a neutral 'medium'. I have already discussed 'inscription' theories of embodiment in several places. In this context what is inscribed is to be interpreted as a signified, and its signified as gender. The relative clumsiness of 'throwing like a girl' could be taken to connote, rightly or wrongly, practical inferiorities of other kinds.

REFERENCES

Aquinas, St Thomas 1964: *Summa Theologica* III. Q.25, a.6. Oxford and London: Blackfriars and Eyre and Spottiswoode.

Arens, W. 1987: *The Man-Eating Myth*. New York: Oxford University Press.

Augustine, 1950: *De Civitate Dei*, trans, J. Healey. London: Dent

Barthes, R. 1985: *The Responsibility of Forms*, trans. R. Howard. New York: Hill and Wang.

Clarke, K. 1956. *The Nude: a Study of Ideal Art*. London: John Murray.

Daniel, E. V. 1989: In B. Lee and G. Urban (eds), 1989, *Semiotics Self and Society*. Berlin and New York: Mouton and De Gruyter.

Dooley, E. A. 1931: *Church Law on Sacred Relics*. Washington DC: Catholic University Press.

Douglas, M. 1970: *Purity and Danger*. Harmondsworth: Penguin.

Dürer, E. 1537: *De Symmetria Humani Corporis*, ch. 27, 28. Nuremburg.

Faris, J. C. 1972: *Nuba Personal Art*. Toronto: Toronto University Press.

Grosz, E. 1987: Corporeal Feminism, *Australian Feminist Studies* 5, 1–15.

Harris, M. 1977: *Cannibals and Kings: The Origins of Culture*. New York: Random House.

Hudson, L. 1982: *Bodies of Knowledge*. London: Weidenfeld and Nicolson.

Hunt, E. 1977: *The Transformation of the Humming Bird*. Ithaca, NY: Cornell University Press.

Lee, B., and Urban, G. (eds), 1989: *Semiotics, Self and Society*. Berlin and New York: Mouton and De Gruyter.

Lyman, S. M., and Scott, M. B. 1968: *A Sociology of the Absurd*. New York: Appleton-Century-Crofts.

Meigs, A. S. 1984: *Food, Sex and Pollution: A New Guinea Religion*. New Brunswick, NJ: Rutgers University Press.

Peirce, W. S. 1931–66: *Collected Papers*, Vols 1 and 5. Cambridge, Mass.: Harvard University Press.

Polhemus, T. (ed.) 1978: *Social Aspects of the Human Body*. Harmondsworth: Penguin.

Reeves, W. P. 1898: *The Long Quiet Cloud*. London: George Allen and Unwin.

Sahlins, M. 1978: Culture as Protein and Profit, *New York Review of Books*, 25 (18), 45–53.

Sahlins, M. 1983: Raw Woman, Cooked Man and Other 'Great Things' of the Fiji Islands, in P. Brown and D. Tuzin (eds), *The Ethnography of Cannibalism*. Washington DC: Society for Psychological Anthropology.

Sanday, P. G. 1986: *Divine Hunger: Cannibalism as a Cultural System*. Cambridge: Cambridge University Press.

Saussure, F. de 1929: *A Course of General Linguistics*. New York: Philosophy Library.

Short, T. L. 1986: David Savan's Peirce Studies. *Transactions of the C. S. Peirce Society*, 22, 59–124.

Singer, M. 1984: *Man's Glassy Essence: Explorations in Semiotic Anthropology*. Bloomington, Indiana: Indian University Press.

Turner, B. S. 1984: *The Body and Society*. Oxford: Basil Blackwell.

Young, I. M. 1980: Throwing Like a Girl: A Phenomenology of Feminine Body Comportment, Motility and Spatiality. *Human Studies*, 3, 137–56.

CHAPTER 12

ANTHROPOGRAPHIE

Man is all symmetrie,
Full of proportions, one limbe to another,
And to all the world besides:
Each part may call the furthest, brother
For head with foot hath private amitie,
And both with moons and tides.

George Herbert

INTRODUCTION: SIGNIFYING BY ANALOGY

In this final chapter I propose to bring out some degree of refinement within the broad Barthian notion of connotation. If it is in the signified that what could roughly be called 'the meaning of the sign' (as signifier) resides, then it is to the properties of the signified that we must look for an analogue of the tropes we identify in a traditional analysis. It is there we would expect to find metaphor, metonymy and simile. It seems to me that the Peircian/Barthian semiotics cannot serve as the foundation for a theory of metaphor, or any other trope, since it is such tropes that constitute Thirdness for any sign. A study of some anthropographies should permit the illustration of some of the connotative tropes that would be involved in use of the human body as signifier. I propose to suspend the question of whether body talk is ever metaphor. My four brief case studies will illustrate connotative possibilities that are, I think, deeper.

I shall look at two cases in which the connotative aspect of the use of the human body as a sign system – that is, as the complex semiotic 'object' 'signifier/signified' – is rooted in analogy. In the case of the body as microcosm the anthropographer is building the connotation of the body conceit as an analogue of the universe in its grandest aspects, the cosmos at large. The principle 'as in the microcosm, so in the macrocosm' was used to explore the properties of the macrocosm by virtue of an analogy that the body as microcosm bears to the cosmos. Some anthropographers, notably St Hildegard of Bingen, assumed that the macrocosm stands to the microcosm in the reciprocal semiotic relation to that in which the microcosm stands to it. We can consult the cosmos to gather the significance of God's other major work of art, the human body. An analogy is always a set of similitudes and dissimilitudes, so there will be a pair-reciprocal relation which plays a meaning engendering role in the constitution of the human body as a system of signs, creating the connotative aspect of what the body as signifier signifies. When the macrocosm was no more than the earth, reciprocal exchange of sign function from micro to macro was a common poetic device. So geographical connotations served to elaborate the significance of anthropographical similitudes and vice versa. Sometimes the connotation of the body as signifier is elaborated through a reciprocal analogy. That significance is itself partly constituted by the highlighting of the analogy relation. The head signifies the king not only because it is the seat of the biological hegemony of the nervous system, but also because it is the seat of the governance of the body itself.

The second pair of tropes underlying the signifying power of the body and its parts are both metonymies. In simple metonymy a body part signifies through its location in the material or organic grounding of some process, for instance, of which it is an emblematic part. The blood would be a signifier in such a way were it used to explicate the meaning of money. Compare its role in an analogue in which it might be used reciprocally with corn, in a dual explication of the economies of the body and of an agrarian state. Cases of the use of a bodily organ in tropes of that sort I shall treat as cases of double metonymy. In the use of phallic imagery by feminist authors, in particular, in which the male generative organs are used as images or signs of social power, the penis serves in just such a double role.

The complexity and the unity of the human body makes it a particularly apt vehicle for a semiotics of the two large-scale environments within which humankind knows itself to live, the physical cosmos and the political state. This signifying relation can run either way. The body can be used as a 'figure for the worlds complexity' (Barkan, 1975: 6) or the body in its cosmic reading can be used as a figure for the complex nature of humanity itself. Reviving a sixteenth-century term, I shall call this use of the body as a semiotics, a system of signs, *anthropographie*. I shall follow Barkan's classification of anthropographies into three 'comparisons': the body and the cosmos, the body and the commonwealth, and finally the body and human artefacts (such as buildings).

Barkan points out that the 'oneness' of the human body with the cosmos is largely imaginary, if the 'comparison' is taken in the sense of using the one as an iconic model of the other. Literary studies have resolved the problem of how this almost ubiquitous style of comparison is to be analysed by invoking metaphor. Barkan (1975: 3) remarks that 'the act of drawing truth out of literal falsehood is the making of metaphor.' But there is another way in which an iconic disparity between the terms of a comparison can be understood, namely through the theory of signs. The letter 'D' is not much like a railway station yet the sequential layouts of 'D' on the Oxford–Paddington railway timetable signifies the changing of trains at Didcot station *in the same order as the trains themselves run*. The 'D's are a kind of icon of the day's trains, yet neither are they a picture of people changing trains at just this station, nor would it be at all appropriate to treat the time table as a metaphor for a train service. The timetable as a physical layout differs from a discursively presented story about the trains. It is neither icon, nor story nor metaphor. It is a semiotic system, a structure of signs. That is how I shall take the anthropographies to be studied in this chapter.

That the human body is particularly apt as the basis for a cosmic semiotics was well understood in the seventeenth century. It was both familiar and yet strange. As the Fletchers (1908) put it, it was 'a foreign home, a strange though antique coast, most obvious to all and yet unknown to most'. But the feature of the body that fits it so well for a role as a cosmic, political and architectural sign system is the fact that it is, of all available physical domains, the most striking example of unity in diversity. The organic parts, such as the divisions of the torso, the limbs and their appendages, organs of perception and of generation, the internal organs and their diverse functions, real and imaginery, form a vast lexicon. At the same time no one of these parts or organs can be understood in isolation from the bodily unity in which it has a well-defined and defining part to play. This special feature of the human body as sign system is not registered in any of the categories of semiotics that I laid out in the last chapter. Anthropographies illustrates a distinctive feature of corporeal semantics.

MICROCOSM–MACROCOSM: MEDIATED CORRESPONDENCES

The semiotic duality of the human body is already clearly manifest in the medieval and renaissance uses of that body in the semantics of anthropographies. Read in one direction, the body can be used as

sign system with which the cosmos can be 'read'. But the correspondences can be taken in the contrary sense. The meanings of the bodily
parts, organs and functions are not given. The body is made meaningful by being read as a cosmos in miniature. However, the correspondences are not always immediate. I quote at length a poem of John
Donne's in which, in a way familiar in the rennaissance, the mapping
of body onto cosmos proceeds by a more immediate anthropographie,
body onto earth and earth onto body.

> Since I am coming to that Holy roome,
> Where with thy Quire of Saints for evermore
> I shall be made thy Musique; As I come
> I tune the instrument here at the dore,
> And what I must doe then, thinke now before.
>
> Whilst my Physicians by their love are growne
> Cosmographers, and I their Mapp, who lie
> Flat on this bed, that by them may be showne
> That this is my South-West discoverie
> *Per fretum febris*, by these streights to die,
> I joy, that in these straits, I see my West;
> For, though theire currants yeeld returne to none,
> What shall my West hurt me? as West and East
> In all flatt Maps (and I am one) are one,
> So death does touch the Resurrection.
>
> Is the Pacifique Sea my home? Or are
> The Eastern riches? Is *Jerusalem*?
> *Anyan*, and *Magellan*, and *Gibraltare*,
> All streights, and none but streights, are ways to them,
> Whether where *Japhet* dwelt, of *Cham*, or *Sem*.
>
> We thinke that *Paradise* and *Calvarie*
> *Christs Crosse*, and *Adams* tree, stood in one place,
> Looke Lord, and find both Adams met in me;
> As the first *Adams* sweat surrounds my face,
> May the last *Adams* blood my soule embrace.
> So, in his purple wrapped received mee Lord,
> By these his thornes give me his other Crowne;
> And as to other soules I prech'd thy word,
> Be this my Text, my Sermon to mine owne,
> Therefore that he may raise the Lord throws down.

The pun on 'streights' as predicaments and 'straits' as channels con-
necting sea with sea ties the anthropographical imagery together. But

the larger cosmic reading requires a further allegory, the identity of geographical East and West through which death and resurrection, the former presided over by the first Adam and the latter by Christ, the last. Another geographical image can be found in Donne's writings. The well-known line 'No man is an island, entire of itself; every man is a piece of the continent, a part of the main' is also by Donne. But the investigation of this imagery is not part of my project here since it is not a corporeal semantics. In Donne's poem we see, I believe, the familiar duality of the human body as signifier, the source of meaning, and the human body as a complex physical being the meaning of which is to be revealed through anthropographie. Donne's body is both a map and something to be mapped. It gives sense to the geographical East and West while the ultimate identity of East and West gives sense to the body as the locus of the Divine in the mundane and material world.

The device of an anthropographie based on the microcosm/macrocosm isomorphism mediated by a common referent in the earth itself, is given detailed realization in the principles of anthropometry. Before a semiotics in the Barthian manner can be constructed for the body as microcosm, some way of analysing the body as a system of signs is required. This is supplied by anthropometry. The body is marked out in a set of proportionalities, and these are located through the interpretation of body structure in terms of simple (and so perfect) geometrical figures. The basic principles of anthropometry are nicely summed up by the sixteenth-century poet Spenser. On the subject of the human body he says:

> The frame thereof seemed partly circulare,
> And part triangulare, O worke diuine;
> Those two the first and last proportions are,
> The one imperfect, mortall, fœminine;
> Th'other immortall, perfect, masculine,
> And twixt them both a quadrate was the base,
> Proportioned equally by seven and nine;
> Nine was the circle set in heauens place,
> All which compacted made a goodly diapase.
>
> *Faërie Queen* II. ix. 22

The last line introduces a feature of anthropometry that was of great importance in the history of science, namely the link between the microcosm/macrocosm proportions and the musical forms. Kepler's *Harmonice Mundi* (1500) was perhaps the most elaborate and mathematically sophisticated presentation of the musical/cosmical analogies via the notion of universal principles of harmony. But in that book the proportions of the human body are noticeable by their absence. It does not draw on the anthropometric proportions as a mathematical basis at all. The Spenserian stanza expresses a more typical view, the same view that can be seen in the frontispiece of Fludd's mystical cosmogeometry (see plate 14).

In the exposition that follows I am largely dependent on a fascinating essay by Barkan (1975). Medieval anthropometry used two analytical systems. The Gothic scheme was based on simple geometrical figures to provide a formal representation of the human form. These shapes were then interpreted both cosmically and morally, to create a semiotic system through which the meaning of the body could be read, and from which a bodily meaning could be given to isomorphic structures, wheresoever they might be found. The Byzantine system used numerical proportion to the same end, basing the measures on a unit one-ninth of the body height. (The significance of the choice of one-ninth cannot but be of some importance. In teaching drawing the module for laying out the structure of the body is one-seventh, which is approximately the ratio of the vertical span of the head to overall height. 'Nine' is of greater cosmological significance than 'seven' perhaps. But given the entrenchment of seven in such important matters as the days of the week, the choice of nine does need to be accounted for.)

I shall exemplify the principles of Gothic and Byzantine anthropometry from the writings of St Hildegard of Bingen. Her visions are structured by elements drawn from both traditions. Her proportionalities are based on threes. The three spheres of the cosmos correspond to a threefold division of the limbless torso, into head, chest and abdomen. The outermost sphere of the cosmos is further subdivided into the three regions of fire, ether and air. This threefold division is matched by the division of the head into three equal parts, divided at the eyebrows and the base of the nose. As Barkan remarks, the limbs have always been something of an embarrassment for anthropographers and stand outside St Hildegard's elegant, but empirically implausible, system. In this way anthropometry provides one who would read either the body or the cosmos with an integrated repertoire of signs. Where are we to find the lexicon by which the sign system will become a semiotics through the building up of denotative and connotative associations? One part of the answer lies in the general application of the principle that the microcosm (the human body) and the macrocosm (the universe at large) are formally – that is, structurally – isomorphic. Another part of the answer lies in what has been called the 'moralizing' of the distinctions. The key to this moralizing lies in the realization that the geometrical shapes and the numerical

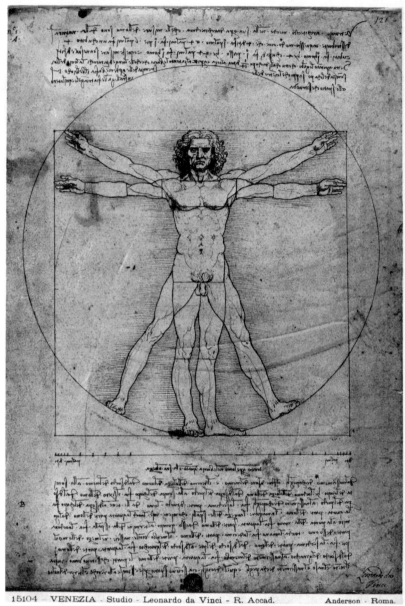

12. Leonardo figure.

(Reproduced by kind permission of The Mansell Collection, London.)

proportions themselves had a kind of moral quality, namely degrees of perfection and an ultimately Pythagorean significance. The circle, the equilateral triangle and the square are the most symmetrical, with the Platonic solids in reserve for the kind of project that Kepler undertook in his *Mysterium Cosmographicum*. In that work he tried to express the structure of the solar system in a series of mathematically harmonious, though complex, proportionalities based on the tetrahedron, like centre, etc. Our anthropometrists needed only the simplest of plane figures. Hildegard, Pacioli (Barkan, 1975: 128) and Giorgi (Barkan, 1975: 129) go no further geometrically. The next step must be to sketch the semiotics through which anthropometry contributed an anthropographical interpretation of humankind's place in the universe and of the moral significance of the body in its relation to the cosmos.

HUMANOID BY DESIGN: ANTHROPOGRAPHIE AND ARCHITECTURE

The term 'anthropographie' was coined by John Dee (1570) in his famous preface to Euclid's *Geometry*. It occurs in an enumeration of the skills needed for architecture.

> Anthropographie [says Dee] is the description of the Number, Measure, Waight, figure, Situation, and colour of every diverse thing, conteyned in the perfect body of Man: with certain knowledge of the Symmetrie, figure, waight, Characterization, and due locall motion, of any parcell of the sayd body, assigned, and of Numbers, to the sayd parcell appertainyng.

If other mathematical specialities such as cosmography have their appropriate name, should the being for which the whole universe was created and 'who is made in the Image and similitude of God' not have its 'peculiar Arte and be called the Arte of Artes', anthropographie?

'Anatomists, physionomists, chyromantistes and metaposcopistes can contribute to this art. One can also consult the excellent Albert Durer as well as Pythagoras, Hippocrates, Plato, Galen and Meletius.' But one can also improve one's knowledge of anthropographie from a study of the heavens and the earth, as well as of other creatures. 'Whereof, good profe will be had, of our Harmonious, and Microcosmicall constitution' and the 'outward Image and vew thereof'. Why should an architect devote such a proportion of effort to the study of the mathematical properties of the human body? The microcosm–macrocosm principle asserts that the structure of that body, as microcosm, must be isomorphic with the structure of the whole universe, the macrocosm. So if one wants to construct one's buildings to reflect the macrocosm, the divine order at large, one need simply adopt the principles of geometrical and numerical proportions of the human body as microcosm.

Classical authority for this reading of the human body as a divine semiotics was there for all to see in Vitruvius, Book 3, chapter 1. According to Vitruvius, temples, as the earthly abodes of the Gods, should of all buildings be proportioned according to the principles of divine order. So via the micro-/macrocosm principle, the use of the principles of symmetry and proportion of the human body in designing the symmetry and proportions of any temple should ensure its isomorphism with the cosmos itself. Vitruvius claimed that a man's body with arms and legs extended would fit into a circle and into a square. This anthropological principle is surely familiar to everyone from the oft reproduced drawing by Leonardo (plate 15).

Examining Leonardo's drawing closely, one sees immediately that the square and the circle are mathematically independent of one another. The circle is not circumscribed around the square, nor is its radius a rational proportion of the side of the square. Furthermore, it is easy to see that while the figure in the square is a proper figure of a man, the superimposed figure in the circle has disproportionately long arms. The anthropometrie is, one might say, pretty forgiving. However, in the previous section we saw that there were other ways to fit circles, triangles and squares to the figure of the human frame. The essential point of all this was indeed those geometrical shapes. The design of temples should be based on some interrelation between square and circle. Wittkower (1949) has shown how this aspect of the formal semiotics of anthropographie was the architectural basis for the crop of round churches constructed during the renaissance.

THE BODY POLITIC

The semiotic role for the body seems to have developed through the need to find an analogy that would enable a commentator to explore the concept of 'unity in diversity'. Wherever there seems to be such a unity, there the corporeal analogy has flourished.

Barkan (1975: 77) expresses the principle of unity succinctly: 'as each member is only a part of the whole body, and therefore less than the whole, but the whole can only exist as the totality of its members.' In like manner he expresses the correlative principle of diversity as the concept of co-operation, that while there is 'an equal commitment of all the members to the well-being of the whole body', nevertheless 'both bodies politic and natural are unions of elements which are unlike in form, function and significance' (p. 78).

The State is analogous to the human body. But it is also part of the working structure of this semiotic scheme that the human body is analogous to the State. The same principle of reciprocity was evident in the micro-/macrocosm semiotics. The human body gets meaning because it is conceived as a little universe or state; it gives meaning because the universe or the State is conceived as a large body. In the semiotic scheme described in this section the body gets its role as the source of the analogies because it seems to be given as a unity in diversity. However, there is some reciprocity. For organicists among political theorists the 'obviousness' of the unity of the State and the differentiation of function and form within it, encourages the use of the State as an analogy for the description of the body. For instance, Aristotle, in *De motu animalium* (703ª) runs the analogy the other way:

> And the animal organism must be conceived after the similitude of a well-governed commonwealth. When order is once established in it there is no more need for a separate monarch to preside over each several task. The individuals each play their assigned task as it is ordered, and one thing follows in its accustomed order . . . there is no need of a soul in each part, she resides in a kind of central governing place in the body.

This direction of fit of body to State is not uncommon, as for instance when one thinks of the head as governing the body. There are several specific parallels through which a semiotics of the body politic has been worked out.

The three analogies that I shall sketch depend on a prior adherence to some version of the organicist view of the state. That is, the body is being drawn upon as a source of meaning, just in so far as the ruling principle of unity in diversity needs illustrating and supporting. One would hardly draw on the body as a root analogy if one were setting out to portray the State as a utilitarian democracy.

The simplest analogy is that in which the concept of injustice in the State is elaborated and made intelligible by analogy with disease in the body. But the body/State analogy is mediated by considerations of the soul. A sick soul is the source of injustice. In *Republic* 444 Socrates says that injustice and justice 'are like disease and health; being in the soul just what disease and health are in the body.' In *Republic* 424 he compares not states, but citizens, to invalids whose illness is a lack of self-restraint. Again in 444 he says that the creation of health is 'the institution or a natural order and government by another in the parts of the soul'. '... virtue is the health and beauty and well-being of the soul and vice the disease and weakness and deformity of the same.' So in Plato's use of the corporeal semantics it is vice and virtue of individual people that is given meaning in terms of the concepts *and theories* of bodily health and illness. The defects of an unjust state are derived from the moral sickness of its citizens. Shakespeare, however, expresses a parallel that ties the sickness of the body to the troubles of the State as a whole. The comparison is whole to whole. For instance, in *Henry IV* Part I the following exchange occurs:

> KING: Then you perceive the body of our kingdom
> How foul it is, what rank diseases grow,
> And with what danger, near the heart of it.
> WARWICK: It is but as a body yet distemper'd,
> Which to his former strength may be restor'd
> With good advice and little medicine.

Much more elaborate than this simple analogy is the comparison of the *structure* of the State with the *anatomy* of the human body. Two features of the organicist State tend to be highlighted, unity and hierarchy. One of the most elaborate versions of this conceit is to be found in the writings of St Paul (*Corinthians* 12: 8–31). The 'State' is the community of Christians, whose unity is rendered problematic through the diversity of roles that different members of the Church must play. Paul declares 'For as the body is one, and hath many members, and all the members of that one body, being many, are one body: so also is Christ.' The interdependence, but differentiation, of the parts is a key concept of the analogy.

> If the foot shall say, Because I am not the hand, I am not of the body; is it therefore not of the body? ... If the whole body were an eye where were the hearing?

> And the eye cannot say unto the hand, I have no need of thee: nor again the head to the feet, I have no need of you. Nay, much more, these members of the body, which seem to be more feeble, are necessary.

In this passage one can find almost all the features of the analogy as it was later deployed and developed by other writers. Unity is founded in baptism, but every member has his or her own function, just as the 'members' and organs of the body perform diverse roles. Furthermore there is a differentiation of form in relation to function. Without co-operation between the members, the 'crowd' would not work as a body. There would be no whole. No member, however humble, can be omitted from the body (community), for each has an essential role to play. Yet there is a hierarchy with the head and heart as governors of all.

Barkan shows that the simple analogy, elaborated by St Paul, developed through the image of the Church as the body of Christ. The Church, Christ's body, was a *res publica* of sorts, a community, though not a political association as such. But that very body was also the substance of the Eucharist, the *corpus mysticum*, The body of Christ takes on a double role. It is at once the analogical image of unity giving meaning to the corporate character of the Christian community, and the common substance of the mystical union of the members in Christ, which is celebrated in the mass.

This scheme was further refined in Eizabethan times, since it raised the question of the relation between the sovereign's actual body and the body politic. In Plowden's *Reports* the following analysis is offered:

> For the King has in him two Bodies, *viz.*, a Body natural, and a Body politic. His body natural . . . is a Body mortal, subject to all Infirmities . . . But his Body politic is a Body that cannot be seen or handled, consisting of Policy and Government . . . and this Body is utterly void of . . . natural Defects . . . which the Body natural is subject to . . . what the King does in his Body politic, cannot be invalidated or frustrated by any disability in his natural Body. (Plowden, 1816: 212a)

Further, the Elizabethan judges declared that 'the Body politic includes the Body natural, but the Body natural is the lesser, and with this the Body politic is consolidated . . . and these two Bodies are incorporated in one Person, and make one Body and not diverse.' The natural body is magnified by this conjunction and so includes the political body. Thus the actual king can do things that count as the doings of the king in his status as body politic. It is worth noting that in this treatment the body politic is not composed of the citizens as its members, but of the abstract or functional aspects of the governing part of the body, as we see it in the functional analogy.

Finally, there is the functional analogy between the body and its organs and the State and its institutions. This use of the body as a semiotic source can be quite as elaborate as the anatomical scheme. 'For like as all wit, reason and sense, feelings, life and all other natural power springeth out of the heart, so from the princes and rulers of the state cometh all laws, order and policy, all justice, virtue and honesty to the rest of this politic body' (Starkey, 1989: 57). However, this simple analogical tie can be greatly elaborated, since it can be applied both to political activities and to the officials who initiate or administer them. Once again form and function are tied together, in that the kingly is more often than not assigned to the head, while the more basic activities are analogized to the hands and feet. Barkan, quoting Lydgate (1975: 84) gives us the following (spelling modernized)

> Mighty princes for their high renown
> As most worthy shall occupy the head
> With wit, memory and even of reason
> To keep their members from mischief and dread.

As a final example I quote again from Thomas Starkey (1989: 33) (spelling and punctuation modernized):

> The part of the politic body...hath his parts which resemble also the parts of the body of man, of which the most general for our purpose be these, the heart, head, hands and feet. The heart thereof is the king, prince, and ruler of the state...for like as all natural power springeth out of the heart so from the princes and rulers of the state cometh all laws, order and policy...to the hands are resembled both craftsmen and warriors which defend the rest of the body [and so on].

Starkey adds a further twist to the analogy when he remarks that 'yet though this politic body be healthy and strong, yet if it be not beautiful but foul deformed it lacketh a part of its well and prosperous state. This beauty also standeth in the due proportion of the parts together.' It is in a likeness of function between body parts and citizen roles that the analogy is most illuminating. The differentiated body as a system of parts and organs is the complex signifier and the functions of its components, working well together, that are the signified in this semiotic scheme. The connotation relation is analogy. And we have noticed that in certain cases the analogical relation can run in both directions. It is a semiotics based on the principle of reciprocal analogy.

I owe to Barkan (1975: 89–90) the extraordinary observation that the analogy turning upon itself and reflecting its own reciprocity led to an infinite regress of bodies, each conferring meaning on that which succeeded it. For instance, the stomach can, and often does, appear as a character in its own right. In *Coriolanus* Shakespeare has the belly take on the part of a whole person who says 'Your most grave Belly was deliberate, not rash like his accusers.' If a human being contains a whole society of organs, then a society as an organic association of such beings, is a society of societies. And if the concept of each organ is itself elaborated along the same lines, then each human being is a society of societies in so far as the organs themselves must be pictured as the sites of the diversified functions of whole bodies.

THE BODY AND BLOOD OF CHRIST

Throughout the Christian world the communion or mass involves the ceremony of the Eucharist. In that ceremony bread and wine are offered to and consumed by the congregation with exhortations such as the following: 'This is my body which was given for you and for many. Feed on me in your hearts with praise and thanksgiving.' The wine is presented as 'the blood of Christ'. At the altar rail the Christian congregation is in the centre of a semiotic system of great complexity and importance. I shall use it to illustrate the fourth and last of the tropes through which the 'signifieds' are constituted, the trope of metonymy resting on a two-step constituting of the signifiers.

In Catholic doctrine transubstantiation, the way in which, when consecrated, bread and wine 'become' the body and blood of Christ, there is a 'mystery'. In orthodox Catholicism this means that it is a datum or given. Efforts to explain the phenomenon are quite misplaced. For instance, chemical analysis of the consecrated bread for signs of animal protein is beside the point. The upshot of the instituting of this 'mystery' is the introduction into the human world of a potent sign system, *consecrated* bread and wine as signifiers. As Powers (1967: 147) remarks, 'Sacramentum est in genere signi.' The gift of Christ to the Church (ibid.: 117) amounts to this: 'the gift is in a sign, the sign of bread and wine.' The mystery constitutes these humble comestibles as signifiers. Catholic and Protestant theologians alike can interest themselves in analysing the semiotics of these signifiers. To this issue the controversies over transubstantiation ('In what sense is the consecrated bread actually Christ's body?') are irrelevant.

The first step in deconstructing the sign system can be taken by identifying the immediate signified of the bread and wine as signifiers. It is the body and blood of Christ. Is this signifier/signified pair to be understood via some standard trope, such as metaphor, simile or metonymy? The 'is' of 'This *is* my body' expresses, I am inclined to think, an internal relation between the incarnated Christ and the historical sequence of actual instances of consecrated bread and wine that have figured in all the masses and communion services that have ever been held. I am not of course claiming that there is such an internal relation, only that for Christians that is how the sign system is constituted. The effect of this is immediately to extend the domain of the signifiers. The body and blood of Christ are signified by the material signifiers that are used in the Eucharist and then, as internally related to those signifiers, are directly constituted as signifiers themselves. I refer to Powers (1967: 147) for an explication of the internal relation within the two-step sign structure

'bread/wine: body of Christ/blood of Christ : : X:Y'.

We have yet to identify the ultimate signified, and so yet to reveal the innermost trope of this semiotic domain. According to Powers, 'the prime analogue of the (Eucharistic) sign is human corporeality itself *in* which (not "behind" which) the spiritual "interiority" of the human person effectively communicates itself to its world of persons and things' – 'the human person is experienced directly in the symbolic action.' In like manner Christ is revealed directly in the bread and wine. (This, one notes, is a very Wittgensteinian point!)

The hunt for the constituting trope narrows its focus. What is signified by the body and blood of Christ as signifiers, and how is the signifying achieved? In short, the question is: How are the denotation and the connotation of these corporeal substances constituted? Rohling (1932) surveys the writings of the early Fathers on the topic of the blood of Christ, and compiles a catalogue of Barthian denotations such as the 'bloody sweat', the 'blood and water' that ran from the side of the crucified Jesus, and so on. It is these denotations that determine the direction in which the connotations of Eucharistic 'body' and 'blood' should be sought. For instance, St Cyprian uses the denotation 'blood and water from the side of the crucified Christ' as the source of the connotation of the 'wine and water' in the communion chalice. The 'wine = blood' connotes Christ and the 'water = lymph' connotes the people. So the union of Christ and people in the Church is signified by the mixture of wine and water as signifier, via the two-step relation to what is finally ultimate, via the intermediate denotation of the bodily fluids of Jesus himself, at the Crucifixion. This pattern is widely repeated in the semiotics of the Eucharist, with the equations 'bread = (1) Christ's body = (2) the Church' and 'wine = (1) Christ's blood = (2) Christ'. Our excursion into Barthian semiotics shows that the relations of signifying [=(1)] and denoting [=(2)] are importantly different. The former is internal and constitutive of the sign system itself, while the latter is contingent and depends on the way the events of Christ's life are drawn on in the creation of a Christian semiotics.

But why is this a case of metonymy? Only because between the signifiers 'bread' and 'wine' and the signified 'Church' and 'Christ' lies the body and blood of Christ. The intermediate signifiers are capable of the connotations offered in Christian theology, just in so far as they denote the corporeal parts of Jesus of Nazareth who, as the Christ, is the source of the significant religious connotations. And that corporeal relation is a simple case of metonymy. However, since bread and wine are not tied to the Church and Christ by metonymy a second level of significance, namely Barthian connotation, is required to unravel the full power of the meaning of the Eucharist to Christians.

REFERENCES

Aristotle 1958: De motu animalium. *The Works of Aristotle Translated into English*. Oxford: Clarendon Press.

Barkan, L. 1975: *Nature's Work of Art*. New Haven and London: Yale University Press.

Dee, J. 1570: Preface to H. Billingsby, *The Elements of Euclid*. London:

Donne, J. 1912: *The Poems of J. Donne*, ed. H. J. Clifford. Oxford: Clarendon Press.

Fletcher, G., and Fletcher, P. 1909: *Poetical Works of Giles and Phineas Fletcher*. Cambridge, Cambridge University Press.

Kepler, J. 1619: *Harmonice Mundi*.

Kantorowicz, E. H. 1957: *The King's Two Bodies*. Princeton: Princeton University Press.

Panofsky, 1940: *The Codex Huyghens and Leonard da Vinci's Art Theory*. London: Warburg Institute.

Plato, *Republic*.

Plowden, E. 1816: *Commentaries on Reports*. London:

Powers, J. M. 1967: *Eucharistic Theology*. New York: Herder and Herder.

Rohling, J. H. 1932: *The Blood of Christ*. Washington, DC: Catholic University Press.

Shakespeare, W. *Henry IV* Part I.

Spenser, E. (1966): *The Poems of Spenser*. Oxford: Oxford University Press.

Starkey, T. (1989): *A Dialogue Between Reginald Pole and Thomas Lapset*, ed. T. E. Mayer. London: Chatto and Windus. St Paul: Epistle to the Corinthians 12.

Vitruvius, P. 1960: *The Ten Books of Architecture*. New York: Dover.

Wittkower, R. 1949: *Architectural Principles in the Age of Humanism*. London:

Yates, F. 1969: *The Theatre of the World*. Chicago: Chicago University Press.

POSTSCRIPT

GENERAL RESEARCH MENU

Unlike the field of personal psychology, much research into the role of the human body in all sorts of human activities has already been undertaken. Much still remains to be done, not least because of the enthnocentricity and implicit Cartesianism of even some of the most interesting studies. Suggestions for projects through which body studies can be given cultural breadth can be found in plenty in the survey article by Scheper-Hughes and Lock (1987). Gillis (1988) has opened up a historical dimension showing us just how modern are many body assumptions. A persistent weakness in much published research is the surviving influence of the outdated and historically particular ideas of Sigmund Freud. Only in the chapter on gender mappings have I completed a modern case against Freud by a detailed exposition of Connell's comprehensive alternative account of the acquisition of masculinity. Much clearing away of Viennese cultural and social particularities remains to be done.

The most fundamental difference between the academic tradition of experiment in psychology and the new emphasis on the study of discursive practices lies in the attitude of the investigator to the human beings who are the subjects of study. The old psychology assumed a passive being driven this way and that by forces and influences both 'internal' and 'external'. The new psychology takes for granted that people are active beings, making use of all sorts of material to try to create orderly lives, or at worst at least the appearance of orderliness. People *use* what they have to hand to accomplish the tasks of everyday living. Everything in this book could be presented as studies of various uses of the body. Not all are consciously managed uses. We use our bodies for grounding personal identity in ourselves and recognizing it in others. We use our bodies as points of reference in relating to other material things. We use our bodies for the assignment of all sorts of roles, tasks, duties and statuses. We use our bodies for practical action. We use our bodies for the expression of moral judgements. We use the condition of our bodies for legitimating a withdrawal from the demands of everyday life. We use our bodies for reproducing the human species. We use our bodies for artwork, as surfaces for decoration and as raw material for sculpture. We use human bodies for the management of the people so embodied. We use our own bodies and those of others to command the cosmos. We use our bodies as message boards, and their parts as succinct codes. We use our bodies for fun, for amusement and for pastimes. This book could be read as a catalogue of some of the uses to which human bodies can be put. Taken this way, a corporeal psychology is just another branch of the tree of activity psychology – the study of human projects and the means adopted to realize them. This book has been concerned with just those projects for the realization of which the human body is the main instrument, either in itself or vicariously in discursive practices in which body concepts are central. Whatever research has been done under the various headings I have used to bring order to such a mass of material has mostly been framed within metaphysical schemes in which the people are passive. Kretschmer and his successors write as if people just found themselves with the temperaments their bodies called for. But what if the presentation of a temperament were an active use of one's body type to display oneself as a certain kind of person? Are most girls passive recipients of gender typing or do they actively take it up as a way of being? Is a male body something one can use to create the impression of masculinity? The aids and props that convert bimodal distributions of secondary sexual characteristics into the bipolarities that reflect the either/or of the primary distinction suggest as much. In this work, rather than propose research menus chapter by chapter, I can simply point to the enormous range of possibilities for study that open up once we start to think of the human body as an instrument for use. What are the main body projects of this and other cultures? My proposals are a sketch of one possible way of identifying ours. How are these projects realized? How is the body managed in these activities? Do the uses of body concepts parallel the uses of bodies? Is there any primacy amongst them?

NAME INDEX

SUBJECT INDEX